Race and Role

Race and Role

• •

The Mixed-Race Asian Experience in American Drama

RENA M. HEINRICH

Rutgers University Press

New Brunswick, Camden, and Newark, New Jersey

London and Oxford

Rutgers University Press is a department of Rutgers, The State University of New Jersey, one of the leading public research universities in the nation. By publishing worldwide, it furthers the University's mission of dedication to excellence in teaching, scholarship, research, and clinical care.

978-1-9788-3554-2 (cloth)
978-1-9788-3553-5 (paper)
978-1-9788-3555-9 (epub)
978-1-9788-3557-3 (web pdf)

Cataloging-in-publication data is available from the Library of Congress.
LCCN 2022041146

A British Cataloging-in-Publication record for this book is available from the British Library.

rutgersuniversitypress.org

For Paige and Lily
and the next generation of mixed-race Asian
performers, playwrights, and theater artists.
This book is for you.

Contents

Race and Role

1

Stages of Denial

• •

The third annual National Asian American Theater Conference was a historic event for the Asian American theater community in 2011. Held in Los Angeles, it was the first time the convening was presented in conjunction with the National Asian American Theater Festival. The joint affair featured a wide array of artists, scholars, and activists from a variety of different Asian diasporic populations, including Cambodian, Chinese, Hmong, Indian, Japanese, Korean, Lao, Pacific Islander, and Vietnamese groups. The Consortium of Asian American Theaters and Artists (CAATA) presented the event with East West Players and TeAda Productions, resident theater companies in Los Angeles, who served as the event hosts. Tim Dang, then producing artistic director of East West Players, spoke to Reed Johnson of the *Los Angeles Times* and asserted, "We tried not to say, 'You're Asian, you're not Asian' or 'You're only half-Asian.' If you self-identify as Asian, then we welcome you into our community."[1] The festival itself thus provided an atmosphere of inclusion and sought to showcase the diversity of Pan-Asian artists within the community.

Nonetheless, at the festival's culminating town hall meeting, a well-known Filipino American film actor stood up and addressed a theater full of conference and festival attendees, contending that mixed-race Asians "were not real Asians," contrary to Dang's statement. He vehemently maintained that these performers stole acting jobs from bona fide Asian Americans, and in his passion and agitation, it was clear that he believed he was speaking to "his people." Award-winning theater artist and Cornerstone Theater Company ensemble member, Shishir Kurup, who was sitting near me, leaped to his feet and publicly confronted the actor, announcing his support of mixed-race Asian artists and calling them "the future" of the community. In the restored church, which had been converted into the theater space that held the oldest Asian American theater company in the country, Kurup pointed directly at me in front of the entire assembly and acknowledged me as a member of the Asian American theater community. As a mixed-race Asian actor and director, it was the first time I felt publicly validated as an Asian American artist in the community.

This ambivalence in the Asian American theater community toward the acceptance of mixed-race theater artists illustrates, I think, the confusion and instability caused by the presence of mixed-race people. If the leaders and members of the Asian American theater community are themselves torn about the validity of the contributions of mixed Asians within their midst, perhaps it does not seem feasible to assign multiracial playwrights and their plays to the Asian American theater canon. If they do not belong there, however, to which category do they belong?

This book examines both the presence and the absence of mixed-Asian playwrights, narratives, and performances in American drama. Western theater scholarship has placed (perhaps correctly) mixed-Asian plays in the purview of the Asian American dramatic canon. However, as the foregoing CAATA example demonstrates, Asian American theater makers in the twentieth and twenty-first centuries have often been reluctant to fully embrace these plays, their playwrights, and the performers who would embody mixed-race characters as authentically "Asian." The fear that mixed-race Asians would infiltrate a space, like theater or film, strictly reserved for "real" Asians reveals a subdominant discourse that "others" these multiracial subjects. At the same time, mixed-race bodies are co-opted by the dominant ideology to fill quotas and act as racial salves without regard for the multiracial's unique positionality. Can mixed-race bodies, performers, and playwrights intervene in the U.S. racial mechanism that would place them outside both Western and Asian American frameworks? Does the denial of the mixed-race body in drama point to the larger ways that racial social structures have penetrated institutions like theater? Can mixed-race performers overturn racial hierarchies and enact racially transgressive performances through dramatized encounters with monoracial bodies onstage? As leading mixed race scholar Naomi Zack contends, "Since human biological race is a fiction, so is mixed race."[2] In other words, does the very acknowledgment of race in a self-proclaimed mixed-race identity ultimately reinforce dominant codes and reify racial categorization?

A multiracial person's choice to claim a mixed-race identity, rather than one that is multiethnic, is perhaps contradictory. By identifying as mixed-race, the subject acknowledges the existence of a racial construct and subscribes to the very mechanism that she desires to resist in claiming mixedness. Therefore, this study explores if and how mixed-race theater makers engage specifically in theater as a tactical maneuver to interrogate and subvert the racial framework in place. Or, has theater foreclosed its generative power—and the promise of collective remembering through performance and theatrical texts—to mixed-race artists, forcing them instead into a monoracial identity?

His book fuses ethnographic methods with archival research and cultural materialist readings of theater texts and their performances to unearth this hidden corpus of mixed-race drama from the Asian American theatrical canon. Specifically, I examine how certain Asian American plays since the nineteenth century have long advocated for the social significance of mixed-race people and their particular dilemma as a subjugated group that has been erased from political discourse. The plays also illuminate a specific positionality that exists outside a monoracial consciousness, a paratopic space I call *double liminality*, which is often not recognized in American society at large nor in performance. These plays studied in the following chapters address major periods in the last two centuries of American performance history from the Progressive Era to the new millennium. I aim to analyze how the bookends of the twentieth century speak to each other and to ascertain how much change in racial classification and performance, if any, has occurred over the span of a century.

The plays and performances in this book also explore the various historical, social, and cultural milestones that have accompanied the rise of mixed-Asian drama in the United States. In investigating the plays, I pay particular attention to how the shifting frameworks of notions of identity in each respective time period influenced the depiction of the mixed-race subject and how mixed-race dramatists responded to these circumstances. Chapters 2 and 3 focus on the life and dramatic work of the curiously overlooked nineteenth-century Japanese German American playwright Sadakichi Hartmann and the yellow face portrayal of the Chinese Irish protagonist in T.S. Denison's 1895 farce *Patsy O'Wang: An Irish Farce with a Chinese Mix-Up* as well as the often-dismissed theatrical contributions of Chinese English, Canadian American author Winnifred Eaton. In chapter 4, I explore the twentieth-century mixed-Asian characters of award-winning Japanese African American playwright Velina Hasu Houston, and finally, in chapter 5, I examine the ways in which cutting-edge playwrights in the new millennium, like Christopher Chen and Frances Ya-Chu Cowhig, continue their key predecessors' important cultural work by contesting the problematic idea of "colorblind racial transcendence."[3] Together, Cowhig and Chen champion theater in the twentieth-first century that validates cultural diversity, particularly the uniqueness of the mixed-race experience.

By focusing specifically on mixed-race Asian drama (as opposed to mixed-race drama more generally), I target the ways in which this hidden oeuvre of the Asian American canon challenges American racial frameworks. Mixed-Asian drama is often overlooked for its failure to fit smoothly into static (i.e., Black-and-white) racial categories, thereby rendering it inconsequential in larger scholarly discourse about race and performance.[4] However, the very invisibility of the multiracial Asian American experience exposes the underlying tensions in the polarization of race and compels us to question the very boundaries with which the white hegemony is so profoundly invested. The dismissal of the mixed-race experience also reveals the invisible discrimination that takes place within minoritized groups like those in Asian America, a landscape collectively coded as the ever-appropriate "model minority."[5] In carefully considering the portrayals and performances of mixed-race Asian American figures, new strategies can be gained in the decolonization of all racialized bodies. As mixed race studies scholar LeiLani Nishime astutely notes, depictions of the mixed-race experience "slow us down to see how race is constituted through discourse" and "through the circulations of cultural meanings."[6] Furthermore, the exploration of the doubly liminal space occupied by the mixed-race Asian body leads to the disassembly of racial codes and enables us, I will suggest, to investigate the very scaffolding that holds subjugated bodies in place.

In the United States, a country sustained by Eurocentric hegemonic ideology, the assignment of races still functions as a way to maintain power for white people. This culture of racialization operates through what Evelyn Alsultany calls a "monoracial cultural logic" that "imposes monoracial identities onto the population" in order to easily maintain a racial social hierarchy.[7] Individuals of mixed-race heritage, like Chin Sum in Denison's play *Patsy O'Wang*, create confusion and disorder in this regimented monoracial system. Because mixed-race subjects cannot fully extract themselves from daily life in a racialized national corpus, they often employ de Certeauian "tactics" to shape shift or move between different racial identities. French theorist Michel de Certeau defines tactics as actions deployed by an individual to circumvent the expectations or laws employed by structural institutions.[8] This means that mixed-race persons use a variety of tactics to outwit the fixed racial codes prescribed by the dominant. Multiracial subjects complicate, subvert, and trouble the tenuous boundaries of monoracial cultural logic. In theater, as I will underscore, mixed-race artists further deploy the art of embodiment and capitalize on their shape shifting prowess to enact racially transgressive performances.[9] Theater is an optimal site for illustrating this complexity and enables mixed-race bodies to talk back to dominant social structures through the audience's encounter with the embodied act of performance. The ability to shape shift empowers the subject to defy racial legibility due to nebulous phenotypical features and facilitates the expression of the race, ethnicity, or culture of the mixed-race subject's choosing. For the multiracial figure, these "performances" can become naturalized over time as a seamless repertoire of behavior. When considered onstage, the embodied performances disrupt systemic racial codes and expand the ways that race is perceived in the United States. They challenge racialized expectations and elucidate the porous boundaries that mixed-race individuals slip across, sometimes with great effort and sometimes effortlessly.

This exploration of the nuanced, mixed-Asian experience extends the fields of critical mixed race studies, Asian American studies, and theater studies and meets at the confluence of all three. Though critical mixed race studies has rapidly become a growing field of academic study, the majority of the work thus far has focused on education, psychology, sociology, history, literature, and media studies.[10] Very little mixed race scholarship has addressed multiracial representation in theater. Likewise, Asian American performance scholarship has keenly elucidated the invisible/visible binary as imposed on the Asian American body but has not extended the examination of this dyad to its unique containment of mixed-Asian identity. For instance, performance theorist Josephine Lee argues that the genre of realism counters stereotypical portrayals of Asian figures, which teaches an audience how to "see" real Asians. Can this notion of recognizing the "real" also extend to mixed-race Asianness?[11] Likewise, performance theorist Karen Shimakawa argues that the abject Asian American figure is othered in American culture even while remaining an essential part of the whole, but this process is further complicated when the mixed-Asian body is invisibilized as other from multiple sub-bodies politic like Asian America. However, I agree that performance is the locus where Asian American bodies—specifically mixed-race Asians in this book—"negotiate the process of coming into visibility."[12] In response, this book traces the depiction of multiracial Asians across a variety of performances in various theatrical contexts from Broadway to smaller theater houses in the Midwest and the West Coast. The book surrounds its study with attention to the aesthetic, theoretical, sociohistorical, and cultural environments that shaped, and are shaped by, these performances. This reclaimed theatrical space sheds light on the doubly liminal consciousness that mixed-race people have constructed inside and outside the dominant and subdominant discourses—a subjectivity that is the center of multiracial, everyday life.

Stage Management: The Construction of Race

Both visibly and invisibly linked, the racialization of the people of the United States and policies and scholarship that institutionalize race have fluidly worked in tandem since the country's inception. The subordination of various ethnic groups based on their physical characteristics has functioned as a way to control non-white people deemed socially inferior while also attempting to keep white bloodlines "pure." Shaped by human "scientific" taxonomies proposed by Carolus Linnaeus and Johann Blumenbach and influenced by the eugenic teachings of Madison Grant, Western hegemonic discourse has historically centered on the assumption that human beings are rightfully divided into different races.[13] Consequently, historian and racial theorist, W. E. B. Du Bois famously observed in 1903 that "the problem of the Twentieth Century is the problem of the color line."[14] This racialized structure places white Westerners at the top of the hierarchy and non-white people from various ethnicities scattered among different classes below. The social stratification also functions through a belief in naturalized hypodescent in which a mixed-race individual is identified by the race of the parent deemed socially subordinate. Hypodescent forces mixed-race people to identify as monoracials who are able to claim only their non-white parentage.[15]

This imposed, hypolineal monoraciality frames "passing"—or falsely posing as white and abandoning one's other parentage—as a form of social and cultural betrayal and leaves multiethnic individuals with seemingly few options.[16] They must choose hypodescent or pass into whiteness, the master monoracial category, and risk facing the cultural consequences. Resultantly, monoraciality has erased many historical narratives about mixed-race people. Such is the case of Anna Leonowens, the real-life governess celebrated in the famed 1951 musical *The King and I*, who hid her multiethnic heritage and was, for decades, believed to be a white woman of purely English descent.[17] Suppressed documentation about figures like Leonowens seems to suggest that interracial marriages and their mixed-race offspring were anomalies in society, rare in previous generations, and only recently on the rise. However, the social mores of previous decades repudiated many interracial unions and often removed them from the discourse. These silenced histories have been replaced by tropes in the social imaginary that depict mixed-race children as defective, deviant, and tragically trapped between two worlds.

One of these is the trope of the tragic mulatto/a, a figure cursed with mental instability, physical weakness, and a compromised morality due to the corporeal confusion of mixed blood.[18] A stereotype "doomed to unfortunate longevity," as Sterling Brown keenly noted, this false rendering of mixedness has narrowly defined the experiences of mixed Blackness within the trope of the tragic.[19] One of the ways that corporeal confusion manifests is in the mixed-race subject's rejection of hypodescent, which underscores the impossibility of passing. Theater has depicted this social phenomenon in dramas like Langston Hughes's *Mulatto: A Tragedy of the Deep South* (1931), in which the son of a Black servant and a white plantation owner declares his right to publicly embrace his white parentage when all other parties, including his own parents, affirm his monoracial Blackness. The protagonist, Robert Norwood, demands recognition for his whiteness, declaring to his brother, "I'm gonna act like my white half, not my black half."[20] His refusal to accept a monoracial identity tragically leads to his demise in the play, elucidating the ultimate penalty for failing to adhere the rigid, racial system.

Often seen through a gendered lens, the tragic mulatta figure is particularly vulnerable as both a Black and white feminine body. In the nineteenth-century melodrama *The Octoroon; or, Life in Louisiana* (1859) by Dion Boucicault, the daughter of a white plantation owner, Zoe, cannot reconcile the "mark of Cain" she bears as a mixed-race person who is one-eighth African descent.[21] This "nearly invisible but fatal blackness" prevents Zoe from achieving happiness as a full-fledged member of white American society.[22] Performance theorist Joseph Roach maintains that inevitably "the invisible presence of blackness marks her flesh as a commodity even as her whiteness changes its value."[23] Resultantly, the omnipresent demands of the one-drop rule tragically lead to Zoe's downfall in the play's original 1859 ending. As a cultural and political artifact of a society concretizing the precepts of whiteness, Boucicault's play demonstrates the inescapable consequences for failing to adhere to the dictates of naturalized hypodescent and the one-drop rule.

Many mixed-race narratives often foreground individuals of Black and white descent, especially because these identities have been deeply rooted and inextricably linked to the history of slavery in the United States and to experiences of rape, coercion, and trauma between slave owners and the enslaved like the characters in *The Octoroon* and *Mulatto*. Notwithstanding these histories of violence, the reality is that there is a broad range of experiences within the mixed-race population among African Americans as well as other racial and ethnic groups. Furthermore, Black and white racial politics permeate the contemporary political understanding of race in the United States. Thus the ethics of passing, as underscored by a Black and white dyad, continue to circulate in popular discourse as a predominant mixed-race narrative.

In the trope of the tragic mulatto/a, the mixed-race figure's precarious biological condition threatens the subject's mental fitness and prohibits full acceptance in both Black and white worlds.[24] Mixed race scholar Cynthia L. Nakashima refers to this belief as the theory of "hybrid degeneracy," which asserts that mixed-race offspring are genetically inferior to the purity of their racial parentage and, as a result, are seen as deviant and strange.[25] Similarly, the tragic Eurasian is characterized as a mixed Asian who struggles with races at war within her mixed-race body, resulting in a weakened mental and physical state.[26] In his 1918 dissertation entitled *The Mulatto in the United States*, Edward Bryont Reuter describes Eurasians as physically "slight and weak. Their personal appearance is subject to the greatest variations. In skin color, for example, they are often darker even than the Asiatic parent. They are naturally indolent and will enter into no employment requiring exertion or labor. This lack of energy is correlated with an incapacity for organization. They will not assume burdensome responsibilities, but they make passable clerks where only routine labor is required."[27] The trope of the tragic Eurasian portrays the mixed-race individual as a biologically impure specimen, in which the incompatible blood from parents of different racial backgrounds causes pathology, deviance, physical and mental weakness, and emotional instability.[28] Correspondingly, these characterizations also play out in cultural artifacts in which despair is biologically determined and physicalized in the body. In Winnifred Eaton's short story "A Father" (1900), Eaton, writing under the pen name Onoto Watanna, maintains that "the immeasurable wistfulness and sadness of the half-breed were stamped indelibly" on her protagonist's features.[29] Similarly, in her short story "The Wickedness of Matsu," half-caste children are described as "unstable, unreliable, incapable of restraint."[30] In other narratives, such as T. S. Denison's *Patsy O'Wang*, the tragic Eurasian most always desires to escape these curses of mixedness through passing and historically has been played by white actors who can supposedly sidestep yellowface and "play race" by portraying mixed-white characters.[31]

Regardless of the supposed risks to their future children, Americans have been mixing and marrying individuals from ethnic backgrounds other than their own for generations, and their children engage in a robust process of identity development that is far more complex than a hopeful reliance on passing. Instances of interracial marriages and the prevalence of mixed families have taken place in significant numbers between a variety of ethnic groups. In this study, I focus specifically on the treatment and experiences of mixed-race individuals with one Asian and one non-Asian parent, and I argue that one of the most critically important ways their mixed-race histories have survived is through theatrical texts. Mixed-race dramas elucidate the external social pressures and cultural limitations that have played a key role in the development of mixed-Asian subjectivity specifically and elucidate an identity construction that resists the false notion of passing and the stereotypes of the tragic. Crucially, plays written since the new millennium present mixed-race subjectivity in a whole new light, which, I assert, is due to the government's formal acknowledgment of the mixed-race population on the 2000 U.S. census. The activism of multiracial groups in the 1990s spurred the U.S. Census Bureau to change its racial categorization policy, allowing persons to identify with more than one designation in the new millennium.[32] The multiracial characters in new work by Obie Award–winning playwright Christopher Chen are, for instance, unapologetic, self-possessed, and befuddled by the crumbling yet persistent stereotypes that surround them in millennial modernity. If, as Edward W. Said so expertly illustrates in his seminal work, *Culture and Imperialism*, literature cannot escape the political world in which it is produced, Chen's plays illuminate fissures in the American racial discourse.[33] As a result, the mixed-race Asian American narrative in theater has begun to shift from one of the "tragic Eurasian" to one of a wholly integrated identity that resists the rigidity of monoracial designation.

Mixed-Asian individuals must navigate the histories of discrimination, hostility, and violence against Asians and Asian Americans as inscribed on the mixed-race body as well as the evolving social contexts that have framed the understanding of the mixed figure in Asian America and the United States more broadly. Beginning with the Page Act of 1875 and the Chinese Exclusion Act of 1882, a series of immigration laws limited the migration of Asian immigrants to the United States in an attempt to engineer a white nativist population deemed more suitable to white patricians with power. In the twentieth century, *The Passing of the Great Race: or, The Racial Basis of European History* (1916), by attorney-turned-pseudoscientist Madison Grant, was the inspiration for the Immigration Acts of 1917, 1921, and 1924, which sharply cut immigration from outside northwest Europe and definitively barred immigrants from Asia. Grant's obsession with interracial sex was behind several anti-miscegenation laws passed in those decades. Due to these policy changes, for two generations afterward, the

American people became steadily whiter and whiter and ever more segregated. Asian figures were marked as undeniably "alien" and unassimilable, and race and culture were understood as so closely intertwined that they were often believed to be synonymous.[34] By extension, race was understood as a natural hierarchy that directly influenced human behavior and cultural practices. These could be understood on a timeline toward a "rational" civilization, which was an accomplishment that Western "culture" had achieved. Miscegenation, therefore, compromised an individual's ability to participate in civilized society, the biological achievement of one's white heritage. Resultantly, the Progressive Era transformed the ideology of nativism into public policies that bestowed its full privileges on individuals of white, European descent. Mixed-race performers, like actress Merle Oberon, shape shifted into whiteness to hide their mixed heritages from public view.[35]

The United States then was a nation grappling with how to categorize a rising mixed-race population, and the U.S. census continued to recognize mixedness to some extent until 1930. For the most part, the classification of multiracial people of African descent has been the focus of government enumeration in the United States. However, this inventory of bodies underscored the country's anxiety and outright obsession with miscegenation in the nineteenth century.[36] As Lawrence Wright contends, the fact that most "every census since [1790] has measured race differently" evinces the fraught relationship the United States has had with its own racial categorization.[37] While acknowledging the existence of multiraciality on the one hand, the 1890 census, for example, also displayed an exhaustive accounting of generational mixedness on the other and identified people as either Black (denoting full African ancestry), mulatto, quadroon, or octoroon, belying the cultural belief in hypodescent.

The one-drop rule, engineered to manage the African American population after slavery, became a legally sanctioned ideology in the 1896 *Plessy v. Ferguson* court decision.[38] The racially ambiguous Homer Plessy, who was predominantly of white descent, was not regarded as white in the eyes of the state. Plessy was one-eighth African ancestry and seven-eighths European descent but was found to be "colored" despite a white-presenting physiognomy due to his mixed-race heritage.[39] Consequently, the court's decision in *Plessy v. Ferguson* formalized an adherence to hypodescent and institutionalized the one-drop rule. Even though subsequent census enumerations in 1910 and 1920 continued to account for individuals of mixed-African descent (these designations were temporarily eliminated in 1900), the categories of mixedness were officially dropped from the U.S. census in 1930.

Reclassifying mixed-African people as monoracially Black consolidated a racially diverse group of people into a monoracial underclass.[40] Government officials believed that three-fourths of all African Americans were already mixed and that individuals of full African descent would eventually disappear. Furthermore, in the 1920s, census officials abandoned their focus on the mixed categorization and concentrated instead on the rise of European immigration in the subsequent decade.[41] This shift, coupled with the antiquated belief that each race had its own blood type that biologically determined a subject's physique, physiognomy, and behavioral characteristics, strengthened America's cultural belief in the one-drop rule. Theories and subsequent blood tests emerged in the 1920s that purportedly determined the race of an individual based on a drop of their blood, an ideology that was challenged at the time and has long been discredited.[42] For the remainder of the twentieth century until the new millennium, the census concretized monoracial categorization and continued to align the process of national enumeration with the nineteenth-century *Plessy v. Ferguson* decision.[43] After 1930, state-sanctioned monoraciality was securely in place and normalized through social acceptance based on hypodescent. This was applied to all minoritized groups, even though racial assignments continued to be arbitrary. The now defunct "Hindu" race category represented South Asians from 1920 to 1940, after which the demographic was deemed white for almost forty years and then placed in the Asian-Pacific Islander group to become Asian in 1977.[44] Furthermore, mixed-race Asian identity, by contrast, has never been recorded on twentieth-century census surveys in any iteration.

Theater, then, has been at the forefront of opening spaces of sanctuary for multiracial acceptance within a racialized United States since the late nineteenth century. This is illuminated, in varying degrees, in Denison's play, *Patsy O'Wang*, a farce about a Chinese Irish multiracial born before the Chinese Exclusion Act, and in the narratives of Sadakichi Hartmann and Winnifred Eaton, whose mixed-race characters foregrounded multiraciality in an America that was already multiracial and intercultural long before the end of the nineteenth century. The selected works of Denison, Hartmann, and Eaton also demonstrate how mixed-race figures employed shape shifting tactics to navigate society at the turn of the century in America. Historian Paul Spickard defines shape shifting as the mixed-race person's ability to slip through the porous boundaries of race.[45] While racial expectation assumes that a perceived phenotype ensures an assignment to the correct racial category, ethnically ambiguous bodies can shape shift and bend racial expectation to adopt multiple racial assignments through performance and reception. The contemporary mixed-race character portrayals of mixed-Asian playwrights Velina Hasu Houston, Frances Ya-Chu Cowhig, and Christopher Chen continue the interventions performed by Denison, Hartmann, and Eaton's protagonists to reveal how shape shifting performances in the late twentieth and early twenty-first centuries expose the fragility of race, especially when confronted by transnational experiences and global migration. Specifically, the plays of Chen and Cowhig interrogate the political and legal systems that hold the American racial framework in place. An understanding of this mixed-race consciousness, constructed and embodied in a liminal space outside monoracial binaries, is crucial for the examination of the mixed-race Asian American stories. These narratives, when transformed into performance texts,[46] can often dismantle the social and cultural assignments that are imposed on mixed-race people.

Multiraciality also illuminates both the dominant culture's desired fixity of race and the co-opting of these constructs by various subdominant groups. By tracing the theatrical depiction of mixed-race persons, we can witness the ways that performance both exposes the systemic parameters in place and also destabilizes those boundaries by constructing performances of racial transgression. Performance theorist Brandi Wilkins Catanese contends that the antidote to colorblind racial "transcendence" is an awareness of the divisions put in place by race, rather than a denial of their existence. Catanese argues that the more humane pursuit is not to ignore race but to acknowledge the division and destruction that racialization has caused. She calls this approach racial transgression, and she advocates for performances that defy racial frameworks to unmask the inherent inability of transcendence to bring about social change.[47] Mixed-race performances of racial transgression exploit the interstitial spaces that allow for shape shifting practices to outwit the strategies of what Rebecca Schneider calls "the monumental."[48] Teresa Kay Williams (now Teresa Williams-León) similarly calls shape shifting the act of "doing race," and she likens the process to the way one "does gender."[49] Williams-León underscores the ways in which the multiracial subject twists and turns in and out of the "racial molds" assigned to her by the monumental hegemony.[50] In theater, contemporary plays, such as Chen's *Mutt* (2014) and Velina Hasu Houston's *Thirst* (1985) and *Kokoro (True Heart)* (1994), demonstrate the ways that Jim Crow and Coolie-era social constructs, which have been enforced by racialized language, attempt to regulate mixed-race people, and how the multiethnic characters in these plays shape shift to illuminate the slippage that occurs between the boundaries of race.

Beyond examining how mixed-race theater disrupts established social categories, I also demonstrate how it offers paradigmatic possibilities for viewing and encountering mixed-race subjects outside our current hierarchical restraints. The theatrical narratives examined in this book address the histories of oppression specific to mixed-race subjectivity and foreground mixed-race figures in central roles. Not only do mixed-race bodies destabilize racial codes as impenetrable but they also choose shape shifting practices to manage their own racial performativity. Most significantly, the acknowledgment of the mixed-race population at the advent of the millennium dilates a new theatrical space for the representation of multiracial identity.

Nearly sixty years after mixed categories were eliminated from the U.S. census, almost 250,000 people identified as multiracial by writing in a mixed-race designation in 1990.[51] Beginning in 1993, the activism of grassroots, multiracial groups spurred the U.S. Census Bureau to change its racial categorization policy in 1997, allowing persons to identify with more than one designation.[52] Resultantly, 2.1 million Asian or Pacific Islander Americans specifically identified themselves as multiethnic when the census allowed respondents to choose more than one box in 2000. Social justice advocate Adriane E. Gamble observes that since this change in racial categorization, a mixed-race community has been emerging, as individuals reject traditional monoracial categories and increasingly identify as *hapa*.[53]

The word *hapa* comes from the Hawaiian term *hapa Haole*, which referred originally to multiethnic individuals with one native Hawaiian parent and one non-Hawaiian parent. *Haole* means "stranger," "foreigner," or "foreign" in native Hawaiian, and after contact with Captain James Cook and the white foreign world in 1778, the word referred specifically to white Europeans or white Americans.[54] *Hapa* is a Hawaiian pidgin term for "half" or "part," in all its iterations, and *Hapa Haole* identified a mixed heritage, native Hawaiian who was half or part white.[55] The Japanese American community—and ultimately the Asian American community—adopted the term in Hawai'i, extending its definition to mean of part Asian and part non-Asian descent.[56] *Hapa* has been popularized as the preferred contemporary term for mixed-race Americans of Asian descent and now often refers to racial mixing that includes both an Asian and a non-Asian parent. While some critical mixed race studies scholars problematize its usage in mainstream American culture, I rely on renowned scholar and native Hawaiian linguist Robert Kaeo NeSmith, who affirms that the term *hapa* applies to mixed-race Asian identity because it correctly defines the notion of mixedness in its usage. The use of *hapa* in this context, according to NeSmith, is relevant and appropriate, rather than appropriated, language. *Hapa* is unique as a term in that it encompasses the notion of "part" without reducing the subject to percentages of ethnicity. Furthermore, NeSmith emphasizes the word's neutral connotation and wide usage in the Hawaiian language, calling it "pedestrian" rather than political.[57] For these reasons, I have opted to employ the term in this study.[58]

In this analysis, I also employ the terms *multiracial*, *mixed-race*, *mixed-Asian*, and *multiethnic*. I use them interchangeably, even though the definitions of *race* and *ethnicity* describe different states of identity and arise from different modes of power. According to sociologists Stephen Cornell and Douglas Hartmann, ethnicity denotes a group of people with a shared ancestry or culture, history, and symbolism, that is, a common homeland, language, or religion.[59] By contrast, race is a socially constructed classification based mainly on phenotypical characteristics. It is a product of perception and is assigned to individuals whose physical characteristics are believed to be inherent.[60] Conceivably, the concept of race maintains a structure of power based on a Eurocentric belief in white superiority. While race is often an imposed construct, ethnicity connotes agency because it allows for self-identification.

While I understand that race and ethnicity are not conceptually the same, I use them synonymously in terms such as *multiracial* or *multiethnic* because the individuals I examine in this book are both. A Hapa who might identify as half-Asian and half-Black can be aptly described—by herself or others—as multiracial or mixed-race. This same person, however, might also self-identify as part Chinese and Thai and part Nigerian descent, thereby accurately characterizing herself as multiethnic. Since many Hapas tend to reject monoraciality, they often skip race identification entirely and lay claim to all the ethnicities in their cultural makeup.

Sociologists Michael Omi and Howard Winant effectively argue that race is not a biologically determined state but an engineered construct supported by national, political, and social structures.[61] Yet Western hegemonic discourse continues to other brown bodies based on racial phenotype and supposedly corresponding indelible character traits. Based on these assessments, persons of color are relegated to a second, subjugated position, while white identities historically occupy the primary position in society. This process denies the secondarily marked individuals access to the same privileges, agency, or personhood available to white Americans.

Furthermore, Claire Jean Kim's theory of racial triangulation suggests that Asians and Asian Americans are judged by a different set of criteria than African Americans, for example.[62] While African Americans may be falsely conceived of as "inferior" based on racial assumptions of character and personhood, they are rightly recognized as American citizens. Asians and Asian Americans, on the other hand, who are perhaps believed to parallel white Americans in terms of "desirable" traits like economic drive or intelligence, are often not considered to be American nationals. As historian Mae M. Ngai affirms, individuals of Asian descent are largely perceived as "alien citizens."[63] They may be American born, but they are almost always presumed to be foreigners and ultimately from elsewhere. This hegemonic assessment of Asians and Asian Americans—politicized racial groups already complicated by diverse cultural and generational experiences—presents mixed-race subjects with a double jeopardy. Not only must they navigate assumptions about hypodescent and differences in cultural practices within racialized group membership, but they must also defend their citizenship and their Americanness. Mixed-race Asian individuals, then, occupy a unique, circumstantial space different from other mixed-race groups. While I in no way mean to compare or qualify the mixed-race experiences of different communities, this question of national belonging brings a unique facet to the multiracial Asian experience.

Setting the Stage: Diverging from the Racial Paradigm

The questions of belonging and of the barriers presented by monoracial cultural logic, which is a dominant discourse, are not the only obstacles that mixed Asians face in the process of self-identification. The subdominant discourse may also refuse to acknowledge and accept racial multiplicity. Coined by Paul Spickard, the term *subdominant discourse* refers to attitudes and beliefs imposed on multiethnic Asians by monoracial Asians and Asian Americans.[64] The subdominant discourse often does not recognize mixed-race Asians as being Asian enough to belong in the monoracial category. Conversely, the dominant discourse also refuses membership to multiracial Hapas, forcing them instead to identify solely as Asian.[65] Therefore, the dominant assigns all individuals to monoracial groups, who then police bodies to hold the system in place. Barred from membership to either group, however, mixed-race people find themselves in a doubly liminal state, on the limen of more than one racial group, without full acceptance in either one. By subscribing to biological, fixed notions of race, both dominant and subdominant cultural thought may trap mixed-race persons within a rigid binary, effectively with no place for them at all.

This untethered space is troubled by cultural expectations that require the mixed-race person to internalize a "double vision." Theater historian Harvey Young's extension of habitus is useful here in considering the construction of non-white identities under a regime of racial conditioning. Young extends sociologist Pierre Bourdieu's theory of habitus to elucidate a double vision within the performance of Blackness.[66] His application of the complexities of habitus is also instrumental in understanding mixed-race subjectivity. As Young explains, habitus can be understood as a "regulated improvisation" where "social expectations are incorporated into the individual, and the individual projects those expectations back upon society."[67] In other words, the theory of habitus evinces an understanding of the body—whether the Black body as in Young's example or the mixed-Asian body as in this book—as socially constructed and as continually reconstructing its own self. External assumptions about the body penetrate the flesh, become inscribed internally, and are ultimately incorporated into the self.

This process of socialization instructs bodies how to behave under a racialized hierarchy, and raced individuals may become unwittingly complicit in their own marginalization. Young's understanding of habitus is contingent upon legible characteristics, such as skin color, hair texture, and other physical features. Upon viewing a body's phenotype, the observer may deploy—in the seeing of the body—racialized assumptions, histories, and violence, which are then mapped onto the body in question. The observed subject internalizes this way of being seen. Young notes, for instance, that a Black shopper might dress up to go shopping to lessen the chances of "being (mis)read as a potential shoplifter."[68] Likewise, an egregious set of barriers and expectations also meets bodies of Asian and Pacific Island descent,[69] including a history of violence, segregation, exclusion, and gross stereotypes—either a hypersexual yet submissive and deadly femininity, or an effeminate, domesticated masculinity, among others.[70] Members of the Asian diaspora also internalize these false perceptions.

By contrast, multiethnic individuals often lack a concrete racial phenotype that would connect them to any particular group. Thus their seemingly ambiguous features potentially place them in multiple communities, including ones with which they may not identify. This is true, for example, for the mixed-Asian actor Paul King from the 2016 Chicago production of *Mutt*, who is continuously mistaken for Latino in everyday life.[71] This presents multiracial people with a paradox. While they incorporate one or more habiti into their personhoods, they may still face rejection from the very groups with which they have been forced to associate. While habitus may assign an individual to a specific grouping, this membership can afford monoracial people a certain assurance of belonging.[72] The mixed-race person is, however, left adrift, anchorless within a prescribed community while simultaneously maintaining an alternate set of habiti that has been externally imposed and internally inscribed.

Nonetheless, multiracial Asian Americans can lay claim to multiple racial experiences because of their inherent ambiguity and because the reception of observers alters how they are received. This unique positionality causes them to operate outside the rules of monoraciality and to inhabit a space apart from dominant and subdominant parameters. Even after they negotiate and aggregate the particular habitus of one racial state, they must then switch and perform the habits of another. They may be rejected by the dominant and fight to control their own identity. Additionally, they are also subjected to a subdominant discourse and othered by monoracial Asian Americans, who may not conceive of them as fully Asian but rather as persons whose Asianness is made murky by another racial background. However, hapa individuals must still navigate their Asian Americanness while, paradoxically, also being marginalized from the Asian American minoritized group. Mixed-race Asians, therefore, must incorporate more than one set of racial habitus and often do so with little sense of inclusion in those corresponding groups.

This dilemma brings me to the precarious place of multiethnic identity construction, which Hapas undertake outside the realm of the dominant/subdominant pairing. I contend that mixed-race Asians form a particular subjectivity that is constructed in response to dominant and subdominant discourses and tempered by lived experience and an individual's own assertion of self. I call this space *double liminality*. Anurima Banerji's concept of paratopia and bell hooks's notion of marginality as center are useful in considering this unique construction of doubly liminal identity. Coined by Banerji, the term *paratopia* is derived from the Greek prefixes *para* meaning "beside or alongside of" and *topos* meaning "place." This "space of alterity" differs from the idealized *utopia*.[73] While it does share similarities with Foucault's *heterotopia*,[74] it differs in that paratopia is specifically evoked through embodied acts. For Banerji, paratopia is a space that exists in tandem with the dominant. That is, it is "another" way of being rather than a place of the "other." While the notion of other implies that there is a primary positionality, which is more correct or more acceptable, "another" points to a space that is equal in legitimacy and exists parallel to the dominant subject position.[75] For mixed-race subjects, this parallel space is claimed neither by the dominant nor the subdominant but exists simultaneously alongside both.

The space of paratopia is not a defined architectural space but is a site enacted in performance.[76] For the doubly liminal subject, it is enacted both onstage and in the performance of self or, in other words, in *beingness*. Onstage, for example as Banerji asserts, the true self identifies neither as solely female nor solely male, as mandated by heteronormative discourse. Banerji offers Indian dance choreographer Chandralekha's *Raga: In Search of Femininity* as an example of a paratopic space where bodies are freed from binaries of gender. In the dance, the "principal duet is unexpectedly . . . composed of two men and their erotic engagement" and is meant to assert that "masculine and feminine elements reside in a single body."[77] Bodily expression in performance—specifically dance performance in Banerji's analysis—liberates the self from the demands of the dominant and provides a site where both genders can coexist.

Whereas Banerji considers gender, I look to paratopia to articulate the site of double liminality, which describes an alternate space where mixed-race subjectivity subverts racialized discourse and where two or more races or ethnicities are expressed within a single body as a perpetual state of being. As with paratopia, double liminality is not constructed as a mode of resistance—though it can serve as one—nor does it necessarily seek to be a direct form of protest. It exists alongside dominant categories of racial identity as one more expression of consciousness that has been acted on by external forces. It describes performances that exist outside the dominant and subdominant realms by expressing an understanding of identity on its own terms.

In theater, these embodied performances become sites of liberation.[78] In Christopher Chen's play, *Mutt*, this is evident when hapa characters Nick and Hanna discuss their racial identities. While Nick does not seem burdened by the rules of hypodescent, his predecessors in previous multiracial dramas do not have the luxury of experiencing this liberated state of being, which demonstrates how theater has documented the shifting of the mixed-race experience over time. Moreover, Nick does not subscribe to one fixed category of race and instead alludes to what he perceives as racial fluidity.

NICK You identify as an Asian?
HANNA If you're mixed race in America, you identify as a minority.
NICK See I never even thought about which side I identify with more. . . . It's funny how we don't really have a "racial" identity, you know? . . . there's just so much, so much evolution going on? Like trying to hit a moving target?[79]

As Chen demonstrates, contemporary mixed-race subjectivity creates a bodily site where two or more racial or ethnic identities freely coexist and where the perception of racial categories undergoes a metamorphosis. While paratopia, as elucidated by Banerji, is not specifically limited to racial expression, I designate those elements of paratopia that resonate with the construction of mixed-race subjectivity as doubly liminal. This in-between but centered position exists outside—and therefore slyly rejects—the dominant and subdominant discourses and relies on its own understanding of the phenomenon we call identity.

Activist-scholar bell hooks claims this same marginal place as a center that, for her, exists as a site of radical resistance.[80] Like Banerji, she also rejects the notion of other, which serves as an erasure, and she observes that living "at the edges" of the dominant culture enables one to "develop a particular way of seeing reality."[81] In this centralized space, the mixed-race subject, I contend, reconciles social habiti with personal experiences and develops an alternate way of seeing.

I extend aspects of Banerji's and hooks's notions of paratopic space and marginality as center to the mixed-race hapa experience I call double liminality. This positionality is doubly liminal from two (or more) racial groups, and it is in this space that the mixed-race person constructs a hapa consciousness. At the threshold of more than one racial group, but perhaps never fully accepted therein, she negotiates each concrete social interaction through a different cultural consciousness, whereby she employs two (or more) worldviews that continuously give way to each other. The mixed-race Asian character Hanna explains this to Nick in *Mutt*:

HANNA Okay. Well, I'm a hapa, like you, so I identify as a minority. And yet I was still conscious of, of being able to fit in, in [a way that] my full Asian brethren couldn't. So it was like . . . maybe I could use this key I'd been given to . . . try and open some doors.[82]

This "another" way of being, of having the ability to use a different "key," is the reason I champion double liminality to describe the fluidity of hapa subjectivity. Hanna's ability to shape shift between two different racial groups, "in [a way that her] full Asian brethren couldn't," affords her a particular access to both.

Mixed-race subjects can also be doubly liminal from each other, since no two multiethnic experiences are alike. For example, the mixed-race characters Len and Nick in *Mutt* have two very different ethnic backgrounds. Nick identifies as half-Chinese and half-white, whereas Len is a mix of every major race in the world. While these personae have mixedness in common, they do not have a similar culture nor upbringing that would characterize them as belonging to the same racial group. Yet literary theorist Stefanie Dunning asserts that "this multiplicity of experience should be looked upon as a strength that destabilizes any essentializing narrative of 'the' biracial experience."[83] In line with Dunning, I seek not to essentialize the experience of multiracials but merely to name the process by which multiethnic people navigate assigned social impositions and blend various cultures and subcultures into one whole identity. For multiracial subjects facing potential rejection from one or both parent cultures, this is a whole new level of complexity with which monoracial individuals do not have to contend. This extraordinary facet of identity construction informs the hapa consciousness.

The constructed, doubly liminal self becomes evident in embodied encounters. Interacting with another individual activates the complex processes of cultural code-switching, or shape shifting, which depends on the circumstances of the exchange. Hence this identity comes into being through the everyday act of performance. Yet, to the doubly liminal subject, this shape shifting process can be seamless since the cultural beliefs, customs, and mindsets of both parent cultures are fully integrated into one identity. That is, she acts as two (or more) self-identified wholes—as opposed to two halves—who maneuver through society as one integrated identity. While mixed-race individuals are able to perform "race," switching effortlessly between one performance to the next, they do so because they encompass both; they have integrated two sets of habiti into their consciousness in varying degrees.[84] In this way, they may participate in acts of "doing race" in their daily performances of self.

This freedom to racially self-identify and express a mixed-race identity in embodied acts elucidates the process of shape shifting. Different than racial passing, ethnically ambiguous mixed-race bodies can slip into many different racial categories, since mixed-race people have the ability to defy preexisting racial codes by easing through the porous boundaries of race. This process is often facilitated by social and historical context, geographical location, the individual's personal genealogical knowledge, and the performance of self and its reception.[85] Personal genealogical knowledge is crucial in this process because it provides mixed-race subjects a particular agency through which to assert control over their own reception. Without knowledge of their personal racial history, multiethnic bodies slip into reified categories of race, leaving their mixed histories inevitably behind. Furthermore, cultural geography plays a key role in the reception of the shape shifter. Racial cartographies provide various cultural expectations that enable the shape shifting process to take place.[86] The ability of the mixed-race body to shape shift across racial lines then becomes contingent on social, historical, and geographical context as well as the reception of the individual in each of these sites.

Crucially, shape shifting differs from passing because passing denotes only one desired racial trajectory. Inherent in the notion of passing is the false assumption that all mixed-race individuals want to be white. Thus, passing reifies the superiority of whiteness and the positionality to which most mixed people aspire, as reinforced by dramas like *The Octoroon*. As the mixed-race playwrights and dramas in this book illustrate, this is not always the case. In reality, the construction of identity yields a much more complicated process, in which social and geographical contexts as well as personal genealogical knowledge inform a mixed-race person's decision to shift from one racial designation to another. Multiracial people shape shift between multiple racial categories, often many times over a single lifetime. This connotes agency in self-expression and identification, whereas passing implies assimilation into an existing, dominant order.

The shape shifting quality of the multiracial figure, whose ambiguous countenance and hapa consciousness enables her to move from one racial group to another, is essential in understanding the racially transgressive nature of double liminality. Monoracial individuals are often confused when they encounter a subject with mixed-race parentage. As Dunning observes, multiracial people "must constantly defend their ethnic heritage and explain their bodies," since their racial ambiguity resists easy categorization.[87] Omi and Winant refer to this occurrence as "a crisis in racial meaning,"[88] in which a mixed-race individual's physical characteristics fail to fit neatly into a prescribed racial category, potentially prompting a monoracial observer to ask, "What are you?" Shape shifting allows the mixed-race individual a certain amount of control over the reception of their racial mutability. Because their phenotypical features are not easily legible, the observer relies on confirmation from the mixed-race subject to complete the assignment of the body to the most superficially correct racial category. Before confirmation takes place, there is a gap, a nebulous temporal space, wherein the observer cannot categorize the observed. For this moment, the observer has a glimpse into the doubly liminal space, a site outside static monoracial categories. In this moment, the observed has escaped the racial framework and exists outside racialization. Furthermore, the mixed-race figure's refusal to respond or offer confirmation about their true multiethnic parentage can bar the observer from completing the process. In this way, the mixed-race figure is able to control how she is racialized within the encounter.

The mixed-race artists and characters discussed in this book actively exercise their ability to shape shift and control these encounters in everyday life. They deploy shape shifting as a tactic in order to navigate the racial limitations of the quotidian. Michel de Certeau characterizes tactics additionally as the "art of making do." These are intentional behaviors or "modalities of action" that take advantage of opportunities as they present themselves. Tactics are used to negotiate the strategies of the dominant.[89] De Certeau differentiates tactics from strategies and defines strategies as calculations, laws, and practices employed by sites of power to regulate the movement of bodies in daily life. For example, de Certeau elucidates the ways in which colonized indigenous peoples used tactics to resist the strategies of the Spanish colonizers. They found ways within the dominant order to subvert the rules without entirely leaving the system.[90] The shape shifting behaviors deployed by multiracial individuals are tactics used to negotiate monoracial cultural logic, which is a strategy employed by the dominant.

This practice of resistance through the use of tactics also disrupts the monoracial logic that governs casting and theater spectatorship. Performance theorist Angela C. Pao defines nontraditional casting as the casting of actors "in roles where race, ethnicity, gender, or physical capability are not necessary to the characters' or the play's development."[91] The use of nontraditional casting can be jarring for audience members, who are surprised by bodies that do not reflect their experiences as viewers. Spectators may experience anxiety if the phenotype of a particular actor prohibits them from affixing certain expectations onto the performer's body or, likewise, if the performer's physiognomy challenges their expectations about the character. Nontraditional casting can intervene in traditional audience spectatorship by hiring ambiguous mixed-race actors to play these kinds of "open" roles to foreground the existence of multiracial subjects and to dislodge racialization in reception. As Pao asserts, "Nontraditional racial casting exposes and destabilizes not just the normativity of all-white casting practices, but more significantly, the normativity of white social and cultural dominance, both of which could be taken for granted until the 1960s."[92] Nontraditional casting also applies to mixed-race characters who are viewed as perhaps more accessible or even more "American" if the actors playing them are part white. This can be seen in the production history of Velina Hasu Houston's play *Kokoro (True Heart)* in chapter 4. Nontraditional casting can be helpful in disrupting audience complacency and can reclaim particular roles from the realm of spectatorial racialization and control, ensuring the representation of all mixed-race people.[93]

Stage Directions: Early Embodiments of Mixed-Race Performance

My purpose in beginning at the turn of the twentieth century is to demonstrate the existence of the mixed-race subject as not merely a contemporary phenomenon but as one who has long occupied a place in American society and, therefore, on American stages. The erasure of mixed-race bodies from drama has produced an unfortunate gap in American popular knowledge. Asians have been present on American soil since as early as 1763,[94] though a large influx of Chinese immigrants began to arrive in the mid-nineteenth century, primarily due to the discovery of gold in California in 1848. Because few of these folks were women and because the Page Act had effectively halted the immigration of Chinese women in 1875, many Chinese men married white—predominantly Irish—brides. These interracial marriages sparked widespread fear among white society about the ensuing racial pollution caused by miscegenation. Resultantly, California expanded its 1850 Anti-miscegenation Law—which prohibited marriage between white people and their Black or Native American partners—to include "Mongolians" in 1880. While this sharply reduced Asian and white interracial marriage in the West, between 1870 and 1910 marriages between Chinese men and white women continued to take place on the East Coast in New York City with more frequency than did unions between Chinese men and women.[95] In 1882, for example, at least seventy Chinese families in New York were composed specifically of Chinese Irish interracial unions.[96] Historian Robert G. Lee asserts that "marriage of Chinese immigrant men to Irish immigrant women, while not significant in a demographic sense, occurred with sufficient frequency to present itself as an imagined threat to working-class whites whose status was precarious and to immigrants whose amalgamation into whiteness was not yet complete."[97] Likewise, Chinese Irish marriages were noticeable enough to gain media attention within the city limits. In 1890, *Harper's Weekly* magazine featured a double-page spread on an interracial couple and their Chinese Irish children.[98] Edith Eaton, who wrote under the pen name Sui Sin Far, further reported on the interracial family life between Chinese fathers, white American mothers, and their mixed-race children in New York as well as in Boston in 1895.[99]

Patsy O'Wang captures the social tension created by these nineteenth-century mixed marriages. The main character, Chin Sum, is half-Chinese and half-Irish. When he drinks tea, he transforms into a subservient, simple-minded Chinese cook. When he drinks whiskey, however, he metamorphoses into Patsy O'Wang, a drunken, belligerent Irishman. Through the monstrous, yet comical, result of such an interracial union, *Patsy O'Wang* documents not only one of the earliest dramatizations of a hapa character but also underscores the public, Coolie-era assumptions that the mixed-race Asian body evoked. Denison's rendering of Patsy foregrounds the popular belief that patterns of behavior were racially inherited and that intermixing created a volatile combination of character flaws. This pathologized treatment of the multiracial figure was common in mixed-race character portrayals penned and imagined by white authors throughout the late nineteenth and early twentieth centuries.[100] As Carole DeSouza asserts, the representation of mixed-race subjects, like the character of Chin Sum/Patsy O'Wang, have not historically been penned by people of multiethnic ancestry.[101]

The life of Japanese German playwright Sadakichi Hartmann offers an astonishing contrast to Denison's mixed-race dramatization. Hartmann (1867–1944), who was also an artist, critic, novelist, performer, and shape shifter, came of age during the fin de siècle movement, which was a period unlike any other in American history. During the Industrial Revolution, Hartmann began writing plays at a time that saw rapid technological change in the West, which, in turn, encouraged global migration. Between the 1880s and 1920s, the West saw the transition from oil and gas lighting to electricity, an accomplishment that also facilitated trans-Atlantic communication and global flows of people, ideas, art, and culture. The continual migration of people contributed to the constant shifting of ideas, as rapid advancements in technology also brought about a multiplicity of identities and upward mobility, especially within arts circles. Hartmann matured as a theater artist in this historical milieu, traveling back and forth from America to Europe multiple times between 1880 and 1920, all while claiming and asserting his Japanese, German, and American identities in the global sanctuary of the fin de siècle. The fact that mixed-race Hartmann, son of a European merchant who traveled across the globe to create a family with a Japanese woman of unknown rank, came of age at this moment in time is perhaps ironic, as it seems to suggest that the era was indeed made by, and perhaps made for, him.

Hartmann's life is provocative because of his sheer range of experiences. His personal history is comingled with the entire cultural, technological, social metamorphosis of the Progressive Era in the late nineteenth and early twentieth centuries. His artistic work and writings, which he kept producing until his death, became one of the cornerstones of American art and photographic criticism. A cross section of his personal history produces experiences and historical memory so broad that it led John Barrymore to sadly dismiss the stories of his life as musings of a drunken old man. Hartmann's life, however, is a sum total of multiple lives lived through multiple identities. This book attempts to shed light on one of those lives, that of a theater maker, which was, in relation to all his others, perhaps his most important personage of all. Significantly, his play *Osadda's Revenge* (1890) dramatized a mixed-race Asian experience, much like Hartmann's own life, as seen at the turn of the century.

Moreover, the mixed-race vaudevillian performers who traversed the globe in the early twentieth century were both a novelty as well a conundrum for global populations. As historian Krystyn Moon recounts, the mixed-Asian bodies who were seen in vaudeville experienced discrimination from white Americans and monoracial Chinese performers because of, as I contend, their doubly liminal ethnic heritages. Their presence on vaudeville stages was a visual reminder of the evils of miscegenation and confirmed white spectators' fears of the threat of Yellow Peril.[102] Performers like George Wong, who was of Chinese and Irish descent, provided physical, bodily evidence of the dilution of the white race. Wong was an acrobat in the troupe the Seven Romas, who had been born in Hoboken, New Jersey. With "light brown hair" and "blue eyes," Wong's shape shifting racial phenotype confused an immigration inspector in Buffalo, New York, in 1915, who noted that, except for Wong's "oblique eyes," his Chinese identity could have gone undetected.[103] At the time, Wong was requesting permission to cross the Canada–U.S. border to perform with the troupe in Toronto. His ability to shape shift troubled the easy categorization implemented by the immigration bureau, which recorded mixed-race Chinese individuals as Chinese and was wary of multiracial figures who attempted to enter the country as "white."[104] Conversely, a Chinese Irish vaudevillian, James Archung, who was born in Salem, Massachusetts, experienced distrust from a fellow monoracial Chinese performer. Archung had a similar parentage to Denison's Patsy O'Wang. His father had immigrated to Salem from Hong Kong and eventually married an Irish woman named Bridget Griffin. In 1912, Archung began singing with the Chung Hwa Comedy Four, one of the first Chinese American vaudeville acts in the United States. The brother of one of the quartet members was Lee Tung Foo, who was a Chinese vaudevillian in his own right. Lee disparaged Archung for being inauthentically Chinese and referred to him as a mulatto.[105] Like the monoracial Asian actor I encountered in 2011, Archung experienced disdain and fear from a monoracial performer who did not see Archung as a "real" Asian.

Perhaps the most striking tale of shape shifting comes from the family history of the vaudevillian Chinese acrobat and magician Long Tack Sam. Long married Austrian Leopoldini Rossler in 1908 after meeting her in Linz while on tour. The couple had three hapa children: daughters Poldi, whose stage name was Nee-Sa; Mina (or Mi-Na); and son Frank, who was nicknamed Bobby. Long incorporated his daughters, who were only a year apart in age, into his traveling revue, billed them as twins, and highlighted their mixed-race heritage to the delight of audiences. Considered "one of the biggest acts in American vaudeville," Nee-Sa and Mi-Na toured and performed with their father and his company all over the world.[106] When they were deemed "too pretty" to appear as monoracial Chinese women in the 1937 film *The Good Earth*, Long denounced Hollywood's stereotypical Asian portrayals and asserted that his daughters would only appear live onstage. Perhaps experience had affirmed that the generative space of theater was elastic enough to allow for their mixed-race identities in a way that film, especially under code restrictions, was not. Bobby was born fourteen years after Nee-Sa in 1924 and was often left with his maternal grandparents in Europe while the family was on tour. In a staggering example of shape shifting, Bobby's mixed-race heritage slipped under the nose of Adolph Hitler when the Führer toured an Austrian boys' school in Linz, the desired future site of the Third Reich. Posing for a picture with an all-boys class in idyllic Austria, Bobby can be seen standing just above Hitler's right shoulder.[107]

Throughout the 1940s–1960s in America, multiethnic performers appearing onstage also shape shifted in plain sight. Mixed-race Asian performer Tony Wing, who had been born Gonzalo Anthony Lagrimas, began performing in Charlie Low's "all-star Chinese revue" at the Forbidden City nightclub in San Francisco after World War II. Wing, who was of Portuguese, Spanish, Filipino, and Chinese descent, had been singing and dancing using the surname Costa, his mother's maiden name. He described his hapa identity as "chop suey," explaining, "They used to ask … what nationality are you? I said, "Oh, I'm chop suey." And they go, "What do you mean chop suey?" This is well, you know, the dish is a mixture of everything. I said, "I'm Portuguese, Spanish, Filipino, and Chinese," and that was it: chop suey."[108] Ever the entrepreneur, Low suggested that Costa change his last name to Wing to fit spectators' expectations of a monoracially "all-Chinese" lineup. Wing's success as a monoracial Chinese performer demonstrated his ability to effectively shape shift onstage, and he continued to perform as Wing at Forbidden City into the 1960s.[109]

White cultural dominance persisted in mainstream theater, however, until the emergence of the national Black Freedom Movement of the 1950s and 1960s, which created opportunities for other communities to mobilize in multiple disciplines, including the arts.[110] Specifically, the student protests during the five-month strike at San Francisco State University in 1968 ignited the Asian American Movement in 1969.[111] In theater, as Angela C. Pao asserts, "Racially mixed companies and productions became instances of the integration of the workplace, schools, and residential neighborhoods that was being legislated and celebrated on one side and often very violently opposed on the other."[112] The first play written by an Asian American to be professionally produced in New York exemplifies the theater born from these movements. Frank Chin, considered to be the grandfather of the first wave, or first generation, of Asian American playwrights, wrote *The Chickencoop Chinaman* in 1971.[113] The play, which premiered in New York at the American Place Theatre in 1972, relentlessly confronts the hegemonic emasculation of the Asian male in popular discourse and features the inclusion of a hapa character named Lee, whose future pregnancy by main character Kenji could potentially redeem her diluted Chinese blood.[114] The following year Chin established the Asian American Theater Company (AATC), one of the earliest Asian American theater companies in the United States.[115] AATC, which began as a playwrighting workshop that grew into a professional company in San Francisco by 1975, resolved to support and develop the talent of Asian American theater practitioners, focusing on the work of its dramatists. Consequently, AATC was the hub of the Asian American theatrical community in northern California in the late 1970s and early 1980s and also supported the work of hapa artists who shape shifted into monoracial Asianness, such as actor Amy Hill and playwright Velina Hasu Houston.

Staging Presence: Mixed-Race Drama in America

The following chapters explore mixed-race performance as envisioned or witnessed in character portrayals in American plays from the late nineteenth century through the early twenty-first century. My analysis of this work explores if, how, and to what extent the dramatic depiction and, in some cases, the performances of these roles, illuminates the racialized experience of doubly liminality and the shape shifting abilities specific to mixed-race persons.

Given the liminal fluidity of this positionality, I focus on the ways in which these characters and, by extension, the playwrights who breathed life into them, contest the fixity of racial classifications reinforced by the dominant and subdominant discourses. These playwrights and their characters detect perforations within the racial scaffolding and create opportunities to capitalize on this slippage. The playwrights also demonstrate how these characters use shape shifting tactics to enact performances of racial transgression and to subvert the systemic strategies that hold monoraciality in place. To what extent do these representations illuminate the calculated negotiations that multiracial people perform on a daily basis? How do mixed-race characters stage ruptures in the current racial hierarchy? How do they resist social expectations about what it means to be mixed without reinforcing the racial codes through a simultaneous assertion of monoracial group membership? How can these performances and characters be identified as mixed-race, when, by the very nature of being multiethnic and doubly liminal, they seem to resist a single, mixed-race group identity? If the contested identity of Asian American is already multiple and hybrid, how does a mixed-Asian identity differ?

The racialized term *Asian* is already fraught as a racial marker that cannot hold the multiple ethnic groups and cultures as well as the generational and linguistic differences it supposedly contains. How then can a mixed-race Asian portrayal be a valid representation worthy of scholarly discussion or analysis? I consider the marginalization that connects multiracial Asians together first as members of an Asian American racialized group, and then specifically how mixedness alters the identity construction and the reception of the diversity within this doubly liminal group. I consider the threads that connect these plays and their mixed characters, including the disparate ethnicities and issues dramatized within each of these depictions.

Specifically, I am interested in three conditions of mixed-race subjectivity and the performance of mixed-race embodiment: the state of being doubly liminal, the ability to shape shift or slip through predetermined racial codes, and the ways in which shape shifting catalyzes a transgressive performativity, which opens up other possibilities of being rather than signifying social betrayal or racial imposture. In light of this, the following chapters trace the relationship between the sociohistorical circumstances and variant ethnic backgrounds that inform how mixed-race figures utilize shape shifting practices in response to their particular contexts. As the case studies in chapters 2 and 3 are situated in the 1890s and early 1900s, respectively, I conduct a semiotic analysis of scripts, photographs, letters, diary entries, reviews, press releases, programs, and other primary sources to ascertain the playwrights' intentions and motivation for creating the work and to glean the possible effect these performances had in social and political arenas. I also rely on secondary sources where appropriate and consider how other historians and performance scholars have interpreted this archival evidence. In chapter 2, I demonstrate the use of shape shifting as a de Certeauian tactic for navigating the U.S. racial hierarchy by examining the life of multiethnic playwright Sadakichi Hartmann and mixed-race characters in the 1890s. My own exploration of the papers of Sadakichi Hartmann is intended to extend this scholarship and, through the understanding of hapa subjectivity, offer a more robust understanding of the intent behind the playwright's work—one that centers and illuminates the calculated agency employed by the playwright who was working within a nineteenth-century racial paradigm. In the case of T. S. Denison's short play *Patsy O'Wang*, I consider the history of the wave of Chinese Irish intermarriage in the 1870s and the Chinese Exclusion Act of 1882 alongside the emergence of the Irish American community as a politically powerful force in white America. The one-act play foregrounds the cultural anxiety surrounding the mixed-race Chinese Irish character Chin Sum and the way he fully shape shifts into an Irish politician by the play's end, much to the chagrin of his many contemporaries.

The plays and performances discussed in chapter 3 focus on the work of mixed-race English Chinese, Canadian American author, playwright, and screenwriter Winnifred Eaton—whose characters appear on Broadway as early as 1903 and in cinema during the transition from silent film to sound—as well as on other mixed-race women who shape shifted midcentury into monoracial Asianness. In this chapter, I elucidate the shape shifting tactics employed by the racially transgressive Eaton and expand on the double liminality of the mixed-race feminine subject, who may not only feel shunned by both dominant and subdominant discourses but on whose body gender normativity and the violent expectations of race land differently. Eaton, like Hartmann, enacted shape shifting performances in her personal life and wrote on a multitude of perspectives that reflected her own mixed-race sensibilities. Sharply criticized by monoracial Asian American scholars for reifying Orientalized tropes and "selling out," the scholarship has been blind to the ways in which Eaton reframed the representation of Asian American women through the lens of the mixed-race figure of the feminine. In this chapter, I also employ semiotic analysis to examine primary sources, such as photographs, press releases, reviews, original manuscripts, and programs, coupled with secondary source scholarship, to elucidate how Eaton centered the racially transgressive, mixed-Asian experience and performance of self in her work. This analysis includes an examination of the 1903 playscript *A Japanese Nightingale*, previously believed by some scholars to be lost.

Chapter 4 chronicles the ways that mixed-Japanese and African American playwright Velina Hasu Houston captured the expansion of the mixed-race movement onstage in the 1980s and 1990s and considers select works of Houston's—*Thirst* and *Kokoro (True Heart)*—paying particular attention to how her portrayals of mixed-race characters reflect the political periods in which they were written. Houston accomplishes this by constructing dramas that display a hapa sensibility in their theatrical forms. By mixing familiar narratives from classical Western or Japanese drama, Houston is able to craft plays with dramatic structures and aesthetics that mirror a hapa cultural consciousness.

This chapter also references an archive of photographs, press releases, reviews, directors' notes, correspondence, original play manuscripts, and filmed footage, combined with ethnographic interviews, to illuminate how the scripts evolved in response to the growing awareness of the mixed-race subject in the late twentieth century. These primary sources also illustrate naturalized concepts embedded in contemporary racialized language, such as the term *American* as being synonymous with whiteness. This is revealed both in the confusion of the characters and in the casting of the performers in Houston's roles. Finally, this chapter examines the ways in which Houston's work galvanizes our understanding of double liminality. Like Hartmann and Eaton so many decades earlier, Houston engages in drama as a tactic to navigate the racialized body politic. For Houston, the theater provides an interstitial space where all expressions of multiraciality are possible. While Hartmann and Easton use performance as a vehicle for shape shifting in their daily lives, in Houston's theater, the plays also become shape shifters.

Chapter 5 focuses on the radically transgressive plays of the emerging fifth wave of Asian American mixed-race playwrights as a means to gauge the zeitgeist of mixed-race accessibility in American theater in the new millennium. These playwrights do not focus on the imperialism that creates the mixed-race body, the mixed body as monstrous, nor a need to be understood or validated by society. They do not pen identity plays, but begin from a naturalized, hapa identity, where mixedness is taken for granted. The plays of Christopher Chen and Frances Ya-Chu Cowhig fiercely challenge the political and legal frameworks that maintain a social hierarchy, which will only grant personhood on its own terms. These dramatizations reject the transcendent seduction of colorblindness and critique the West's appropriation of shape shifting practices as a means to reify the racial status quo. In this chapter, I combine semiotic analysis with ethnographic methods, utilized in a short-term study of the 2016 Midwest premiere of Chen's play *Mutt*, to analyze how the political climate has shaped the evolution of hapa subjectivity into the twenty-first century. Using Ric Knowles's triangular framework, which examines how the performance text, the conditions of production, and the conditions of reception equally and reflexively work together to produce meaning, this chapter demonstrates how the prismatic perspective in Chen's writing interrogates the racial status quo and current race relations.[116] Concretely, Chen lays bare a racialized landscape in the supposedly post-race era that foreshadowed the political unrest of 2020 and provided fertile ground for the overt racism of the Trump era. Chen additionally questions and dismantles the messianic "Face of the Future" imaginary, which delivered no relief at all. Building on Brandi Wilkins Catanese's performance theory of racial transgression and pairing Spickard's racial theory of shape shifting with Joshua Chambers-Letson's keen observation that the legal creation of personhood occurs through the performance of race (specifically monoraciality), I consider how Christopher Chen's *Mutt* and Frances Cowhig's *Lidless* demonstrate the ways in which the fluidity of mixed-race identity becomes co-opted and erased by polarizing monoracial cultural logic. Together, this critical analysis exposes the disconnect between imposed monoraciality and the reality of the mixed-race subject as a liminal outsider, encumbered by an American cultural dependence on prescribed racial codes and the naturalization of hypodescent.

These chapters and the theoretical analysis of their respective plays and reception significantly expand critical mixed race and Asian American scholarship in theater and performance studies. Mixed-race subjectivity, formed in response to and outside the dominant and subdominant discourses, elucidates a process of identity construction unique to the mixed-race experience. This process can be traced through theatrical texts and performances not only in dramas that expose the beliefs of the dominant and subdominant but also in the ways this critical sampling of contemporary mixed-race plays actively calls these discourses into question. The hapa playwrights of this work bequeath their own doubly liminal subjectivities to their fictional characters and continue to speak to each other on either side of the twentieth century.

2

Tragic Eurasians

· ·

Mixed-Asian Dramas in the
Late Nineteenth Century

The confession scene begins with a knife. In the 1890 unpublished play, *Osadda's Revenge*, the mixed-race Japanese protagonist, Hidetada, reveals a dagger hidden beneath his clothing.[1] He discloses to his lover, Clarissa, his plans to find and murder his white father to avenge his mother's death. Hidetada is later confronted by Clarissa, whom he discovers is his half-sister. Distraught over their forbidden love, she is desperate to save their father from her brother's deep-seated vengeance. For almost a century, this symbolist melodrama by Japanese German playwright Sadakichi Hartmann lay in obscurity. After it was first produced in 1890, Hartmann himself lost the manuscript and recovered it again fifteen years later; thereafter it remained among his papers. Until the twenty-first century, some scholars believed that the play had actually never been produced, but descriptions of the 1890 production reveal that not only was *Osadda's Revenge* Hartmann's debut as a playwright but Hartmann himself performed the role of the half-Japanese protagonist out for revenge.[2]

The character Hidetada in *Osadda's Revenge* could easily be interpreted as a reinforcement of the tragic Eurasian trope, where the pathological "half-breed" character engages in deviant criminality, in this case in premeditated murder and an incestuous relationship with his sister. However, a closer look reveals multiple interpretative threads in the dramatic narrative, including the use of shape shifting as a tactic to manage the limitations of racial hierarchy as well as a reconsideration of mixed-race identity, an experience that existed among communities of color in the nineteenth century rather than as a solely contemporary phenomenon. The existence of *Osadda's Revenge* stands as a testament to the visibility of Asian multiracial people onstage in the United States at the fin de siècle. This is significant because other theatrical narratives, such as the seminal *Madame Butterfly* (1900), have dramatized the mixed-race subject—a child named Trouble—as an object rendered invisible.[3]

Furthermore, the Orientalist narrative of *Madame Butterfly* has dominated the performance opportunities of Asians and Asian Americans in the West throughout the twentieth and twenty-first centuries. It is perhaps ironic that *Osadda's Revenge* has languished in obscurity, since the play itself dismantles the romanticization of "East meets West" in *Madame Butterfly*. Never in the Orientalist drama or any of its other iterations, including David Henry Hwang's play *M. Butterfly* (1986) and the musical *Miss Saigon* (1989), does the mixed-race child of the interracial union speak.[4] The hapa child has remained silenced by those who would write about her, monoracial voices with particular political agendas. This has been the erasure of the mixed-race Asian voice in theater.[5]

Few studies have surveyed mixed-Asian characters in nineteenth-century drama. Theater scholar Joyce Flynn has examined multiraciality in the depiction of mixed-race Black characters in narratives such as *Uncle Tom's Cabin* (1858), *The Escape* (1858), and *The Octoroon* (1859).[6] While Flynn briefly mentions the play *Patsy O'Wang: An Irish Farce with a Chinese Mix-Up* (1895), she does not include multiracial Asian roles in her survey but focuses primarily on period narratives that explore Black and white hybridity, American Indian mixed-blood, and Jewish assimilation. What then of the mixed-race Asian figures? Does theater also serve as an archive for the mixed-Asian experience in the nineteenth century?

The plays discussed in this chapter illuminate exactly this. These competing discourses dramatize the existence of the mixed-race hapa figure in nineteenth-century society and highlight the ways in which multiracials employ various tactics to "make do" and capitalize on the racialized circumstances in which they are presented. Sadakichi Hartmann, arguably America's first hapa playwright, wrote about the mixed-Asian experience in *Osadda's Revenge* ten years before the multiethnic child in *Madame Butterfly* appeared on American stages in 1900, five years before T. S. Denison penned the aforementioned yellowface comedy, *Patsy O'Wang*, and six years before Winnifred Eaton's hapa characters began appearing in newspapers in 1896.[7] As a mixed-race figure, Sadakichi Hartmann moved through many different identities and contexts in nineteenth-century America. Throughout his lifetime, he adopted different personae and wrote under a myriad of pen names, and, though culturally German, performed his Japaneseness in elite, social circles that were accessible to him because of his mixed-Asian identity.[8]

Hartmann's ability to permeate different social contexts elucidates his use of shape shifting as a tactic in order to navigate the racialized landscape of daily life. Historian Paul Spickard defines shape shifting as the mixed-race person's ability to embody different racial identities. While racial expectation assumes that a perceived phenotype ensures an assignment to the most superficially correct racial category, ethnically ambiguous mixed-race bodies can also shape shift and slip into many different racial designations. This process is influenced by sociohistorical contexts, geographical location, known family history, and the performance of self and its reception.[9] I argue that shape shifting behavior is what Michel de Certeau has defined as a tactic. Mixed-race figures employ tactics to navigate the racial limitations imposed by society. De Certeau differentiates these tactics from strategies. While he defines strategies as calculations employed by sites of power to regulate the movement of the quotidian, he characterizes tactics as the "art of making do," noting that a tactic is an intentional action that takes advantage of opportunities as they present themselves.[10] Elizabeth Bell notes how de Certeau's tactics are "especially important to explain the making do of marginalized groups and peoples."[11] Rebecca Schneider further concludes that in the banal detail of the tactic, we can interrupt the "agendas of the monumental."[12] In his life and in the play *Osadda's Revenge*, Hartmann demonstrates how he capitalizes on his ambiguous racial phenotype and "makes do," using the opportunities that materialize to his advantage. Rather than simply passing, a maneuver that articulates a singular movement from a subjugated category of color into whiteness, Hartmann shape shifts and moves ambiguously between multiple racial identities. To extend de Certeau's observations, I suggest that Hartmann's use of shape shifting as a tactic in his writing and in his performance of self follows Bell's notion of tactics that embody a creative resistance to dominant structures by marginalized individuals and dispels, as Schneider astutely asserts, "the myth of the monumental," or the larger, hegemonic grand narrative, to which racial passing ultimately subscribes.[13]

Hartmann contended with a fraught association with his status as mixed-race. His experiences and his circumstances as a multiethnic shape shifter shed a special luminosity on the period in which he lived, in which mixed blood was often viewed as producing an impure biology and a wayward mind. One famous example is Edward L. Price's melodrama *In the Tenderloin* (1894), which capitalized on the criminality of the infamous half-Chinese, half-Irish thief, George Appo. In the 1894 New York production, Appo appeared onstage as himself in a narrative partly based on his real-life experience as a pickpocket and an informant for the Lexow Committee, a New York State Senate–empaneled commission investigating police corruption in New York's Tenderloin district.[14] While Appo's mixed-race body onstage no doubt afforded him an opportunity to wrest a certain amount of spectatorial control from a stereotypical portrayal,[15] his performance within a theatrical framework controlled by white theater makers reenacted representations of otherness and reinforced society's belief in the mental degeneracy and immoral behavior of the pathological half-breed.[16] Hartmann's play *Osadda's Revenge* intervenes in theatrical spaces where the depictions of mixedness have been manipulated by monoracial playwrights. In many ways, the work parallels contemporary performances in which mixed-race dramatists and performers also disrupt the co-opted multiracial representations evident in twentieth-century theater.

The perilous association of mixed race as an unstable, biological state is particularly evident in the 1895 farce, *Patsy O'Wang*, by European American playwright Thomas Stewart Denison. In Denison's yellowface comedy, the mixed Chinese and Irish character Patsy O'Wang transforms from a docile Chinese cook to an ambitious, self-righteous Irishman. The metamorphosis dramatizes the supposed hyperbolic instability of the tragic half-breed and exposes the anxiety surrounding the miscegenation of immigrant populations in the United States, especially between peoples of Irish, African, and Asian descent, who were thought of as co-conspirators and capable of corrupting the national values of honesty, ingenuity, and moderation, among others.[17] Denison's play specifically underscores the prevalence of multiracial Asians in nineteenth-century America, many of whom were the children of Irish and Chinese interracial relationships.[18] Not only does *Patsy O'Wang* display the social confusion over these undesirable offspring, it also foregrounds an Orientalist attitude toward Chinese immigrants and dramatizes the Irish transformation from poor, working-class laborers into a free, middle-class white demographic with political power.[19] The play is particularly compelling because the character Patsy tactically uses his unusual shape shifting ability to physically transform from one race to another, enabling him to embrace a white persona and reject his Asian identity. As Denison seems to assert, whiteness is the preferred racial state in Patsy's nineteenth-century world. For Sadakichi Hartmann, it is not.

Hartmann's play *Osadda's Revenge* creates a powerful rupture in the nineteenth-century discourse perpetuated by white authors of dramas like *In the Tenderloin* and *Patsy O'Wang*, who depict mixed-race subjects as objects or half-caste creatures.[20] Like Hartmann, the multiethnic protagonist, Hidetada, experiences an agency that had not been previously seen on American stages. Hartmann's thoughts and approaches for engaging with a society that, at times, both accepted and shunned him feels relatively contemporary and closely resembles the same thought processes and challenges undertaken by hapa subjects in the late twentieth and twenty-first centuries. This is significant, as it indicates that the mixed-race experience is not just a modern-day phenomenon. Hartmann's work reveals an alternative way of being in monoracial spaces and an ability to navigate the normative narratives that persistently demonized mixed-race bodies and certain ethnic groups. In Hartmann's own voice, in both personal essays and theatrical texts, he writes about an experience where his ethnic backgrounds both arm him with an extraordinary agency and prevent him from being fully accepted in society. In the unpublished play, *Osadda's Revenge*, actor and playwright Hartmann uses theater to also "make do." He writes not from the margins, but from his own center as a mixed-race subject actively participating in a society where his mixedness garners a variety of reactions from the community at large. The voice of his multiethnic character Hidetada reflects Hartmann's keen understanding of mixed-race subjectivity.

The two dramatic texts analyzed in this chapter, *Osadda's Revenge* and *Patsy O'Wang*, illustrate a striking contrast between the different discourses around mixed-race Asians at the fin de siècle. Though not strictly comparable, these competing representations of mixed-Asian subjectivity aver the polyvalent landscape of hapa portrayals in nineteenth-century theater and of hapa populations in America. Both protagonists are multiracial with different Asian ethnic backgrounds—Chinese and Japanese—that are inscribed with different histories of oppression. That is, these two figures are doubly liminal not only from the respective cultural groups of their parentage but also from each other. The reception of the mixed-Chinese individual is different from that of the mixed-Japanese subject. Furthermore, this is amplified by disparate ethnic European backgrounds where Irish, English, and German people experienced the complexity of whiteness in different ways. For the Irish in the early to mid-nineteenth century, the category of whiteness and their respective claims to it were still evolving. Denison's play emphasizes the transformation of the Irish from poor agrarian immigrants into a white, politically powerful Irish American class, while in Hartmann's play the mixed-race Japanese Hidetada moves through elite cultural circles with ease. These disparate representations reveal contrasting mixed-race experiences, which disrupt the conflation of mixed-race Asians seen in American popular culture in the early twentieth century. These depictions sparked an early public dialogue on miscegenation and racial mixing vis-à-vis performance.

The Art of Being in Between

Jolie A. Sheffer's analysis of late nineteenth- and early twentieth-century mixed-race fiction reveals a multiethnic America in which race mixing and miscegenation were much more prevalent than contemporary discourse suggests. I focus specifically on Sheffer's consideration of the "multiracial nation-family" trope as explored in mixed-race writer Winnifred Eaton's short stories.[21] Per Sheffer, the fictional aesthetics of multiraciality began decades before the advent of the civil rights movement of the 1950s–1960s. Sheffer contends that despite a persistent rhetoric of nativism, mixed-race narratives elucidate a "model of a nation as always already multiracial and multicultural."[22] According to Sheffer, the roots of this idea can be found in the mixed-race romances popular at the end of the nineteenth century and into the twentieth century, like those written by Eaton.[23] Of Chinese and English descent, Eaton published under the pseudo-Japanese pen name Onoto Watanna. As Watanna, she is well-known for her collections of short stories and romance novels, which often depicted the mixed-race experience at the turn of the century.[24]

Multiracial romances like Eaton's work dramatize mixed-race characters who, trapped in liminal space, grapple with finding their place in white society. As

Sheffer contends, this need for acceptance and belonging is realized in the romantic relationships.[25] The play *Osadda's Revenge* similarly functions as a multiracial romance. The play employs a melodramatic twist that indulges in forbidden interracial and incestuous desires. Hidetada's lust for his sister provides him with an unlikely tactic that recognizes him as an undeniable member of his family of origin. His sister's full-fledged acceptance of Hidetada as her brother validates him as an equal and reinstates the privileges he lost when his father abandoned him. In the play, we also see Hartmann's early explorations with symbolism, which dominate his later dramas and position him as a significant contributor to the genre in theater. Through his craft, the doubly liminal Hartmann utilizes various tactics—his European theater training and the themes of his dramatic narratives—both to establish himself in white society and to differentiate himself in the landscape of American drama.

In *Patsy O'Wang*, the main character Patsy also employs tactical shape shifting to obtain equality, not in the dramatization of a multiracial romance but in an assertion of white dominance in the evolving political and legal landscapes of the nineteenth century. The play reveals the ethnic stereotypes associated with immigrant populations, like the Chinese and Irish, and the cultural misgivings over race mixing, especially between the two ethnic groups. As Robert Lee contends, Chinese Irish miscegenation "occurred with enough frequency to present itself as an imagined threat to working class whites."[26] Like Hartmann's protagonist, Hidetada, Patsy O'Wang also expresses his desire to belong, as he asserts his whiteness and stereotypically consumes whiskey as a tactic to permanently solidify his white Irish identity.

The performances of mixed race in Sadakichi Hartmann and T. S. Denison's plays offer us contrasting ways to witness the encounters between differently raced bodies onstage. The embodied presence of the multiracial body and the stark contrast between a white actor in yellowface in *Patsy O'Wang* and an actual mixed-Asian body in *Osadda's Revenge* offers us a cogent way to examine mixed race in the nineteenth century. Through these depictions and their performances, we can observe how the contemporary acceptance of hapa identity in the late twentieth and early twenty-first centuries has its roots in the multiracial society present in the late 1800s and the anxiety this mixedness aroused in white America. Hartmann's Hidetada strives for racial equality in the multiethnic landscape of America, while the yellowface character, Patsy O'Wang, under the positionality of a white playwright and a white performer, seeks to liberate whiteness from his mixed-race body.

Half-Butterfly, Half-Caste: Sadakichi Hartmann and the Mixed-Japanese Drama, *Osadda's Revenge*

Sadakichi Hartmann's life (1867–1944) illustrates the shape shifting tactics he employed to navigate normative social structures in nineteenth-century America. By 1905, for instance, he had published under the names Sidney Allan,

A. Chameleon, Caliban, and Chrysanthemum, among half a dozen others. He aligned himself with luminaries, penetrating their social circles while occupying different professions. He was Walt Whitman's secretary and Alfred Stieglitz's lifelong friend. He corresponded regularly with Ezra Pound and Stéphane Mallarmé. He appeared as the Court Magician in Douglas Fairbanks's 1924 silent film *The Thief of Bagdad* and was frequently found drunk with John Barrymore in John Decker's studio in Los Angeles. Hartmann is most famously known as an art critic and a pioneer in the burgeoning field of photography at the beginning of the twentieth century. Historian Jane Calhoun Weaver has noted that "American art and photography in the United States simply could not have become what they are today without his remarkable presence."[27] The prolific Hartmann was also a poet, a novelist, a journalist, and a short story author. When the desire to produce work in all these other genres left him, he inevitably returned to his lifelong passion. His first love was theater.[28] He continued through the end of his life to write plays and perform in staged readings of his own work and those of beloved authors, such as Henrik Ibsen and Edgar Allan Poe, whose middle name he adopted for one of his personae, Sidney Allan.[29] As English scholar Linda Trinh Moser notes, "Of all his creative efforts, Hartmann seemed most interested in drama."[30] As a dramatist, Hartmann is most well-known for his realist play, *A Tragedy in a New York Flat* (1896), and five symbolist plays about religious figures: *Christ* (1893), *Buddha* (1897), *Mohammed* (1899), *Confucius* (1923), and *Moses* (1934). A careful consideration of his papers at the University of California, Riverside, Special Collections, however, reveals the manuscripts of seventeen other plays and the outline for an eighteenth. This does not include the plays Hartmann recounts writing in his early years in Boston, the manuscripts of which appear to be lost to history.[31]

In this chapter, I focus my analysis on Hartmann's mixed-Asian character, Hidetada, in the play, *Osadda's Revenge*. Asian American performance scholar Esther Kim Lee has suggested that Hartmann is perhaps the first Asian American playwright, noting that while "his plays do not address Asian American issues, they are rare symbolist plays with intercultural themes."[32] However, perhaps due to the vast volumes of literary work produced by Hartmann, very little attention has been paid to his life as a theater artist, much less to his work as an Asian American dramatist. Yet his love of theater quietly, persistently dominates the literature on Hartmann's life, his accomplishments, his dark, troubled moments, and his very own words. Hartmann is, I argue, America's first mixed-race hapa playwright, writing about mixed-race Asians in America as early as 1890. In Hartmann's plays *Osadda's Revenge* (1890) and *Boston Lions* (1890–1896), he explores Asian American identity through mixed-race hapa characters, who are based on his own experiences.[33]

Hartmann's obscurity as a playwright, however, was not a fact lost on him. He lamented his own lack of success as a theater maker and a dramatist. As he dolefully writes in his unpublished essay, "Aspirations of a Playwright,"

The trouble is that a playwright cannot work independently, he has to write a play specially for a specific purpose, for an actress or actor, cater to the box office and the fads of the time. So what's the use.

My real ambition in the dramatic line was so remote from ordinary facts and conditions. If a man writes *Christ* he should not meddle with writing a popular play. So I am really glad that all my attempts are buried in oblivion, and aside from my religious dramas none remain but my *Boston Lions* and *Tragedy in a New York Flat.*[34]

Hartmann may have believed he was a failure as a dramatist, but his early plays stand firmly in the confluence of melodrama, naturalism, and symbolism in theater. His later works, such as *Christ* and *Buddha*, reveal a theater artist who developed and expanded the symbolist movement. The symbolists were not interested in an accurate depiction of the natural world, which they considered to be an illusion. Instead, they sought to uncover obscured, deep-seated truths, which they believed were revealed onstage through symbols and accessed through the senses.[35] Furthermore, what Hartmann's plays reveal about the representation of multiracial subjectivity continues to resonate with us today. It is his plays alone that exist as a theatrical archive for mixed-Asian subjectivity in the late 1800s. The actions and choices of both Hartmann and characters like Hidetada demonstrate the ways in which mixed people have sought to navigate and interrogate monoraciality since the nineteenth century.

The circumstances surrounding Hartmann's birth and childhood informed his choices to use shape shifting as a tactic to traverse the social strategies or systems in place in the nineteenth-century world. The child of a German father and a Japanese mother, Carl Sadakichi Hartmann was born on the island of Dejima in Nagasaki Harbor around 1867.[36] Dejima was a manmade islet well-known for having first housed the interracial, multiethnic families of Portuguese traders and Japanese women and their mixed-race children in 1636.[37] The island was solely designated as a Dutch trading post in 1641 during Japan's period of isolationism before Commodore Matthew Perry successfully "opened" Japan to foreign trade in 1854. This pivotal moment quickly innervated the industrialization of Japan and spread Japanese cultural products to the West. Hartmann's father was among the many German merchants who continued to dock at Dejima during the advent of the Meji restoration in 1868. Carl Hermann Oskar Hartmann was a multilingual German official from Hamburg, a city crucial to Germany's overseas economic prosperity.[38] Hartmann's mother was known only as Osada, and her class and her status in society are not entirely known. Historians disagree over whether she was of the servant or merchant class and even whether she was Carl Hartmann's mistress or wife. Osada died when Hartmann was less than one year old.[39] He and his older brother, Hidetaru Oskar, were taken back to Hamburg to be raised by their paternal grandmother and their uncle, Ernst. There Hartmann was baptized Lutheran and raised in considerable wealth. Known in his youth as Carl, he was well-educated and credited his uncle for instilling in him a lifelong interest in the arts, of which theater was an early interest. Sadakichi Hartmann, however, would reinvent the personae of his parents many times over the course of his entire life. He was especially consumed with the vision of his unknown mother and the circumstances of the early death that robbed him of her guidance and care.[40]

Racial bias was a constant in Hartmann's life. Culturally, he was German. In fact, there is little evidence that he interacted with the Japanese community in Europe or in the United States.[41] Phenotypically Asian, however, Hartmann was not fully accepted as a member of German society. Hartmann recounted that his father had been "hauled over the coals socially for having indulged in a liaison with a woman of another race," and consequently, the "mention of Japan was somewhat taboo in [his] household."[42] In his youth, despite his luxurious upbringing, Hartmann was shunned by his peers for being Japanese.[43] Of mixed marriage or "intercopulation," Hartmann remarked that though it was one of the "best character molders . . . I do not particularly recommend it from personal experience or the adventures of my children."[44] Not accepted as entirely German and unable to fully embrace a Japanese identity or parentage, Hartmann often referred to himself later in life as the son of Madame Butterfly, "an innocent haunted by a tragedy he could not set right."[45] This is significant, as Hartmann often identified with the narrative, even though he was born thirty years before John Luther Long's short story "Madame Butterfly" (1898) was published.

His father's marriage set the stage for *Osadda's Revenge*. In 1873, his father married Helena Mayer, a widow with two daughters, who inevitably wanted nothing to do with her adopted "half-breed" sons. In his thirteenth year, Hartmann was sent to a preparatory naval school, though he ran away from it because he "hated everything like discipline."[46] Resultantly, Hartmann was disinherited (after being recovered) and sent to live with a great-uncle and great-aunt in Philadelphia.[47] He arrived in America with three dollars in his pocket on a hot summer day in June 1882.[48] As a result of his banishment, his stepmother was able to secure an inheritance solely for her own daughters, Elsa and Rosa.[49] Hartmann later compared his stepmother to the character Laura in August Strindberg's play *The Father*, musing, "She was willing to wait as long as she was sure to conquer eventually." His uncle's entire fortune ultimately went to Mayer's daughters.[50]

The acting profession intrigued Hartmann, who perhaps came to view it as an extension of the shape shifting he employed in his everyday life. Perhaps he recognized the power of his racially ambiguous body early in his days in America as a German adolescent who was often mistaken as being from South America.[51] While in Philadelphia, he took a series of odd jobs and voraciously continued his education at public libraries and secondhand bookstores. He read on a variety of topics and, though he focused mainly on the fine arts, he recollected that his "greatest urge was for the stage."[52] He took voice lessons to prepare for an acting career and spent precious funds on theater tickets. His favorite playwright was the controversial Norwegian naturalistic writer, Henrik Ibsen, whom Hartmann considered to be "the greatest dramatist of modern times."[53] Hartmann was astounded that Ibsen was still virtually unknown in the United States when he first arrived, which also sparked his interest in directing and producing.[54] He eventually left his guardians in Philadelphia and moved to Boston.

Japan's "opening" to the West in 1854 enabled the global spread of Japanese cultural products and aesthetics, and the Japanese success in the Sino-Japanese War (1894–1895) further spurred a widespread curiosity about Japanese culture in Western contexts.[55] In the United States, the Japanese were embraced as far more appealing and exotic than the sinister and menacing Chinese, whose imagined threat was galvanized by a growing immigrant population. Progressive Era America was eager to consume Japanese culture, purchase Orientalized Japanese goods, and participate in Japanese customs like tea ceremony, however superficially. In the late nineteenth century, a cult of Japonisme seemed to provide the social and geographical context necessary for Hartmann to successfully shape shift into a Japanese persona as an adult.

Hartmann capitalized on America's Japanese enthusiasm and used his racial ambiguity to his advantage. He tactically engaged in shape shifting to create opportunities he might not otherwise have had. For instance, in 1884, Hartmann knocked on the door of American poet Walt Whitman in Camden, New Jersey, at the suggestion of a friend who disclosed where the writer lived. Hartmann was then just sixteen years old. When the poet opened the door, Hartmann simply said, "I would like to see Walt Whitman" to which Whitman responded, "And you are a Japanese boy are you not?" Hartmann explained his ethnic background, replying, "My father is German, but my mother was Japanese, and I was born in Japan."[56] He would later remark that Whitman was "the only person who recognized my nationality at first glance."[57] Hartmann was, of course, thoroughly German. He had a German accent, and though his phenotypic characteristics marked him as an Asian, he had no cultural connection to Japan. Though he and Whitman talked about Japan and "the beautiful bay of Nagasaki," Hartmann later remarked, "I did not know much about it from personal recollection."[58] While people saw Hartmann as authentically Japanese, and no doubt he was by birth, they read his visage as exotic rather than as simply European. This demonstrated white society's reliance on hypodescent and its tendency to see race as synonymous with culture and nationality. Hartmann was well aware of this social bias, for he admitted, "I had pliable material to work with and used it to the best advantage."[59] Hartmann's words elucidate his positionality in a doubly liminal state and his overt decision to deploy his abilities to shape shift.

Whitman, though intrigued by Hartmann, also expressed confusion over his racial background and his desire to pursue a career in performance. During their first meeting, they spoke not of poetry but of theater. Hartmann introduced

Whitman to the work of Ibsen. They spoke earnestly about Shakespeare's fools, and Hartmann asserted that he was "too tall" to play any of them, though he was committed to developing an acting career. Whitman discouraged Hartmann from pursuing this passion, citing Hartmann's mixedness as a deterrent to his possible success: "I fear that won't go. There are so many traits, characteristics, Americanisms, inborn with us, which you would never get at. One can do a great deal of propping. After all, one can't grow roses on a peach tree."[60] Over the course of their relationship, Whitman racialized Hartmann many times, often citing his Japanese heritage as the dominant, biological force driving Hartmann's personality. When he was agreeable to Whitman, Hartmann was Whitman's "old friend the German-Japanese." When Whitman was enraged, Hartmann was simply, "that damned Japanee."[61] Whitman's struggle in classifying the ambiguous Hartmann further emphasizes the cultural propensity to see race as a determining factor in othering certain individuals and underscores the monoracial attitudes Hartmann encountered as a mixed-race figure in late nineteenth-century America.

Despite Whitman's discouragement, Hartmann's forays into theater continued to pepper his everyday life. In each city where he lived, he engaged in theater. He had trained in technical theater in Germany during the age of *Gesamtkunstwerk*, or "the total work of art."[62] His experimental sensibilities reflected his training in Richard Wagner's total theater, which fused the artistic elements of music, drama, dance, light, and spectacle into a complete artistic vision. Hartmann spent eight months in 1885 as an apprentice in the court theater in Munich, learning set design from Kurt Lautenschläger, who designed the architecture for the innovative "Shakespearean stage."[63] He received acting training in Dresden and studied dance in Paris.[64] He wrote extensively on theater and dance for various arts magazines and gave acting and voice lessons in New York.[65] He turned to journalism as a means to make money, and he considered the myriad of lifestyle essays he wrote to make a living to be menial work. When he was twenty-three, he published 400 copies of his first symbolist drama, *Christ* (1893), which he dedicated to August Strindberg.[66] In the drama, Hartmann depicted Christ in scandalous scenes of sexual temptation. Of the play, the leading French symbolist poet, Stéphane Mallarmé, whom Hartmann had met in Paris in 1892, said, "You painted . . . a vast fresco as I have dreamed of, decorating the popular palaces of this time and future times. The beauty of it is that its colors are those of the dream, delicate and powerful at the same time so that even a lonely soul amidst the acclaim of the masses has his exquisite share of beauty. In this manner, the book is human because of its expression as well as its artistic value."[67] But, in Boston, the play was considered blasphemous. It was immediately banned, and copies of the script were publicly burned. Theater critic James Gibbons Huneker described the play as "absolutely the most daring of all decadent productions."[68] Hartmann was arrested for publishing and selling obscenity on December 21, 1893. He spent the subsequent Christmas Day in jail and was not released until January 2, 1894. He pleaded guilty two days later and paid the hundred-dollar fine.

Hartmann, influenced by his European training, persisted in his exploration of symbolism in theater making. This was often misconstrued as eccentric behavior brought about by a weak mind and impure biology. In his next play, *Buddha*, Hartmann included in its stage directions guidelines for the use of colors and various perfumes that would extinguish "the illusion of reality" and ignite the raw emotions and pure imagination of the spectator.[69] In November 1902, he produced a perfume concert at the New York Theatre under the pseudonym, "Chrysanthemum," a name he wielded when he wanted to assert his Japanese cultural identity.[70] The performance, called "A Trip to Japan in Sixteen Minutes, a Melody of Eight Odors," reflected Hartmann's desire to cultivate a performance for the senses that did not privilege sight. Symbolist theater had begun to employ the use of smells via perfume fountains, incense, and even scented programs to influence the mood of its audiences.[71] Hartmann's creation of symbolist "olfactory art" also mirrored personal experiences. He had worked as a perfume peddler in his early years in Philadelphia and had perhaps been influenced by Whitman, who explored the connection between smell and memory in his poetry.[72] The perfume concert was billed as "the chief attraction"[73] in an evening of vaudevillian performances that included the Rossow Midgets and the can-can kicking Meredith Sisters, who later assisted Hartmann costumed as "Japanese twin geisha girls."[74] In the concert, Hartmann attempted to create the experience of traveling from New York to Japan by submerging large sheets of cheese cloth in various perfumed scents. Using industrial fans, Hartmann blew the aromas into the audience while delivering a travel monologue of the journey. He called the aromatic contraption, the "Hartmann Perfumator," and *The New York Times* review provided the following description of his creation: "Two boxes about the size of beehives were placed on the stage. Behind them were powerful electric fans, and the conductor was going to put in the boxes linen saturated with perfumes, the extracts of flowers from different nations. The air currents were to drive the odors into the theatre."[75] An announcement for the much-anticipated affair declared, "the Nose will be guaranteed arrival in Yokohama."[76] The evening's audience was filled with a menagerie of patrons that included those with hay fever, who wanted to enjoy the pollen-free scent of flowers, as well as a group of "deaf-mutes," who were attracted to a sensorial event they could experience with their noses.[77]

The early modernist performance of smellscapes, however, was largely a failure. Hartmann's aromas failed to travel farther than the first few rows of the theater, which led to brutal heckling from the balcony. His perfumes also competed with the thick tobacco smoke that had filled the theater during the previous acts. After only two "travel stops" in New York and Germany, Hartmann "could not go on. He bowed, and with his face filled with very real pain said in a broken voice that he would have to be excused; he could not give the concert under such conditions."[78] The disappointed allergy-ridden spectators trickled out of the theater with the deaf audience members, whose fingers rapidly proclaimed their horror at the audience's treatment of the artist.

Publicly, Hartmann's failed attempt at creating a concert of scents was largely attributed to his impure ethnic parentage, signaling a popular belief in the mentally weak and unstable psychological state of the mixed-race body.[79] As Christina Bradstreet observes, *The New York Times* announcement of the performance indirectly referred to Hartmann a "weakling and . . . a degenerate."[80] Bradstreet notes that "his art, it was inferred, was as unhealthy as his exotic mixed-race persona . . . since olfactory imagination was linked to mental degeneracy."[81] Hence Hartmann's impetus for creating a symbolist performance, typical of smaller theaters in Paris at the time,[82] was linked to the inferiority of his mixed-race biology. While this kind of exploration of the senses was on the rise in symbolist theaters in Europe, in America, Hartmann's cutting-edge aesthetics became racialized. His European influences together with an ambiguous Asian countenance made him appear odd to American theater critics and audiences, but his strangeness was attributed not to his Europeanness but to his mixed Asianness.

Similar unfortunate failed attempts at experimental theater continued throughout Hartmann's life and were attributed to his eccentric character. In March 1917, he produced a controversial performance of Ibsen's *Ghosts* (1881) in the Russian Hill neighborhood of San Francisco. Hartmann rented the old Hanford Mansion and dubbed it "The House of Mystery."[83] The program for "The House of Mystery" performance series featured two performances of *Ghosts* and one presentation of Hartmann's plays *Buddha* and *Confucius* on subsequent nights. The performance of *Buddha* was billed as a "Color Drama of the Future" to be presented "with special color settings," while *Confucius* would be fully realized with Chinese dancing and music.[84] Hartmann played the role of Osvald in *Ghosts*, a performance he considered to be "twenty-eight years late," since he was fifty when he played the young artist character.[85] During the show, Hartmann directed that fire be ignited in the yard to correspond with the burning orphanage in the play's second act. When the fire spread to the house and almost burned the audience inside alive, Hartmann was again arrested and banned from producing the play in San Francisco. In the timeline for his autobiography, Hartmann simply referred to the incident as "The House of Mystery' episode."[86] More than likely, Hartmann canceled the other two plays on the bill, although an ad for the remaining "House of Mystery" performances ran in the *San Francisco Chronicle* the following week.[87]

However eccentric his theatrical experiments were, theater remained central to Hartmann's artistic aesthetic and seemed to facilitate his personal life as a shape shifter. To make a living, Hartmann was often found lecturing in a Japanese kimono, capitalizing on his Asian visage and educating audiences on "authentic" Japanese perspectives (see figure 2.1). As he mused, "I personally never

FIGURE 2.1 Sadakichi Hartmann in kimono, 1889. Sadakichi Hartmann Papers (MS 068). (Special Collections & University Archives, University of California, Riverside.)

think of myself as a German or Asiatic. Others do it for me. I am supposed to be a Eurasian and all my early amazing success and enterprise is due to that fact. The first Eurasian in Boston, lecturing—how interesting! All doors opened!"[88] While he was often racialized for his multiethnic parentage, his mixed ancestry also granted him access to opportunities he might not otherwise have had.

Hartmann's use of shape shifting as a tactic enabled him to further widen his access to employment on the lecture circuit. By 1902, Hartmann had created an alter ego named Sidney Allan as a pseudonym to write in Alfred Stieglitz's photography magazine, *Camera Notes*.[89] Soon thereafter, Sidney Allan began appearing in public and lecturing throughout New England. The dignified Allan wore a three-piece suit and donned a derby hat and a monocle. He was far more sartorially put together and, as a writer, more controlled and serious than the bombastic, bohemian Hartmann.[90] He also physically resembled the German Stieglitz, whom Hartmann considered a kindred spirit. Allan lectured on a variety of topics that seemed beyond Hartmann's personal code of ethics, such as his most famous lecture entitled "Good Taste and Common Sense," and by 1911, Allan's calendar was filled with national lecture tours. Over the years, many newspaper reporters interviewed Sidney Allan, unaware that he was, in fact, Sadakichi Hartmann.[91] George Knox and Harry W. Lawton observed that the "mobility of Hartmann's features lent themselves to almost any treatment,"[92] which enabled Hartmann to shape shift into a variety of different personae of his creation. However, though the versatility and illegibility of Hartmann's visage often served him, in his personal essay, "In Search of My Likeness," Hartmann lamented his easily shifting countenance: "Can you imagine anything more embarrassing than offering your portrait to a friend and he answering ... 'a very nice picture that, but who is it?'"[93] Each attempt to capture his physical likeness on film was, as he put it, "a pictorial transfiguration."[94] A favorite subject of photographers, Hartmann's ability to shape shift has been captured numerous times on film. Knox and Lawton have asserted that no other literary figure was photographed as much as Hartmann at the turn of the century.[95]

In *Osadda's Revenge*, therefore, Hartmann blended many aspects of his life: the loss of his mother, his anger toward his father, his dismay at being displaced by his stepsisters, and his longing for a family to which he could return. Like Hartmann, Hidetada in *Osadda's Revenge* moves through society as a mixed-race Asian shape shifter and uses his racialized identity to his advantage. With it, he gains access to different social circles as he seeks to murder his father and avenge his mother's death. Hartmann described his assessment of the play in his essay, "Aspirations of a Playwright," reflecting, "A strictly amateurish, but by far, more serious effort than all of them is my Japanese romance, a lurid three act melodrama, one half tragedy, and the other pure caricature and horseplay. The hero was a young half-breed who falls in love with his stepsister. I wrote it for my first stage appearance, and it was performed with me in the leading part in Patterson [New Jersey]. The serious part of the play contained much fervor and poetic imagery, and as far as plot and actor are concerned, it was well constructed."[96] In *Osadda's Revenge*, Hartmann created a theatrical romance that drew on his many European influences. Hartmann leaned on his European training as a means of making do since he knew no Japanese dramatists. This is significant because he was considered Asian, although he was raised as a European, demonstrating society's false belief in biology, rather than culture, as the determining factor in shaping an individual's character. Employing similar plot points and character relationships, Hartmann alludes to Shakespeare's *Othello* (1604) and to Ibsen's *Ghosts*.[97] These plays, written by two European dramatists whom Hartmann admired and respected, seem to have carried a special meaning for him.

Jolie A. Sheffer analyzes how incest serves to disrupt race and racial hierarchy and put mixed-race siblings and white family members on equal footing.[98] Similarly, the plots of Winnifred Eaton's short stories "A Half-Caste" (1899) and "A Father" (1900) loosely resemble Hartmann's play and feature abandoned mixed-race adult children, who also confront their white fathers.[99] When considering the character Clarissa, Hidetada's love interest, as a possible representation of Hartmann's stepsisters, the analysis of what Sheffer calls an "incest-recognition plot" proves useful here. According to descriptions filed with *Osadda's Revenge* in the archive at the University of California, Riverside,[100] Hartmann was disillusioned by the loss of his inheritance to his stepsisters. In his relationships with a series of mentors, who were replacements for his father, he constantly revisited the need for revenge that consumed his thoughts in Philadelphia.[101] Theater scholar Peter B. Hodges notes the "naked way [Hartmann] exposes" his own personal demons within the narrative of the play.[102] Hartmann's Hidetada asserts his desire to belong as he proclaims his whiteness and strives for equality in the multiracial nation-family in nineteenth-century America.

Hartmann's first task seems to be to upend the tragic Eurasian trope by displaying an educated superiority over his white counterparts. *Osadda's Revenge* begins at a debutante ball at a hotel in Newport, Rhode Island, widely regarded as a summer resort town for the New England upper class. Edith Dayton arrives with her merchant father, Mr. Dayton, anxious to see her beau, a medical student named George van Bos. Her sister, Clarissa Fulton, enters carrying a bouquet of chrysanthemums. Though married, she is smitten by a Japanese suitor named Hidetada. Dayton and his daughters are joined by a cast of characters who represent a privileged elite, including an older, pretentious socialite named Helena Blueblood and Baron d'Epignol, who repeatedly tells his companions that he is a member of the Académie Française and a poet.

Blueblood is the first character to provide a description of Hidetada, the half-Japanese gentleman with whom Clarissa is in love. After detailing his handsome physical aspects, she coos about his literary prowess:

BLUEBLOOD How well he is poised in literature. He made some very sagacious
    quotations, for instance he allowed himself to say "She loved me for the danger
    I had past, and I loved her that she did pity them." I naturally knew at once that
    my favorite poet Browning had written those lines.[103]

Blueblood, of course, mistakenly attributes these lines to the wrong writer. They are from Shakespeare's *Othello* and not the work of the English poet Robert Browning.

Through Blueblood, Hartmann potentially references *Othello* for a variety of reasons. Firstly, Hartmann foreshadows Hidetada's exchange with Clarissa and, through intertextuality, evokes the presence of the famous interracial couple, Othello and Desdemona, in the text. The interraciality of their relationship not only foreshadows the mixedness present in Hidetada's romantic relationship with Clarissa but it also conjures and reconstitutes another couple who haunt the text: Hartmann's own interracial, biological parents. Conversely, Blueblood's allusion to Shakespeare allows Hartmann to foreshadow Hidetada's encounter with Clarissa and creates a shorthand through which to experience their relationship. The nod to *Othello* is also meant to foreground the hypocrisy of the privileged American elite, whose ignorance of European writers and culture Hartmann found shocking. Hartmann's frustration here is obvious as the arrogant and pompous Miss Blueblood mistakes William Shakespeare for the more contemporary Robert Browning.[104] Furthermore, Blueblood misquotes Shakespeare, saying "danger" instead of "dangers" as in the original text. In the play, Hartmann thumbs his nose at a high society that could not recognize Shakespeare and knew little of Ibsen. Hartmann claims his intellectual superiority over white mainstream culture to prove that he is far from, as Christina Bradstreet notes, the mentally defective offspring often thought to come from an impure, interracial union.

Hidetada's incestuous advances seem to be a way for Hartmann to make do in an effort to win back his inheritance, even in a fantastical realm like theater. When Hidetada and Clarissa finally meet alone, Hartmann directly references *Othello*, establishing Clarissa as Desdemona and Hidetada as Othello. Clarissa speaks to Hidetada saying, "Therefore tell me what sorrowful story lies hidden in your heart. Be assured that I would appreciate your trust in me; it is not curiosity which prompts my tongue to speak, but a burning desire with my soul that is akin to yours."[105] Her words mirror Desdemona's show of adoration and devotion to Othello in Shakespeare's drama. Like Desdemona, Clarissa is drawn to her love interest's troubled past. Clarissa continues, imploring Hidetada to "speak to me. Let me be no longer ignorant of the great torturing passions of your existence."[106] As Othello recounts in act one, scene three, "She loved me for the dangers I had past, and I loved her that she did pity them,"[107] and Hidetada also loves having Clarissa as a devoted and empathetic confidante.

Within the dramatization of an incestuous relationship, Hartmann asserts himself as an equal to his own stepsisters. When Clarissa affirms that she and Hidetada are similar, describing her soul as "akin" to his, she foreshadows their blood ties as siblings.[108] Sheffer refers to this as an incest-recognition plot, in which a romantic relationship establishes siblings as equals. The incest taboo cannot ignore the fact that the lovers are related. Later in the play, this prevents Hidetada from consummating his romantic relationship with his sister, but it undeniably positions him as an equal member of the family and his father's son. Clarissa's affection further negates Hidetada's illegitimate status as her mixed-race brother. When Hartmann hints that the lovers are "kin" in Clarissa's innocent declaration, he also proclaims himself an equal to his own stepsisters and, therefore, rightfully deserving of his inheritance.

Hartmann further displays his cultural and intellectual prowess through his creation of the character Clarissa. As a composite of many influences in Hartmann's life, she seems to be an amalgamation of Helene Alving and Regina Engstrand from Ibsen's *Ghosts*. Like Helene Alving, Clarissa is married to a philanderer. Clarissa's husband, Clay, is in prison for fraud during the course of the play, and he eventually dies there, also leaving Clarissa a widow like Helene. Yet Clarissa also resembles Regina Engstrand and enters into a romantic relationship with her brother, unaware that they are related.[109]

Hidetada's connection to Clarissa fulfills an emotional void for the protagonist, but the relationship also rectifies a financial discrepancy as well. The love interest is perhaps reminiscent of Clara, a young woman with whom Hartmann was in love in Boston in 1887. Despite their apparent devotion to each other, Hartmann recounted that the affair was "purely osculation," much like the relationship between Hidetada and Clarissa.[110] The relationship ended abruptly and seemingly irreparably later that year to Hartmann's dismay after he returned from another trip to Europe in the fall of 1887. It is no coincidence, however, that Hartmann's first love in the United States was named Clara. The character Clarissa may be inspired by her, but the name's meaning also serves another purpose in the text. Clarissa is a related form of Clara or Clare, meaning "clear" and "bright." Later in the narrative, it is Clarissa who tries to talk sense into Hidetada, vehemently denying her approval of their incestuous relationship. However, Hidetada's choice for a romantic partner is clear. She is the only spot of clarity and brightness in his life. As the white legitimate daughter, she is guaranteed financial security and belonging. Hidetada finds a way to be equal to his rival heir, however, by demanding recognition as the abandoned and forgotten half-breed son. When Clarissa tries to reason with him, she offers her love as a sister. Hidetada counters, "I want a nearer tie!"[111] as he knows he will not receive the equality he deserves if he settles for being her sibling. Eventually in this exchange, Clarissa relents, replying, "Take me. I am yours," signaling her acceptance of him as an equal.[112]

In *Osadda's Revenge*, the mixed-race child, now an adult, speaks, penned by an author who lived through an experience not unlike Trouble or Sorrow in *Madame/a Butterfly*.[113] Yet, in the *Butterfly* narratives, the mixed-race subject has remained silenced, a dismissed object, peripheral to a story undergirded by Orientalism and essentialized notions of race. In *Osadda's Revenge*, however, Hidetada admonishes the white imperialist privilege that has led to his abandonment:

HIDETADA The great crime which so many foreigners committed who settled there. Women were good enough for them while staying in Japan, but when they returned, their children were forgotten. How many . . . hearts have been forsaken? How many tears were shed for them? . . . How many a child had to suffer for this—father's wrong?[114]

In his lifetime, Hartmann was critical of the white imperialist project. He referred to white colonizers as "devils [who] claim that they come as benefactors as they relieve the natives of the tsetse fly, when they themselves are worse than any plague of flies."[115] While both Blueblood and Clarissa identify Hidetada as a "foreigner" earlier in the text, the protagonist also uses the word when referring to his white father and other Europeans like him who refuse to claim their mixed children.[116] Dayton feebly replies that he is not the only one to have ever committed such a crime, but Hidetada refuses to accept that as an excuse:

DAYTON That is happening every day all over the world.
HIDETADA Sad if it is true. But no man can defend such villainy.[117]

Speaking not from the margins, therefore, Hidetada's use of the word *foreigner* decenters the West's positionality in the text. Through *Osadda's Revenge*, and with the aid of the European dramatists who raised him, Sadakichi Hartmann confronts his father's rejection and claims Japan and Europe together as the center from which he speaks. This assertion of self through the embodied act of performance reveals the paratopic space occupied by Hidetada as a mixed-race subject.

Though not helmed by professionals, newspaper accounts reviewed the production favorably, like the 1890 review in the *New York Clipper Annual*, which reported that the author made "a stellar debut."[118] Peter Hodges notes that Hartmann assembled a cast of amateur actors in New York for the show and opened the performance at the Apollo Hall in Paterson, New Jersey, a city often remembered as the place where East Coast actors received their first big break.[119] Hartmann's leading ingenue, a night watchman's daughter, was "naivete personified" with an abundance of wavy hair for which Hartmann would evidently forgive anything she did.[120] Though apparently well received according to surviving newspaper accounts, the production seems to have had a predictable outcome since Hartmann made do with an amateur cast and a leading lady whom he cast for his own self-interests rather than for her acting ability.

Newspaper descriptions of the production illuminate the racialized landscape that perhaps led Hartmann to capitalize on his Japanese phenotype. Hartmann is identified in a review in *America: A Journal for the Americas* as a "gentleman," who is encouraged as a Japanese foreigner who writes in English: "As long as these foreigners do not insist in writing plays in their native lingos they are welcome to scribble as much as they please. After all a play written in English by a Japanese is far better than a paper printed in German in this country."[121] The article further describes Germans, perhaps ironically, as "imported citizens who have wit enough to dispense beer but not enough to learn the language of the country they fatten upon."[122] Hartmann's decision to fully shape shift into a "Japanese Gentleman" also reveals an understanding of the American negative sentiment toward Germans and an attempt to capitalize on the admiration and attention poured upon Japanese people in the late nineteenth century. No doubt the audience's encounter with the mixed-race body of Sadakichi Hartmann onstage aroused a burgeoning attraction to Japanese people and cultural products. Hartmann's Germanness lent itself to the project of making Hartmann seem more exotic and, in a subversive move on Hartmann's part, assisted in making him more Japanese.

Hartmann's rejection of his Germanness continued well into the 1930s and 1940s with the advent of World War II. Not surprisingly, his steadfast devotion to his Japanese identity dissipated under the looming threat of Japanese internment. America's modernist obsession with Japonisme gave way to a growing suspicion of the menacing Japanese nation in the 1930s, which grew into full-scale fear, distrust, and contempt after the bombing of Pearl Harbor in 1941. In response to the attack, Franklin Roosevelt signed Executive Order 9066 in February the following year, calling for the immediate removal and incarceration of all persons of Japanese ancestry from the West Coast, including the *nisei*, or second-generation Japanese American citizens. The U.S. government's stance was that these American-born, "full-blooded" Japanese children who had been raised by Japanese immigrant *issei* parents were culturally more Japanese than American and, therefore, impermeable to assimilation. They were, in the minds of the American public at large, first and foremost, Japanese whose loyalties, by *nature*, lay with the Japanese nation. The incarceration of the Japanese Americans was an act defined solely by race, which was conflated with culture and nationhood. By the time the U.S. concentration camps officially closed, approximately 120,000 people of Japanese descent, two-thirds of whom were U.S. citizens, had been forcibly removed from their homes without due process in the western United States. However, not one Japanese nor Japanese American had been convicted of espionage by the war's end.

By March 1942, the process of removal had begun across the American West, which was deemed vulnerable because of its proximity to the Pacific Ocean and the nation of Japan beyond. This removal of all persons of Japanese descent included mixed-race Japanese people. By then, the aged and sickly Sadakichi Hartmann was living with his daughter, Wistaria, and her family on the Morongo Indian Reservation. Hartmann was asthmatic and addicted to alcohol to manage pain, though he was still acting and had been giving dramatic readings of the work of his favorites—Whitman, Ibsen, and Poe—as well as of his own, in private salon performances in Los Angeles deep into the 1930s. In March 1942, however, the Riverside County sheriff and investigators from the FBI came calling. They questioned Hartmann about his Japanese identity, prompting the racially mobile figure to shape shift, not back into Germanness but into a white Americanness.

In multiple statements drafted in 1942, Hartmann asserted that he was not Japanese and emphasized his Americanness since renouncing his German citizenship and becoming legally naturalized in New York in 1894. In chronicling

his early speaking career, he underscored his lectures on "European art, literature, music, Walt Whitman, and the slums of Paris," further clarifying that he
"*posed* as a 'Eurasean'" strictly "to attract attention as a personality."[123] For someone who knowingly deployed his Asian ethnic background to open doors he
could not have accessed otherwise, his shift to whiteness occurred with the same
bombastic bravado characteristic of his younger days in Boston, New York, and
San Francisco. Seeming to enjoy the challenge, he denounced the very inquiry,
declaring, "How at this late date can I be ranked as Japanese? I also entertain
doubts (ready to testify under oath) whether my mother was Japanese. . . . I came
to the conclusion, years ago, that my mother was a Korean."[124] Moreover, he
reverted back to Carl Sadakichi Hartmann and cited Sadakichi Hartmann as
an alias along with the moniker Sidney Allan.

Hartmann relied on his easily shifting countenance, once a source of embar-
rassment, to prove that he was not physically Japanese. The now infamous 1941
article from *Life* magazine, "How to Tell Japs from the Chinese," instructed its
readers to read the racial differences between Chinese and Japanese people
through certain telltale signs. The essay was meant to serve as a balm for widespread white panic and to address the rising incidents of violence against Chinese Americans who were mistaken as being of Japanese descent. The article
featured a comparison of the photographic images of General Hideki Tojo and
Chinese minister of public affairs Ong Wen-hao, whose faces had been dia-
grammed and annotated to supposedly differentiate their physical features. As
a racial primer, the annotations focused on eye shape, bone structure, facial hair,
and characteristics of skin. The Chinese visage was described as long and fine-
boned, whereas the Japanese prime minister was noted for his "massive cheek
and jawbone" and "broader, shorter face."[125] The article maintained that the Japanese physique exhibited a "squat, solid, long torso and short stocky legs," belying its "aboriginal antecedents," and thereby characterizing the Japanese as less
evolved, uncivilized, and subordinate. This supposed lesser biology was conflated
with culture, encouraging the interpretation of bodily expressions as identifying markers of race. Hartmann, no doubt, was familiar with these racial met-
rics.[126] Standing nearly six feet tall and keenly cognizant of his ability to shape
shift, he challenged the investigators to "take a good long look at me. Do you
discover anything strikingly Oriental: in my sparse figure, the structure of the
skull, the position of the eyes, my features (upper jawbone), skin texture, hair,
my gestures and intonation of voice? Did you ever meet a Japanese who resembles me? No, you haven't, as it is biologically impossible."[127] Perhaps it was not
Hartmann's tall, angular frame, his narrow jaw, nor his aquiline nose that con-
vinced investigators of this racial status as much as his confidence in his racial
illegibility.

An exploration of the U.S. policy toward exemptions to internment provides
further insight into Hartmann's ability to successfully evade incarceration. It was

not enough that he did not qualify as phenotypically Japanese according to the racial primers of the era. Hartmann also had to demonstrate that he was not culturally Japanese—which his mixedness had allowed him to claim—and could verify his full assimilation as a white American. The United States implemented the Mixed Marriage Policy in 1942, which spared interracial couples and their mixed-race children from internment so long as they could prove that their households were devoid of a Japanese cultural influence.[128]

In order to qualify for exemption, applicants successfully proved that they were fully assimilated into American life. Emphasis was placed on gender as well as race because the male head of household was believed to direct the culture of the home. Race and ethnicity were seen as directly tied to culture and nationality because diasporic ethnic groups were thought to be inextricably tied and therefore loyal to the geographic origins of their ancestors. If the male head of the household was Japanese, the culture and upbringing of the children were thought to be Japanese, and the wife, especially a white woman, was seen as a traitor to her race and country. However, if the male head of household was white, the culture and upbringing were considered to be "Caucasian" and provided an avenue to exemption for the family in order to protect the children from being tainted by the Japanese in camp. While there was an emphasis on loyalty, this was a euphemism for race since race and ethnic background inherently connected one to culture and nation. One's only recourse then was to prove assimilation.

In light of these parameters, Hartmann successfully proved his full assimilation by disassociating himself from Japan entirely. Not only did he deny his Japanese heritage and claim that his mother was Korean, but he also asserted that he was born not on Japanese soil but on the politically inert island of Dejima. He affirmed that he had never returned to Japan after having left as an infant, never learned the language, and never associated with Japanese people in Europe or the United States. He had been raised, according to the qualifications of exemption, in a "non-Japanese environment." Further, he emphasized that not only was he a loyal American but he had also written the authoritative tome on American art, thereby establishing himself as the arbiter of American culture itself.[129] In his final act of shape shifting, Hartmann concretized his racial ambiguity through assimilation, neutralized his mixed-Japanese status, and shape shifted, essentially, into an old, infirm "Caucasian" man—already living in containment—on an Indian reservation on the outskirts of Banning, California. His investigation was closed in May 1943. His FBI case file affirms that in May "all outstanding leads [had] been covered" with "no indication of any un-Americanism or subversive activity on the part of the subject." Hartmann was described as an "invalid," who was "employed as an actor and writer in Hollywood from 1923–1935." Ultimately, his decisions to shape shift from German to Japanese—a culture with which he did not identify—to an assertion of whiteness vis-à-vis the racial ambiguity of assimilation illustrates the complexity

FIGURE 2.2 Sadakichi Hartmann, 1899. B.J. Falk. Sadakichi Hartmann Papers (MS 068). (Special Collections & University Archives, University of California, Riverside.)

of a doubly liminal identity in the late nineteenth through the mid-twentieth centuries.

In the final moments of *Osadda's Revenge*, Hartmann's desires to reconcile his relationships with his father and his stepsisters begin to coalesce. At the play's end, it is Clarissa's maid, Cora, whose name invokes the "core," "center," or "heart," who dissuades Hidetada from carrying out his plans for revenge. In her cri de coeur, she reasons that if Hidetada killed his father, he would dishonor the love his mother had for both of them.

CORA If your mother has ever cherished the memory of your father with all the
    tenderness a woman has, then she has forgiven him long, long ago.
HIDETADA It is true, she never blamed him for his crime, she pardoned him and
    loved him still.
CORA And then her son will kill that man who she so loved, who was the greatest
    joy of all her life? That can never be right.[130]

Cora acts as a mother-surrogate and as the final arbiter in Hidetada's quest for revenge. Hidetada's ultimate refusal to destroy the only man his mother loved, along with his father's long-awaited recognition, eventually eases his need for vengeance. He addresses Dayton and Clarissa as his father and sister, having finally gained acceptance into the family that he had lost. Then, perhaps as a final olive branch to Clara, Hartmann speaks through Hidetada in his last lines to his sister: "Clarissa, our love has not been in vain, it taught me some great lesson . . . to find life worth living."[131] This lesson learned is what Hartmann consistently, fearlessly endeavored to do: to pursue a life worth living.

Of his stepsisters' inheritance Hartmann closes his personal essay "Erb-schleicherei," saying, "Now in 1933 it is all a dead issue—the world's war and the shift of mundane possessions—I do not know what has become of them and do not particularly care. I stop here abruptly as all this really does not belong to the part of my career which I endeavored to describe, only that it played such an important influence and intangible force in the development of my early life."[132] Whether or not Hartmann had truly forgiven them in the 1930s, perhaps in those early years in Boston and Philadelphia, he desired to bury his thoughts of revenge and dreamed of reconciliation. At the end of *Osadda's Revenge*, Hidetada relinquishes his dagger to Cora's outstretched hands and pledges to begin a new life.

The Most Affectionate Creature: The Mixed-Race Body of Patsy O'Wang

Nineteenth-century mixed-race drama often dramatized and reified coolie-era stereotypes.[133] Unlike the initial admiration enjoyed by the Japanese, Chinese laborers were the recipients of popular resentment and a widespread fear of the "Yellow Peril," the belief that white America would be overrun by a horde of an inferior race.[134] This contamination would extend not only into the white American body through disease but also into the moral fabric of white American culture through the seduction of immoral, deviant behavior. Meanwhile, white America was also grappling with an immigrant Irish population that had a history of mixing and intermarrying with the Chinese, even as it sought to affirm its whiteness. In 1895, American playwright Thomas Stewart Denison published a one-act play, *Patsy O'Wang: An Irish Farce with a Chinese Mix-Up,* which underscored the American public's opinion of Chinese labor, the evolving Irish underclass, and the continued threat of miscegenation. The farce featured a protagonist with "a remarkable dual nature."[135] Chin Sum, a half-Chinese, half-Irish cook, has the uncanny ability to transform himself into a "true Irishman" named Patsy O'Wang.[136] This metamorphosis occurs whenever Sum consumes whiskey, "the drink of his father."[137] Tea, "the beverage of his mother," can restore him to his docile, Chinese temperament, the state preferred by his employer, Dr. Fluke.[138] When Sum's excessive drinking releases the "spirit of Hibernia," Fluke endeavors to recover Sum's obedient Chinese body by continuously feeding him tea. A struggle between Sum's Chinese persona and his Irish character creates chaos for Fluke and the rest of the household and emblematizes the confusion and anxiety produced by the mixed-race body in nineteenth-century society. The play foregrounded popular ethnic stereotypes ascribed to the Chinese and the Irish at the turn of the century and, consequently, dramatized the Irish community's transformation from poor, working class to full-fledged members of white American society with substantial political power.

A former high school principal, Denison was a prolific publisher and playwright, who wrote vaudeville scripts and commercial plays as well as one-acts for schools, churches, and other community groups. His aim had primarily been to tap into the amateur market, which often lacked the resources and experience necessary to produce professional scripts.[139] As historian Hsin-yun Ou notes, the absence of a sufficient performance history of *Patsy O'Wang* further suggests that the play was not intended for commercial use.[140] One amateur production of the play is detailed in the "Clubs and Women's Societies" column in the *Washington Post* in February 1908, which asserted that the show was "one of the best performances given this winter."[141] Performed by St. Mark's Sunday school at Pythian Temple in the District of Columbia, the show "won much applause," and John E. Tyler, the yellowface actor in the title role, impressively "kept everybody laughing."[142] The performance of the farce seems to align with nonprofessional school productions typical of the era that served as a white middle- and upper-class form of entertainment. These performances often satirized various immigrant and ethnic groups and, in a display of Eurocentrism, highlighted white superiority.[143] Additionally, yellowface roles like Chin Sum gave white audiences a "sanctioned space through which to view the unknowable," the immoral, contaminated Chinese body and the unnatural result of an interracial union.[144] In *Patsy O'Wang,* the mixed-race Chinese body is contained and put on display for viewing pleasure.

Both historians Gregory T. Carter and Hsin-yun Ou elucidate the ways in which the play dramatizes the antagonism that existed between the Chinese and the Irish populations. As the Irish struggled to find their place in American society, they found themselves in competition with Chinese immigrants for working-class jobs. In the play's opening, the Irish domestics balk at the idea of sharing the household with a Chinese cook, and when Chin Sum later shape shifts, presumably into one of their own vis-à-vis the transformative effects of whiskey, Norah and Mike remain skeptical. Performance scholar Krystyn R. Moon elucidates the tension that existed between the supposed brutish and masculine Irish, especially Irish women, and Chinese men, who were often rivals in domestic work. The anti-Chinese sentiment was expressed in songs of the era like "Since the Chinese Ruint the Thrade" (1871), which describes the plight of an Irish laundress who struggles with the loss of her husband and daughter, as well as with harsh working conditions and competition from other Chinese laundries.[145] These songs, as Moon argues, championed anti-Chinese immigration policies and worked to solidify Irishness as synonymous with whiteness.[146] Similarly, Norah and Mike's hostility toward Chin Sum further evinces the Irish disdain and mistrust of the Chinese.

The close contact with the Irish and Chinese in domestic service and menial labor, however, also resulted in intermarriage and miscegenation. Although Denison penned *Patsy O'Wang* as a comedy intended for a white audience, the play foregrounds the existence of the mixed-Asian body in the nineteenth century that was a threat prevalent enough to create anxiety. It also provides evidence of an awareness of the phenomenon of shape shifting and the desperate attempt to force the mixed-race body to adhere to the rule of hypodescent. The fear that Patsy would successfully and wrongly shape shift into whiteness is a constant fear in the entire Fluke household, which serves as an analogue for the American cultural landscape. The play revolves around every effort to restrain his shape shifting body and impede his transformation. The character, which made its way onstage and into performance, evinces the presence of white-Asian interracial relationships and their resulting offspring, serving as a reflection of the zeitgeist and, like *Osadda's Revenge*, as an archive of the mixed-race body. Specifically, *Patsy O'Wang* assures us of the prevalence of Chinese Irish unions like those found in significant numbers in urban centers, such as New York and San Francisco. Historian Robert Lee notes that Chinese Irish marriages were more commonplace on the East Coast and that "Chinese-Chinese households in New York were so rare that, in 1875, *Frank Leslie's Illustrated Weekly* reported on the first such marriage in the city."[147] Historian Jack Kuo Wei Tchen further maintains that "at least one quarter of all Chinese men who lived in New York between 1820 and 1870 were married to, or lived with, Irish women" as opposed to only a dozen Chinese-white interracial couples residing in San Francisco's Chinatown.[148] While one dozen Chinese interracial relationships in San Francisco may not appear demographically significant, the existence of these relationships demonstrates that they were perhaps more common than contemporary discourse affirms. Furthermore, these unions took place with enough frequency to be a concern for California delegates, who, in 1878, proposed an amendment to the California constitution that would restrict Chinese and white marriages. Consequently, the California Assembly successfully expanded its 1850 anti-miscegenation law and passed Assembly Bill 261 in 1880, making it unlawful for a white person to marry "persons of other races," including Asiatic "Mongolians."[149]

The play *Patsy O'Wang* also dramatizes SanSan Kwan and Kenneth Speirs's observation that the mixed-race body houses competing histories of oppression within the same corporeal subjectivity. As Kwan and Speirs remind us, no mixed-race body is the same as another, and they challenge the cultural tendency to relegate mixed individuals to one all-encompassing group.[150] Within Patsy's body, according to Denison, wages an unnatural war of blood between the docile Chinese servant and a loud-mouthed, drunken Irishman. Though undoubtedly stereotypical renderings, Patsy's character must navigate the discriminatory oppression endured by both the Chinese and the Irish underclasses. The play also evinces a mixed-Asian experience that is quite different from that of the protagonist Hidetada, for example, in *Osadda's Revenge*—a man of Japanese descent, who enjoys the privilege of tolerance born of a Western fascination with Japan. Although both are of Asian ancestry, these two characters ultimately remain doubly liminal from white society and from each other as mixed-race subjects of different ethnic backgrounds. Additionally, Patsy O'Wang actualizes the negative assumptions attributed not only to Chinese immigrants but also to the Irish immigrant community, who were seen as "savage, brutish drunks" and as "co-conspirators with other non-white groups," which only magnified the social belief in the travesty of miscegenation.[151] The Flukes' efforts of containment of Chin Sum's body as seen in *Patsy O'Wang* evince the fear that miscegenation evoked in the American body politic.

The competing histories within the body are what make mixed-race individuals doubly liminal, or racially separate, from each other. While Hartmann's Japanese-white character, Hidetada, and Denison's Chinese Irish Patsy are both half-Asian and half-white, they do not share a common personal experience other than the marginalization of their mixed-race status. Hidetada, abandoned by his father for being half-Asian, chooses to shape shift into a Japanese persona. This enables him to walk through elite social circles with a certain kind of agency and freedom that allows him to hunt for his mother's supposed murderer. Patsy's lower socioeconomic status as a Chinese man assigns him to domestic labor often relegated to the Chinese immigrant population in the mid- to late nineteenth century. In response, Patsy shape shifts into whiteness, which ultimately affords him the agency and power he desires.

While *Patsy O'Wang* provides us with evidence of a mixed-Asian role in the 1890s, the Patsy character does not have a mixed-race subjectivity of his own. Unlike *Osadda's Revenge*, the play was written by a white playwright, who uses mixed-race identity as a comedic gag rather than a serious dramatization about multiraciality because Patsy's racial selves are not integrated but expressed as separate, embodied personalities. In the character of Patsy O'Wang, we observe a forerunner of mixed-Asian characters like Trouble or Sorrow in iterations of

Madame Butterfly or of The Engineer and Tam in *Miss Saigon*. Like Patsy, these successors are creations of white playwrights who deploy them as devices in the theatrical narratives in which they appear. Apart from The Engineer, these other hapa characters devolve into objects that have no voice. I would argue that the point of view emanating from The Engineer does not reflect a mixed-race subjectivity, either, but that of the European theater artists who created him.[152] In Patsy's case, the Chinese Irish role serves to entertain a white audience in a racialized fantasy and perpetuates coolie-era stereotypes that have relentlessly persisted into the twentieth and twenty-first centuries.

The racialization is first apparent in Denison's descriptions of his characters' accents. At the top of the script, the playwright carefully outlines how the white characters intonate, and he differentiates between the conventionally Irish Mike and Norah, who speak with "a thick brogue," and the Irish Patsy, who, having interacted with British officers in Hong Kong, has "acquired the language of gentleman."[153] Of Chinese character Chin Sum, however, Denison asserts that "no instructions can be given here concerning the Chinese part except that the timbre and tones of the Chinese voice are very peculiar, and can be heard only by listening to Chinamen. The Chinese dialect as written here is ... good enough to be funny, which is the only object in view."[154] Denison's treatment of a Chinese accent is perhaps no surprise. The use of an Orientalized, simplified pidgin English legitimized characterizations of Asians—specifically of Japanese and Chinese people—and became commonplace in vaudeville and scripted drama during the Progressive Era. Misspellings in dialogue like "Vellee nice mission gull (girl)," Patsy's response to meeting the local Sunday school teacher Miss Simper, were the norm.[155] The mispronunciation of certain letters like "r" in the words "very" or "girl" emphasized the Chinese as ignorant, inferior, and incapable of assimilation.[156] Moreover, the addition of English "translations," such as "girl" for "gull," marked the Chinese as perpetually foreign. It is doubtful, however, that Denison would have questioned this performative function of pidgin. Besides his many plays and publications, Denison's lifework and self-proclaimed masterpiece was an etymological history of the Nahuatl language and its supposed links (in Denison's mind) to Aryan roots, belying a lack of linguistic scholarship that seems to be prevalent in Denison's oeuvre. His unsubstantiated philological study has been largely debunked, and he admittedly was not a trained linguist.[157] His dismissal of an accurate portrayal of the Chinese accent, save for its ability to garner a comedic response from a white audience, underscores the prevalence of anti-Chinese sentiments vis-à-vis Asian stereotypes and Denison's use of Patsy as a mere device within the narrative.

The presence of Chinese domestic labor in a male-dominated Gold Rush contributed to the feminization of Asian men, a stereotype that persists in the American imaginary in the twentieth and twenty-first centuries. *Patsy O'Wang* elucidates a variety of Chinese stereotypes of the 1890s and foregrounds the early immigrant history of the Chinese. Approximately 250,000 Chinese migrated to the U.S. West Coast in the 1800s. The majority came midcentury, lured by

California's Gold Rush beginning in 1848. Historian Paul Spickard observes that though gold production had decreased by 1870, nearly 9,000 of the still remaining California miners were Chinese. While many turned to railroad construction for work, significant numbers of Chinese men sought employment in domestic professions, opening laundries and serving in white, middle-class households as servants, cooks, and nannies. These domestic tasks were most commonly considered to be feminine labor.[158]

Dr. Fluke's attitude toward Patsy highlights the emasculation of Chinese men in domestic service. The play opens with Fluke announcing that he has hired Patsy O'Wang to be the family's new cook. The doctor reads a letter of referral from his friend, Major Barker, who glowingly recommends Patsy by characterizing him as feminine and childlike. Barker describes Patsy as a "most obedient servant" and "the most affectionate creature," and Fluke refers to Patsy in this same vein, calling him "a treasure" and "as peaceful as a lamb."[159] Later in the farce, Fluke adopts Barker's sentiments and frequently refers to Patsy as a "most affectionate creature," which others the mixed-Chinese masculine body as oddly and unconventionally feminine. Furthermore, Patsy's impure status as a mixed-race "creature" challenges the white hegemonic belief that a "full-blooded" Chinese subject can be contained. Fluke recognizes that Patsy is not an ideal find. He has a "flaw in his [Chinese] pedigree," which is tainted with barbarous Irish blood.[160] This strange combination produces a not-quite-human creature.[161]

The play additionally reinforces the Orientalist belief that Chinese character flaws are directly related to paganism, which can only be cured by Western imperialist intervention. Christian conversion alone can save the heathen Chinese according to Miss Simper, and she confesses to Dr. Fluke that her "heart bleeds for all the millions of Asia who sit in outer darkness."[162] Simper's sentiments highlight the Western, Orientalist conflation of the many regional differences, cultures, and communities of Asia into one irreligious, uncivilized populace.[163] Her attitude also underscores the belief that Asian cultures need the protection and salvation that their white, Christian neighbors can supposedly provide. Cultural theorist Edward Said contends that the Western imperialist desire to dominate distant lands, which seemingly have no valid cultural history, is sustained and reified in objects of culture, specifically in literature where imperialism becomes normalized in fiction.[164] Denison's play reinforces this imperialistic vision, which justifies its actions in the proselytization of "lesser," colonized peoples. The acceptance of Western dress is often seen as evidence of a complete conversion. As Simper continues to inquire, she asks Fluke if Patsy has "doffed the Chinese garb . . . and donned the raiment of civilization."[165] There is a clear differentiation between "Chinese garb" and Western attire, which makes physical the distinction between the cultured, educated Christian West and the Asians "who sit in outer darkness."[166] Simper believes, however, that all subalterns are worthy of salvation and benevolence, especially the Chinese, whom she later describes as having "such lovely dispositions."[167] Denison's play contributes to the notion of empire through Simper's evangelical mission as a backdrop in his work of dramatic fiction.

The conversion to Christianity was also thought to entrain the Chinese to adopt a respectable, normative domesticity, reinforced by white Christian ideals. Often misinterpreted as deviant behavior, Chinese economic decisions revolved simply around saving money. Bachelors chose to share lodgings and live together in single-family dwellings.[168] Because women were prohibited from immigrating to the United States vis-à-vis the Page Act of 1875, common living spaces were the norm for a single-male population with limited economic resources and scant opportunities for marriage. These unconventional circumstances created an acute anxiety for the white middle class, who found the behavior non-normative and threatening to middle-class values, though American immigration and anti-miscegenation laws had forced this dilemma onto the Chinese.[169] Instead, the popular nineteenth-century belief among white government officials maintained that the Chinese immigrant population preferred these abnormal conditions, which were intensified by opium addiction, gambling, and prostitution.[170] In the play, Mrs. Fluke embodies and reifies this middle-class anxiety and fear. Before Patsy's transformation into an Irish gentleman, she condemns her husband's decision to hire the shape shifter, retorting, "Well, Dr. Fluke, I shan't take the responsibility of having a Chinaman in the house. . . . Who knows but he may poison us all."[171] She later confesses her fear that Patsy will bring opium into the household.[172]

Denison emphasizes the construction of the Chinese as pollutants, who were believed to be unhygienic and, therefore, uncivilized and inferior. After Simper attempts to assure Mrs. Fluke that the "poor boy" is nothing to be afraid of, the doctor's wife clings instead to "those horrid stories of rats and opium."[173] The Irish servants, Mike and Norah, echo Mrs. Fluke's sentiments and express their disdain and mistrust of Chin Sum.

NORAH It's a disgrace, I'll give notice, I will—
MIKE I'll not ate a bit o' his dirty cookin', faith I'll not.[174]

As Nayan Shah notes, local authorities in San Francisco equated the Chinese with animals and, by extension, poor hygiene due to their unfortunate circumstances with overcrowding. This, in turn, fed a perception that the Chinese were inhumane and inferior to white communities.[175] Racist comparisons particularly linked the community to rats and pigs, underscored by the animals' association with filth and waste.[176] Chinese domestic spaces, like those in Chinatown, were often under sanitary inspection and thought to need constant regulation from lurking disease. Government officials further believed that the Chinese were harbingers of drug addiction and sexual depravity, luring white women into "dens" or "joints," where opium addiction would compromise their sexual morals.[177] Domestics who provided childcare were particularly suspect, since they were thought to be vessels of contamination and disease.[178] As Shah asserts, "The living densities of Chinese 'dens' demonstrated Chinese indifference to human comforts."[179] Like farm animals crowded into small spaces, the Chinese capacity to attract disease seemed to triple according to health officials.

Patsy's ability to shape shift dislodges the Asian stereotypes inscribed on his body and asserts his desire for Irish whiteness. By extension, this assertion of whiteness inadvertently challenges the rule of hypodescent. In the narrative, Chin Sum comes across a bottle of whiskey while in the Flukes' employ. After he consumes the liquor, he becomes briefly confused. In Denison's text, he physically shape shifts into a different persona onstage. Like Dr. Henry Jekyll, he completes a metamorphosis into his alter ego, Patsy O'Wang—aided by a linguistic shift to unaccented English. No longer speaking in a Chinese "pidgin," Patsy speaks with no accent. He has no Irish brogue like Mike and Norah, for he has bypassed their lower social status entirely, which he demonstrates by speaking in an elevated Anglo-American dialect. He could perhaps be English, but it is clear from the text that he is and remains Irish. Denison hyperbolizes Patsy's shape shifting abilities to dramatize the evolution of the burgeoning Irish political ascent in American politics. Rather than merely foregrounding the tensions that existed between the Irish and Chinese working classes, Patsy's character also dramatizes the transformation of the Irish immigrant population from that of a poor, oppressed class to one of the most powerful, ethnically white groups in America.

As the newly minted Irish version of Patsy, his unequivocal transformation fools even the anxious Mrs. Fluke. After Patsy's transmutation is complete, she is the first person to encounter him. Though the performer has not physically changed, Mrs. Fluke's character does not recognize Patsy's corporeality as the Chinese Chin Sum. He has effectively shape shifted into whiteness, and Mrs. Fluke initially mistakes him to be a patient of her husband. When he identifies himself as Patsy O'Wang, even Mrs. Fluke cannot deny that he has changed, remarking, "He's very polite, at any rate."[180] Patsy notices her alarm and graciously gestures for her to sit and rest. Remarkably, the scene dramatizes the ability of the hapa figure to shape shift onstage. Unlike racial passing, which denotes a singular shift to whiteness, shape shifting connotes a "multifaceted passing," like the many racial embodiments performed by Sadakichi Hartmann. The Patsy O'Wang audience understands that if the shape shifting Patsy were to consume tea, he would morph again into his Chinese persona, a choice available to him if it were in his best interests to do so.

It is interesting to note that although Patsy has morphed into a "full-fledged Irishman," losing his Chinese accent and his docile manner, Mike and Norah still refuse to accept him. He is, in fact, a different "creature," a term Dr. Fluke uses to describe the cook multiple times in the play. Instead, Patsy speaks in standard, unaccented English instead of an Irish brogue, which differentiates him linguistically and elevates him above the rough and obstinate Mike. Even

Mrs. Fluke, who refuses to be alone with the Chinese Chin Sum earlier in the play, seems taken with this new, Irish persona. Her comment that Patsy is "very polite" belies her bias as his gentility was one of the many qualities she failed to recognize earlier when he was Chinese.[181]

Patsy's desire to shape shift into an Irish persona demonstrates the way he uses his transformative ability to his advantage. As an Irishman, he, too, affirms the negative stereotypes heaped upon the Chinese, further illustrating the Irish community's need (and his own) to separate from the imagined lesser Chinese population. In an attempt to disassociate himself from the indecency of his Chinese identity, Patsy conflates assumptions about Chinese immorality and depravity with a tale of cannibalism. In the play's final moments, he admits that, as the Chinese Chin Sum, he cooked and served human flesh. Recounting his ocean voyage from Hong Kong to America, Irish Patsy confesses that seasickness forced him to take green tea as a curative, completely turning him into his Chinese persona, Chin Sum. Patsy refers to Chin Sum as a "haythen Chinaman," who assumed the role of cook, made pudding, and boiled the "captain's mate" during the sea-crossing.[182] In Patsy's complete rejection of his Chinese identity, we see Denison's use of the multiracial condition as a device to elevate whiteness above other racial classes.

The contrast between the Irish servants, Norah and Mike, and the polished, ambitious Patsy demonstrates the political rise of the Irish from the early to the late nineteenth century. In contemporary popular imagination, the Irish are still remembered as a destitute, agrarian underclass that immigrated to the United States to escape famine in the 1840s and 1850s. Though their origins were as farmers when they arrived in America, their poverty confined them to urban centers on the East Coast. Desperate for work, these Irish immigrants took a myriad of menial jobs, including domestic employment in middle-class, white homes like the Fluke household. Mike and Norah embody this wave of Irish immigrants. For many Irish Americans, as well as the American cultural imaginary at large, this mass exodus from Ireland persists as a "self-defining collective diasporic memory"[183] regardless of when one's particular Irish ancestors arrived.

In the character Patsy O'Wang and in his assertion of whiteness, we see the emergence of a strong, politically connected middle class that characterized the latter wave of Irish American immigrants in the years between 1870 and 1930. Like Hidetada, Patsy capitalizes on his mixedness and makes do, shape shifting beyond two ethnically inferior options. Ou acknowledges that toward the end of the nineteenth century the Irish people had attained a social and political status not enjoyed by the Irish who came to America in the mid-1800s. However, Ou asserts that Patsy embraces his Irish identity during a period when the "whiteness" of Irish immigrants was still being contested.[184] She maintains that "despite the rights granted to the Irish . . . there was still, at this point and for years to come, a clear conception of the Irish as not white, and Patsy's efforts to assimilate accentuate that situation."[185] But the period in which *Patsy O'Wang* was written, the 1890s, reveals a different story. Beginning in 1870, the Irish were no longer poor, rural farmers turned menial laborers, but rather an influential middle class. As historian Paul Spickard observes, "By the late nineteenth century, the Irish Americans were poor no more, whether they were immigrants or born in America. They were mainly middle-class people with property. As a group, Irish Americans had risen to a position of influence in the Catholic church, the ranks of labor, and the Democratic party."[186] Patsy's physical differences from Mike and Norah, in both speech and demeanor, emphasize this assimilation of the Irish community. Patsy behaves more English than Irish in the minds of individuals like Mrs. Fluke, who represents respectable American middle-class values, and this transformation is met with her praise and acceptance. In other words, as an Irishman, Patsy solidifies his nativist whiteness.

Significantly, Carter and Ou argue that Patsy has the freedom to choose whiteness, a luxury that many mixed-race subjects do not have.[187] Although I would contend otherwise, considering that Sadakichi Hartmann successfully shape shifted into whiteness when it suited him in his livelihoods or when necessary during the Japanese internment, because Patsy's personal genealogical knowledge and mere assertion of heritage do not necessarily ensure that he will be accepted as white. As is characteristic of the shape shifting process, this assertion requires confirmation and agreement from the observer. After all, Fluke's Irish assistant Mike has not forgotten that Patsy is mixed. When Patsy announces his plans to run for a municipal office, Mike retorts, "I'll niver vote for a shplit ticket, half Irish half Chinay."[188] Patsy may lay claim to his whiteness, but an outsider's knowledge of his Chinese parentage poses a threat to his best-laid plans.[189] In other words, Patsy will ultimately remain liminal to white society long after Mike has successfully attained the privileges of whiteness, including the power to vote.

Sadakichi Hartmann's *Osadda's Revenge* and T. S. Denison's *Patsy O'Wang* illuminate the polyvalent landscape occupied by the mixed-race Asian figure in nineteenth-century America. Together, the protagonist of each play demonstrates the hapa figure's ability to shape shift as a tactical means of making do, each challenging the myth of the monumental and using racial fluidity to reclaim power. Additionally, *Patsy O'Wang* demonstrates how the mixed-race body is often manipulated by monoracial writers to reify stereotypes and to assert white superiority for Eurocentric audiences. By contrast, *Osadda's Revenge* reveals a poignant and sensitive portrayal from a mixed-race author attempting to reconcile with his circumstances and personal history as a multiethnic subject. The drama and, more broadly, the practice of theater also foreground Hartmann's decisions to perform shape shifting across multiple racial categories. These function as tactical responses to the acceptance and abandonment that he experienced simultaneously. In both plays, Patsy and Hidetada's shape shifting performances defy the normative discourses that fail to contain their mixed-race bodies and serve as dramatic traces of a multiracial America in the nineteenth century.

3

Shape Shifting Performances in the Twentieth Century

• •

Yuki is not in love with Jack Bigelow. Though she has many motives for marrying the blond, blue-eyed "barbarian," love is not one of them. She goes where she wants, disappears for days on end, and seems to have little regard for her husband. This is strange for an ostracized, mixed-Japanese woman with limited social freedoms, yet this is precisely what makes her so appealing to Jack. At the end of the 1901 novel, *A Japanese Nightingale*, Yuki eventually leaves her husband for two years and is immediately taken back upon her return. When compared to her contemporary, Cho-Cho-San from David Belasco's 1900 play *Madame Butterfly*, Yuki is a rare figure: a racialized Japanese, multiracial woman imbued with so much agency she seems to overturn the lotus blossom trope before it even took hold in the twentieth century.[1] Why then is her creator, author Winnifred Eaton, so disdained by ethnic studies scholars for the best-selling novel? *A Japanese Nightingale* went on to be adapted into a high-profile production on Broadway in 1903 and a 1918 silent film.[2] Yet Eaton's characterization of Yuki, along with many of her other mixed-race heroines, has been dismissed by scholars as disposable and Orientalist because Eaton wrote within the genre, and many fail to see her early literature as executing any serious intervention in racial discourse, subverting tropes from within. In some ways, Eaton fits in with other writers of the period who committed acts of imperialist betrayal, because her work is frequently disregarded as belonging to the same Orientalist travelogue narratives seen in Pierre Loti's novel *Madame Chrysanthème* (1887).[3] However, a careful examination of Eaton's work reveals interventions often misread by Asian American scholars, who apply the same paradigmatic expectations to Eaton that they do to other monoracial Asian American writers, which include Eaton's older sister, Edith Eaton, among them. As cultural scholar Eve Oishi contends, the insufficient critical scholarship does not concentrate on Eaton's literary contributions but fixates on "the dubiousness of her ethnic identification."[4] The shape shifting, multiracial Winnifred Eaton, however, wrote not about Asian American themes but about a mixed-race consciousness, and I suggest that she shape shifted into a Japanese persona, Onoto Watanna, to do it.[5]

This chapter analyzes the mixed-race feminine figure and considers how gender intersects with race to change the ways in which racial oppression affects the body. The chapter explores the work of Winnifred Eaton, specifically the novel and its adapted play *A Japanese Nightingale*, who is most widely known as a novelist, short story author, and screenwriter. Eaton, a mixed-race Chinese woman in the early twentieth century confronted by the era's Chinese prejudice and violence, chose, like Sadakichi Hartmann, to shape shift in Japaneseness. When the Japanese nation fell from cultural and political favor in the United States, Eaton (also like Hartmann) dropped her Japanese persona and fluidly moved through society as white or mixed-Chinese.

Eaton's performance of self, often a conundrum for monoracial scholars, transgressed the edicts of racial hierarchy and monoracial cultural logic. Specifically, Eaton rejected the idea that she must adhere to social expectations and identify as monoracially Chinese as dictated by hypodescent. Instead, she embraced her mixed-Asian identity and chose mixed-Japaneseness for herself, capitalizing on the fascination and popularity of Japanese culture in the zeitgeist of the nineteenth century in the West.

In this chapter I compare aspects of Eaton's novel *A Japanese Nightingale* with the popular Madame Butterfly narrative vis-à-vis David Belasco's 1900 play and then explore the ways in which the protofeminist novel differs from its theatrical adaptation, which was written by William Young in 1902. The latter strays from the interventions performed by its namesake and aligns more closely with the Orientalist feminized stereotypes of *Madame Butterfly*, concretizing characterizations that the novel precisely rejects. I will triangulate these three works to elucidate Eaton's doubly liminal positionality as a mixed-race subject and demonstrate the ways in which her work has been misconstrued as ethnic and political betrayal. I argue that Eaton's choice to shape shift is not an act of betrayal nor a failure but instead is evidence of Eaton's refusal to subscribe to easy categorization and stagnant, monoracial malaise.

I discuss the background of the novel within the context of Eaton's multiracial upbringing in order to illuminate her racially transgressive decision to foreground mixedness in her work. To the degree that monoracial theater makers have misunderstood the centrality of mixedness in her novel, monoracial literary scholars similarly misinterpret the crucial inventions Eaton made in racial discourse. Moreover, the categorization of Eaton as a race traitor denotes a mis-contextualization of her cultural position amid the anti-Chinese rhetoric of Progressive Era America and a misreading of the complexity of her multiracial identity. Eaton's positionality as a doubly liminal subject meant that she incor-porated two different sets of social habiti, which influenced her subsequent deci-sions and produced a consciousness separate from a monoracial Asian American subjectivity.[6]

An exploration of Eaton and her limited options in an ever-evolving racialized landscape assists us in understanding the erasure of the mixed-race subject in the mid-twentieth century. Specifically, theater and film have been complicit in reinforcing concomitant monoraciality for mixed-race individuals in both dominant and subdominant discourses. This can be seen in the transformation of mixed-race figure Anna Leonowens into a white English governess in multi-ple adaptations of *The King and I* as well as the mixed-race character Lee in the Asian American play *The Chickencoop Chinaman*, who appeared onstage embod-ied by a white actor in the 1972 production. These depictions of mixedness in the mid-twentieth century illustrate the abject invisibility of the mixed-race subject.[7]

An investigation into contradictory ontologies inevitably produces a turn to failure. These failures in the articulation of alternative paratopic spaces generate their own kind of combustible energy that unsettles conventional notions of Asian American subjectivity. Performance scholar Sara Jane Bailes contends that in its status as a wrongdoing, "one of [failure's] most radical properties is that it operates through a principle of difference rather than sameness."[8] I suggest that, for Eaton, difference reveals itself as a monoracial nonconforming identity, whose ability to shape shift foregrounds a betrayal in Asian American discourse. Some Asian American scholars hold that Winnifred Eaton failed for two reasons. First, they believe she failed to publicly embrace her Chinese heritage and to write about Chinese diasporic themes. Instead, Eaton "masqueraded" as a mixed-Japanese woman and chose to write within the Orientalist genre. This failure is a particularly insidious betrayal as the genre concretizes the objectifi-cation and hypersexualization of Asian (specifically Japanese) women and romanticized the sexual tourism normalized on nineteenth-century Japan's island of Dejima. Praised among white, Western, early twentieth-century readers for her "authentic" voice and insider knowledge, Eaton has been characterized as a traitor who betrayed the Asian diasporic community by contributing to the proliferation of femme fatale stereotypes, such as the lotus blossom in stories like *A Japanese Nightingale.*[9]

The second failure is Eaton's Broadway play *A Japanese Nightingale* itself, an adaptation of her best-selling novel, whose production was panned in the press and closed after only forty-six performances.[10] This is significant when compared to Belasco's play *Madame Butterfly*, which was a Broadway success before being transferred to London and on whose coat tails *A Japanese Nightingale* was riding. For all intents and purposes, in the midst of the Progressive Era's preoccupation with Japonisme, there was little reason for Eaton's play to flop.

Eaton's failures suggest that her work was misread through monoracial Asian American literary expectations that do not apply to it. It is precisely through Bailes's "difference" that Eaton's novel *A Japanese Nightingale* resists the trappings of Orientalist literature and the reason that the book's play adaptation did not succeed. As Bailes articulates earlier in this discussion, I suggest that sameness is the criterion curated by monoracial Asian American scholars, who deem Eaton's questionable intentions as a "wrongdoing"—a betrayal of her Chinese heritage and of the Asian transnational diasporic community—rather than an intervention, a rupture in discourse about race and culture in the early twentieth century. It also showcases the sameness by which Asian figures were represented onstage in Progressive Era America and the expectations through which spectators had been culturally conditioned. Bailes contends that in its status as wrongdoing, "a failed objective establishes an aperture, an opening onto several . . . other ways of doing that counter the authority of a singular or 'correct' outcome."[11] I agree with Bailes that a wrongdoing calls into question the criteria expected by an established authority.

What then and according to whose authority is the correct outcome for an Asian American identity? Cultural theorist Crystal Parikh in *An Ethics of Betrayal* further suggests that traitors "offer a crucial and unique perspective on the complexities of belonging, assimilation, and exclusion in U.S. culture and politics."[12] Parikh, like Brandi Wilkins Catanese, underscores the generative potential of racial transgression to transform the paradigms that govern racial discourses. While Catanese interrogates the dominant's aggrandizement of racial transcendence, Parikh dislodges the expectations and edicts of the subdominant. She astutely observes that betrayal signals "social agency and decision making" and asserts that by "foregrounding an ethical account of transgressions, especially as they reconfigure the cultural politics of minority discourse . . . we must account for the values that are established or undermined when . . . traitorous, agents contest social identities and formations."[13] Eaton's work destabilizes the vetting criteria that has governed the authenticity of Asian American literature. A closer examination of the mixed-race perspective in her work reframes Eaton's shape shifting decisions as a woman and as a mixed-race author in a profession that was largely accessible only to white men in the early twentieth century. This investigation also reclaims Eaton's place as an Asian American author of mixed-race descent, who expands the contemporary understanding of the multitude of experiences, histories, and identities belonging to Asian America. Eaton's shape shifting performance as a mixed-Japanese woman undermines the privilege of whiteness embedded in the act of passing and expands the umbrella of monoracial Asian American identity and racial formation.

Shape shifting allows mixed-race individuals a certain amount of control over the reception of their racial mutability. Because their phenotypical features are not easily legible, the observer relies on confirmation from the mixed-race subject in order to assign the body to a suitable, though superficial, racial category. The mixed-race person's refusal to respond or offer confirmation about their multiethnic parentage can bar the observer from completing this process. In this way, the mixed-race figure is able to control how she is racialized within the encounter, which serves as a source of agency. If racialization is an unjust containment, then Eaton's decision to shape shift signals a tactic deployed to navigate a monoracial hierarchical system rather than a betrayal of her racial identity.

Cultural geography plays a key role in the reception of the shape shifter, too. Racial cartographies provide various cultural expectations that further enable the shape shifting process to take place. For example, mixed-race playwright Sadakichi Hartmann, who was partly of Asian descent, successfully shape shifted into a Japanese persona in America during the height of Japonisme, even though Hartmann was not culturally Japanese. The ability of the mixed-race body to shape shift across racial lines then becomes contingent on the geographical context as well as the reception of the individual at each of these sites.

Most of the literature on Winnifred Eaton passes judgment on her shape shifting performances as unethical racial imposture. In other words, she is "passing," thus seemingly compromising her place in the Asian American canon, even though her biographer Jean Lee Cole reminds us that she is impossible to ignore as the first novelist of Asian descent in the United States.[14] Yet her shape shifting has foreclosed her right to be crowned the "godmother" of Asian American literature—a title bestowed instead on her (equally deserving) sister Edith Eaton. Winnifred Eaton has been criticized as a sellout for abandoning her own Chinese ancestry, while her sister Edith publicly embraced their parentage and, in fact, has become memorialized as a champion of fair treatment for Chinese communities. Jolie Sheffer characterizes the younger Winnifred's shape shifting persona as "a kind of drag performance," whereas other scholars, like Amy Ling and Yuko Matsukawa, refer to it, respectively, as "put[ting] on ethnicity" or as an even more improbable "trickster figure" who overtly mocks authority and uses deception to balance the scales.[15] While the shape shifter, as articulated by Spickard, does share some characteristics with the trickster, the latter still denotes a false representation or an impersonation of identity and a direct challenge to the dominant. The shape shifter instead illuminates another way of being, that, like Anurima Banerji's paratopia, merely exists alongside the dominant monoracial articulations of being.

Mixed-race artists like Eaton deploy shape shifting as a tactic to navigate the racial limitations of the quotidian. This is fraught because Eaton's early writing not only participated in Orientalist literature but was also instrumental in driving its popularity. Moreover, Eaton's work also presents a conundrum because, as a mixed-race author, she has written through the lens of multiple ethnic and cultural perspectives, such as that of a working class Irish domestic as in "The Diary of Delia" (1907), or of white ranchers in Alberta, Canada in *Cattle* (1923).

Eve Oishi asserts that "baldly stated, critics of Asian American literature simply do not know what to do with a Eurasian writer of Chinese and Anglo descent who assumed a Japanese identity" and then proceeded to write about mixed-Japanese women.[16] However, even Oishi suggests that Eaton's alter ego was monoracially Japanese. The social expectations of hypodescent that govern the options for racial identification effectively bar Eaton from writing from her mixed-race positionality, a state of being that did not change in any of Eaton's shape shifting personae. Eaton wrote squarely and authentically from a mixed-race subjectivity. Like Sadakichi Hartmann, she shape shifted into Japaneseness and used her shape shifting abilities to capitalize on a market that was ripe for a love of all things Japanese.

Progressive Era America was swept up in an enthusiastic fervor for Japanese cultural artifacts, regardless of authenticity. Cheap goods printed with Asiatic floral designs were available en masse for the commodified consumption of the middle class. The Western understanding of Japanese customs and culture played out in the parlors of middle-class women who lounged in kimonos, consumed tea, and shared their love of Gilbert and Sullivan's opera *The Mikado (1885)*.[17] Even Eaton and her own sisters shared in the obsession with Gilbert and Sullivan as children. Diana Birchall, Winnifred Eaton's granddaughter and biographer, notes a family photograph in which three of Eaton's sisters—Sara, Rose, and May—can be seen, wrapped in kimonos and posing with fans.[18] Experiences with Progressive Era racial prejudice, coupled with exposure to Japanese culture, however peripheral, no doubt influenced Eaton's decision to shape shift into a Japanese persona as an adult.

Eaton made a name for herself early on, writing Orientalist novels that were popular in the early part of the twentieth century, like her first novel *Miss Numè of Japan* (1899) and the subsequent *A Japanese Nightingale* (1901).[19] She capitalized on the cult of Japonisme that overtook Progressive Era America but that had begun to wane by 1910 due in part to the rise of American eugenics as well as the successful Japanese military campaigns of the Russo-Japanese War, which produced anxiety about ramifications of Japanese expansion.[20] She actively exercised her ability to shape shift and to control racialized encounters as an individual of Asian descent. If indeed the mixed-race Asian experience is a part of the Asian American/Asian diasporic experience, then Eaton has more than earned her place.

A Savage in Silks: The Curious Case of Winnifred Eaton

Winnifred Eaton was born in Montreal in Quebec, Canada, to English merchant Edward Eaton and his Chinese bride, Achuen Amoy, christened "Grace" in 1875. Grace Trefusis had been adopted by English missionaries and educated at a Presbyterian college in England before returning to China as a missionary at the age of twenty. According to Winnifred Eaton's sister, Edith, Grace met Edward during one of his business ventures in Shanghai, and they were married in China in 1863.[21] The family was poor and lived its early years with Eaton's family in England before moving and settling in Quebec—after a short residence in New York—in 1872. Winnifred was their eighth child. With twelve Eaton children in all, Winnifred began writing and publishing in her early adolescence to help support her siblings who were still at home.[22]

An initial, racialized curiosity and a more sinister, overt prejudice followed the children as they grew. After the passing of the Chinese Exclusion Act in the United States in 1882, many Chinese immigrants migrated to Canada to find work completing the rails of the Canadian Pacific Railway, which was finished in 1885. This influx of Chinese labor created anxiety in towns like the Eatons' own Montreal, which expressed dismay at its increasing Chinese population. Resultantly, the Canadian government followed American legislation and passed the Chinese Immigration Act of 1885, barring citizenship from Canadian residents of Chinese descent and reifying the growing anti-Chinese sentiment that permeated Canada through the law. Winnifred's older sister Edith—writing under the pen name Sui Sin Far—wrote about the hatred and disdain that legally sanctioned racism condoned in public spaces. In Canada, she encountered French and English children who would "amuse themselves" by taunting her and her siblings and pulling their hair.[23] Moreover, the adults would, in Edith's words, "pause and gaze upon us, very much in the same way that I have seen people gaze upon strange animals in a menagerie."[24] While their mother, Grace, cheered them on in such strife, their father deemed it "wisest to be blind and deaf to many things."[25] The Eaton children experienced continual prejudice in French Canada and in the United States, and to the siblings, the prejudice looked and felt the same. Years earlier in Hudson City, New York, where the family had lived prior to relocating to Canada, a crowd of children taunted Edith, chanting, "Chinky, Chinky, Chinaman, yellow-face, pig-tail, rat-eater," to which Edith retaliated with "I'd rather be Chinese than anything else in the world" before a brutal brawl ensued. This left Edith and her accompanying brother crawling home. The siblings told their skeptical mother that they had "won the battle."[26]

This political climate presented the Eaton siblings with limited options. Racist attitudes cast poor, working-class Chinese laborers as deviant and morally inferior. This was in stark contrast to the tolerance and even admiration of Japanese immigrants and tourists who tended to be from the merchant class and were, therefore, more acceptable in status. Unlike Hidetada and his creator, Sadakichi Hartmann, who were most often met with fascination by their contemporaries, Chinese subjects were mistrusted and blamed for the economic hardships that befell their white peers. Nonetheless, the elder Eaton sister eventually shape shifted publicly into Sui Sin Far, a half-Chinese, Eurasian writer.[27] While Edith made good on this claim that she would rather be Chinese than anything else—adopting a Chinese moniker and writing about the Chinese diasporic experience—her siblings, Winnifred among them, did not share this sentiment.

In a letter, Winnifred's daughter Doris affirmed that her mother "was not particularly proud of the fact that she was *partly* Chinese. As a child she suffered from racial prejudice in Montreal, and I think would have preferred to be all Chinese or all English."[28] This is significant because it debunks the misconception that mixed-race people implicitly desire to pass as white. Eaton understood that the racialized system, more importantly, operated through monoracial categories, and her mixed-race identity subjected her to discrimination within both groups.

This conundrum is especially fraught when one ethnic group is organized lower in the hierarchy. In "Leaves from the Mental Portfolio of an Eurasian," Edith recounted several early twentieth-century instances in which mixed-race Chinese engaged in shape shifting as a tactic to navigate the racial prejudice toward the Chinese: "The Americans, having for many years manifested a much higher regard for the Japanese than for the Chinese, several half Chinese young men and women, thinking to advance themselves, both in a social and business sense, pass as Japanese. They continue to be known as Eurasians; but a Japanese Eurasian does not appear in the same light as a Chinese Eurasian."[29] Likewise, mixed-race figures of Chinese descent also shape shifted into categories beyond other Asian ethnic groups. Edith wrote about her sister May, but hid May's identity, asserting that in San Francisco, she met "a half Chinese, half white girl. Her face is plastered with a thick white coat of paint and her eyelids and eyebrows so that the shape of her eyes and the whole expression of her face is changed. She was born in the East, and at the age of eighteen came West in answer to an advertisement. . . . It is not difficult, in a land like California, for a half Chinese, half white girl to *pass* as one of Spanish or Mexican origin. This poor child does, though she lives in nervous dread of being discovered."[30] Certainly, May had shifted into what she deemed a more acceptable category, based on the opportunities and expectations that the social geography presented to her in California. She did not pass into whiteness as some of her siblings had but rather shape shifted into brownness.

Many of the Eaton siblings shape shifted into whiteness as their own physiognomies and geographic contexts allowed. Sister Grace, who was between Edith and Winnifred in age, became a high-powered attorney in Chicago.[31] Grace downplayed her Chinese ancestry and identified with her English heritage in public spheres. There is also evidence that Grace identified at times as being half-Japanese. Birchall suspects that this was perhaps to corroborate Winnifred's own shift into Japaneseness, as not only did the two remain close but Winnifred often consulted Grace in personal legal matters, thus making it probable that they would have engaged with similar groups of people.[32] Their older brother Edward Charles actively hid his ethnic background and cemented his adamant shift into Englishness with memberships to "whites-only" clubs.[33]

The desire to shape shift into whiteness is understandable due to the doubly liminal state in which the multiracial Eaton siblings found themselves. The misconception built into the notion of racial passing is the belief that individuals reject subjugated group memberships for imposturous associations with whiteness. However, as doubly liminal mixed-race subjects, it is just as likely that they will be met with rejection from the subdominant racialized group. As Edith asserted, "Fundamentally, I muse, all people are the same. My mother's race is as prejudiced as my father's."[34] Likewise, Edith wrote that the monoracial Chinese women she encountered doubted whether or not she could find a monoracial Chinese man to marry her: "They are, however, a little doubtful as to whether one could be persuaded to care for me, full-blooded Chinese people having a prejudice against the half white."[35] Winnifred Eaton shifted into a half-Japanese persona to altogether avoid the negative backlash against and from Chinese immigrants. While many scholars assert that there are "troubling ethical questions of Eaton's decision to 'pass' for Japanese,"[36] I disagree that Eaton's choice was a decision to "pass," and I reframe her actions as in line with the complex identity construction inherent in shape shifting. No doubt if Chinoiserie were a lucrative literary option, Eaton would have claimed and publicly embraced (she did not reject it privately) her Chinese ancestry. Working within social and geographic contexts that conflated many ethnic groups into the highly unstable category of Oriental, Eaton understandably chose the one that garnered the most advantages within her assigned racial group: Japanese. Eaton, like Hartmann, like other figures in this book, deployed shape shifting as a tactic to fulfill professional ambitions and dreams.

After working as a writer in Jamaica, Winnifred Eaton moved to Chicago in 1897, where she worked as a stenographer and wrote fiction after hours (figure 3.1).[37] She delved into the Orientalist Japanese stories made popular by John Luther Long, who gleaned his inspiration from the 1887 novel *Madame Chrysanthème* by Pierre Loti. "Following the vogue of things Japanese," Eaton gained a popularity of her own as the half-Japanese, half-English writer Onoto Watanna, who first appeared in publication the same year that Eaton settled in Chicago.[38] Though Watanna wrote familiar commercialized stories, she abandoned the formulaic "coupling of the big blonde barbarian and a charming little Japanese maiden," a seductive combination for the Progressive Era audience.[39] Capitalizing on this magnetic appeal, Watanna drew a readership to her work and repurposed the form to harshly critique the abandonment of half-caste children left in the wake of interracial encounters or in "Japanese marriages." In Orientalist literature, these Japanese nuptials were temporary contracts that were null and void when white, Western husbands left their wives on the shores of Japan. These "husbands" traded in the arrangements for permanent, legitimate "American marriages." Eaton's stories that explore this narrative arc include "A Half-Caste" (1899) and "A Father" (1900).

Sometimes, Eaton's decision to assume the half-Japanese persona was co-opted without her knowledge, and her own metamorphosis got away from her. Eaton's various editors in Chicago marketed Onoto Watanna with enthusiastic zeal, and

FIGURE 3.1 Winnifred Eaton in Chicago in 1899. (Photo courtesy of Elizabeth Rooney and Diana Birchall.)

Watanna's biography often differed from one account to another, although her origins often matched those of her protagonists. Described as the daughter of a British naval officer, or an English consul, her mother was "a Japanese beauty," and Watanna reportedly lived in Japan until she was fifteen, after which she moved with her family to Canada or the United States.[40] Watanna's biography, published in *Current Literature* in 1897, was the first article that purposely introduced the alter ego to the public.[41] Watanna was identified by her "real" Japanese name Kitishima Kata Hasche, two monikers that were purported to mean the same thing in different Japanese dialects. As Birchall so keenly notes, this assertion was not entirely untrue, as in reality "neither name meant anything."[42] *Current Literature* printed the article with a picture of a Japanese woman who was supposedly Eaton, which was a surprise even to the author. The portrait was of a different person entirely.[43]

These marketing campaigns led by Eaton's publishers served to aid her in her shape shifting. Biographies of the author's life were accompanied by a photograph of the author in a kimono to solidify the author's authenticity, though at times, the rendering was not even that of Eaton. Even more interesting is that these accounts describe the shape shifting process in plain sight. In an article entitled "Onoto Watanna, the Writer," the author makes the following observation: "In modern American trappings she is a charming girl, whose Oriental origin scarcely would be detected. In Japanese kimono, however, all the features of a winning little chrysanthemum belle stand out. While her dark eyes do not slant perceptibly, the Japanese droop at either side of the nose proclaims her race."[44] The article details a crucial aspect of the shape shifting process in which the reception of the racially ambiguous body changes based on the context, in this case the "costume" adorning the subject. The body does not change but, because of the context, the reception of it does. The reportage also provides evidence of an early twentieth-century understanding of race as biologically legible. Watanna's "Japanese droop" purportedly betrays her and gives her away. The irony, of course, is the fallacy of this statement since there is no "Japanese" droop on Eaton's multiethnic Chinese visage. Furthermore, it seems that the context is enough to camouflage Wattana's multiraciality because it can "scarcely be detected," thereby disproving race as being anything that can be read on one's body.

The account goes further to conflate race with culture and intelligence in regard to education, the purview of the civilized West. The article foregrounds Eaton's "little education" and her "uneven" style, highlighting the supposed characteristics of an inferior racial group. Other articles made note of Watanna's "simplicity of speech," but all of these literary shortcomings were forgiven on the assumption that Watanna was writing in a second language, English.[45] Eaton's work, however, would never have met its success without a developed sense of command. Second, due to the public's fascination with Japonisme, it seems that readers hungry to consume Japanese stories would excuse the presence of stilted language, a continuation of Eaton's performance vis-à-vis her text. Eaton's literary prowess lay in her ability to extend the performance of her Japaneseness onto paper.

The novel *A Japanese Nightingale* was Eaton's first major success. The book sold approximately 200,000 copies and was published in multiple countries, including England, France, Japan, Spain, and Sweden. In the novel, Jack Bigelow enters a "Japanese marriage" with the half-caste Yuki Burton (her surname because of her English father). Yuki's Japanese physiognomy is disrupted by "intensely, vividly blue" eyes with "rich red-black hair."[46] Jack muses that the combination makes her "an eerie little creature" and asks if she is, in fact, Japanese, as Eaton tells us, "to make sure."[47] Despite his initial resistance, however, Jack finds himself drawn to the geisha, and though he has no intention of entering marriage, he allows a Japanese matchmaker to arrange a meeting with her. Jack's Japanese friend, Taro, warns him about such engagements and advises him to steer clear of them. However, Yuki is eager to make the match, and Jack is so taken with her that he finally agrees to marry her in spite of himself.

Theirs is an unconventional marriage, even for a "Japanese" one. In their married life, Yuki often disappears for hours, sometimes days on end, never revealing where she has been. She always seems to need more clothes and more money. Jack eventually learns that she has been giving the money to her mother, who uses it to support Yuki's older brother in college in the United States. In a turn toward the dramatic, this brother turns out to be none other than Jack's friend Taro, who is horrified that his sister married a man specifically to support his studies, and worse, that Jack is the American who entrapped his sister. Taro dies from a head wound acquired in a fight with Jack to defend his sister's honor. Yuki flees in shame for two years, while the lovesick Jack relentlessly pursues her.

A Japanese Nightingale subverts many of the accepted tropes in Orientalist stories in the early twentieth century. Like Long's short story and its subsequent theatrical iterations, Eaton's narrative focuses on an interracial couple, in which a Japanese woman and a white American or English man are brought together in a "Japanese marriage" through a matchmaker. Unlike the Butterfly narratives, however, it is the husband who takes the marriage much more seriously than his Asian wife. The common knowledge that Westerners leave their Japanese wives is the one thing that gives Yuki comfort and that which enables her to agree to such an arrangement. Instead of hoping he will fall in love and stay, she is counting on him to leave. For her, the marriage is a means to an end, a personal sacrifice to earn money to ensure the welfare of her brother and one that she enters knowingly and shrewdly. She is deliberate in her agency. Yuki is neither the lotus blossom nor the dragon lady, and in encompassing characteristics of both, she shatters the tropes from the inside. She is a strong, self-possessed, single-minded woman, cloaked in Orientalist garments, a savage in silks, sashaying before the American populace in plain sight. She possesses all the autonomy, intelligence, and savvy of her creator, Winnifred Eaton. As a woman amid financial hardship, who ventured out on her own and built a life on her own terms, Eaton infuses Yuki with this feminist spirit. As Dominika Ferens observes, there is nothing formulaic about Eaton's tales of miscegenation, which successfully "sidestep the Asian equivalent of the "tragic mulatto" narrative."[48] This is a phenomenon we certainly do not see in other Orientalist literature. Seemingly unlikely candidates, Eaton and Yuki demonstrate the possibility of a mixed-race, feminine subject's ability to tactically navigate the status quo and slip between expectations of race, culture, gender, and class.

Eaton's perspective and the novel *A Japanese Nightingale* provide a unique contrast to the work of Sadakichi Hartmann because they both reveal the doubly liminal state of the mixed-race subject in the early twentieth century. Hartmann, who did not know his Asian mother and identified as a German, did not interact with the Japanese community and did not experience rejection as a result of the subdominant discourse. Winnifred Eaton, however, raised by a Chinese mother who infused Eaton's childhood with her culture, encountered discrimination from members of the monoracial Chinese community. These experiences informed Eaton's storytelling and make her works extraordinary among Orientalist contemporary fiction. In the case of *A Japanese Nightingale*, Eaton was not writing a novel solely about the Asian American experience but one that was written from and about a hapa consciousness. The assumption that mixed-race subjects were not at the forefront of the social milieu, actively intervening in the rising conflation of race, culture, and biology nor engaging directly with its cultural artifacts, is simply not true.

Furthermore, even though Eaton is writing in an Orientalist literary genre, her work does not concretize the binary of Orientalism, where the "feminine" East is put in a position of subjugation as compared to the dominant, "masculine" West.[49] Rather than being complicit with this relationship of power and domination, Eaton's work in *A Japanese Nightingale* instead accomplishes two tasks.[50] First, Eaton reclaims power for the East (represented by the geisha figure) by decentering the position of the West in the narrative. Yuki's agency allows her to make her own decisions, economic or otherwise, which she does in an Asian landscape that is deliberately seen through her eyes as an insider. Second, Eaton illuminates the nuanced complexities of a doubly liminal positionality rather than re-creating a two-dimensional femme fatale character as seen in other Orientalist literature. Main character Yuki's physiognomy as the product of a Japanese mother and an English father (similar to Onoto Watanna's parentage) creates what Maria P. P. Root calls an "emotional/psychic earthquake" in the eyes of her observers, since they cannot reconcile her physical appearance with their cultural expectations.[51] Resultantly, both white American and Japanese characters refer to her as a "creature," whom they regard with disdain. She is, as Cynthia L. Nakashima contends, a "mythological multiracial monster."[52] It is as if the multiethnic Yuki should not exist since creatures usually reside in different realms of reality. In other words, the multiethnic Yuki is an anomaly in this monoracial regime. In this way, she simultaneously destabilizes multiple identities. Perhaps it is for this reason that the racial interventions of Eaton, her novel, and its main character altogether have not been recognized in multiple fields.

Yuki's experience as a subject who is liminal from two cultural parent groups is amplified through the rejection of the subdominant discourse. When Jack inquires after the ethereal performer early in the novel, the Japanese proprietor divulges that he distrusts her. Eaton establishes the proprietor as a cultural authority vis-à-vis his ownership of a Japanese tea house, an establishment representative of specific cultural practices in Japan. Even to him, Yuki's singing and dancing seem strange, positioning her as an outsider to the culture. The proprietor describes Yuki thus, revealing his contempt for her. She is "a cheap girl from Tokyo, with the blue-glass eyes of the barbarian, the yellow skin of the lower Japanese, the hair of mixed color, black and red . . . and the heart and nature of those honorably unreliable creatures, alien at this country, alien at your honorable country, augustly despicable—a half-caste!"[53] Although she was born and raised in Japan, he indicates that her behavior is biologically predetermined and tainted by her mixed biology. The proprietor begrudgingly allows Yuki to perform because her "strange" song and dance draw huge crowds of Japanese and foreign patrons. Both groups are drawn to her "weird" performances and her biologically illegible body with equal fascination. Yuki's barbarous blue eyes, typically seen in the West, are unnatural. In the proprietor's description of her, Eaton underscores the rejection and discrimination that mixed Asians similarly encounter from Asian cultural groups, a phenomenon known as the subdominant discourse.[54] Eaton goes further to decenter the West's perspective that Asian cultural groups similarly subscribe to the rule of hypodescent and automatically accept mixed-race subjects as their own. Eaton debunks this misinformed assumption that continues to circulate as a kind of Western knowledge about the East. Through encounters with the proprietor, and with neighborhood children later in the novel—which parallel Eaton's experiences with adults and children she encountered in her childhood—any reinforcement of the East/West dichotomy is thwarted in the description of doubly liminal Yuki and her observers. This demonstrates how the mixed-race subject is relegated to the limens of different monoracial groups, clearly elucidating, in this regard, an identity politics in 1901 similar to that seen in contemporary times.

Furthermore, both racial groups, according to Eaton, subscribe to the trope of the tragic Eurasian, as a "creature," who possesses unstable biological characteristics. Paradoxically, many parties want to capitalize on Yuki's outsider status, transforming her into a commodity. The tea house proprietor benefits from her spectators. An American theatrical manager wants her to perform in his vaudeville revue. The Japanese marriage broker, Ido, is eager to arrange a meeting with Jack for a profit.

Eaton further dismantles the Orientalist dyad by positioning mixedness as a centralized role rather than as a peripheral object. When the matchmaker brings Yuki to Jack's home, the American again appraises her Japanese physiognomy (and her garments, which, according to Jack, seemingly solidify her Japaneseness) that is troubled by "blue-glass eyes" and "black and red" hair.[55] Because of her ambiguous appearance, Jack expresses his skepticism at Yuki's claim of parentage. Her racialized membership is questionable, and her ambiguous physiognomy seems to confirm his doubt. In scenes like these, Eaton communicates the anxiety, distrust, and disdain inscribed on the mixed-race subject that transforms her into a tragic figure in the minds of the public. Later in the novel, when Jack searches for Yuki after her disappearance, he encounters Madame Pine-leaf as he goes from teahouse to teahouse, looking for his wife. When he reveals that he is looking for a half-Japanese girl, Pine-leaf feigns politeness, but her expression of annoyance and disapproval belies her inner thoughts. "Ah-h!—a half-caste," she retorts and "pretends" to consult her memory.[56] The truth, according to Eaton's tone, is that Pine-leaf has not bothered to commit a half-caste girl to memory, further underscoring the subdominant attitude toward "half-breeds" and the subsequent, doubly liminal positionality of the mixed-race subject.

While Yuki defies the trappings of a stereotypical lotus blossom protagonist, Jack, as the dominant, Western masculine figure also differs from Pinkerton, his counterpart in *Madame Butterfly*. Described as "one of the richest foreigners" in Tokyo, he remains "impregnable" to the offers put before him by the numerous matchmakers in the city.[57] Eaton's use of the word *impregnable* is not to be overlooked here, as she makes it noticeably clear that no tragic mixed-race child will cloud the singular vision of the novel. Instead, she offers Taro Burton, Yuki's brother, as the example of a half-caste son who endured the trials of the dominant and subdominant discourses. Taro is a man, not a child, and he talks back directly to the white American husband and, potentially, father-to-be. Like Hartmann's Hidetada, he impresses upon Jack the strife that desertion would bring to a wife and child. In *A Japanese Nightingale*, the understanding comes before the marriage in question and not long after, for Jack pledges to Taro that he would not join "the long list of foreigners who for a . . . *convenient* season cheerfully take unto themselves Japanese wives, and with the same cheerfulness desert them."[58] In this way, Eaton, writing alongside white male authors, provides a counterpoint to the imperialist arrogance rooted in their tales of the exotic and intervenes in the abandonment of "Butterfly."

Eaton further subverts the Orientalist Butterfly narrative through Yuki's agency. It is for Yuki that the marriage is one of convenience and one in which she benefits from the unconditional love of a spouse. It is she who abandons her husband, leaving him in utter turmoil, without a valid explanation. She is also gone, like Pinkerton, for two years, while her spouse "waits" in vain for her. Jack refuses to move on and, like Cho-Cho-San, clings to a belief that he will see his spouse again. Eaton turns the Butterfly narrative on its head and offers an alternative, which instead empowers the feminine body. In this way, Eaton does Asian American literature a grave service, by submerging herself within the trappings of the Orientalist novel and dismantling it from the inside. Furthermore, in an ethical move on Eaton's part, she emphasizes the importance of ensuring that the marriage is sound before bringing a child into it. This seems to be informed by her own life, in which she witnessed a successful marriage between her own interracial parents and through an understanding that the hapa children of such unions are not to be ignored as two-dimensional devices like Trouble or Sorrow (ironically named), the child in iterations of *Madame Butterfly*. Thus Eaton affirms then that such interracial marriages are not unconventional, and that they do exist. Her contribution to Asian American literature has been grossly overlooked, both for its crucial early interventions made but also for her early assertion that mixed-race Asians have a place in the Asian diasporic story.

If Eaton failed to overtly write about monoracial Asian American themes, her second failure was the 1903 production of "A Japanese Nightingale," which dilated Orientalism by embodying it onstage. Eaton was an avid theater spectator who frequently attended performances in New York with her friend Jean Webster (Mark Twain's great-niece). Eaton found her most successful novel adapted into a play and serendipitously produced on Broadway at the height of the Japonisme craze. She had submitted *A Japanese Nightingale* and a synopsis for her subsequent book *The Wooing of Wistaria* to Benjamin Roeder, the manager of "The Wizard" of the American theater himself, David Belasco. Belasco was a consummate theater maker, producer, director, and playwright. (He abhorred the term *dramatist*, contending that he didn't simply write plays, but "wrighted" them into being.)[59] The "Wizard" was known for subjecting actors to long, grueling hours of rehearsal and spared no expense in creating lavish theatrical spectacles, which were, like him, larger-than-life.[60] According to Roeder, Belasco was searching for a new project for actress Blanche Bates, who had starred as Cho-Cho-San in *Madame Butterfly*. Though Roeder promised Eaton a decision on her submission in a few days, after months with no word, Eaton submitted the book and manuscript to the prominent drama agent Elizabeth Marbury, who worked with major play broker Alice Kauser.[61] Clients of their office included Oscar Wilde, George Bernard Shaw, Maurice Maeterlinck, and Gerhart Hauptman. No doubt it was a major steppingstone for Eaton to secure such heavy-hitting representation in the theatrical world. When Marbury insisted that Belasco return the materials, he cited, through his manager, his disinterest in producing a full-length Japanese play and acquiesced.[62]

Marbury turned around and sold the rights for *A Japanese Nightingale* to theater moguls Mark Klaw and Abraham L. Erlanger on June 30, 1902. The powerful producing team had found success with the box office smash *Ben-Hur* (1899) on Broadway, which ran from 1899 to 1920, and they enlisted William Young to pen an adaptation of Eaton's book for the stage.[63] Young had a track record of adapting novels into playscripts that turned their productions into box office gold.[64] Eaton had been trying to put something onstage for four years. The four of them together appeared to be the perfect combination.

Young's adaption transformed Eaton's novel into an Orientalist drama that seemed to pinch aspects of *Madame Butterfly* and to capitalize on Western assumptions about Japan. Young was perhaps re-creating a formulaic copy of the latter in the hopes of mirroring its success. It is crucial to note that Young was a monoracial white writer, who was not making the same decisions as Eaton (or at least not for the same reasons), and this lies at the heart of the problems, therefore the failure, of the play. When Young adapted the novel, he changed Yuki's ethnic background to be one that was entirely, mono-ethnically Japanese, eliminating the complexities of identity and silencing the interventions that the novel made in contemporary racial discourse. This early erasure of a mixed-race character from the Broadway stage illustrates a larger, continued erasure of mixed-race hapa figures from performance, a trend that extends deep into the midcentury and undergirds the play's outcome as a box office failure. The importance of a narrative about a hapa protagonist was missed in the hands of a white male writer who recast Yuki as a monoracial Asian figure.

The play nullifies the central mixed-race subjectivity and centers the experiences of its white subjects in Japan. The linear, chronological narrative is told through an Orientalist, Eurocentric lens, in which the main characters are white, and the Asian characters serve merely as frames for the white protagonists. In the play, Yuki does not appear until page 32 of act 1 (as opposed to the novel where she enters on page 5), and the entire first 30 pages are devoted to exposition for the white characters who do not exist in the novel, save for Jack Bigelow. These characters are benevolent, rational, and empathic, while the Japanese characters are cold, irrational, and callous, quickly establishing the East/West binary in the play's opening pages. Significantly, the presence of an additional ingenue, Theodosia, the only white woman in the group of white American tourists, begins the play by justifying her presence at the tea house, announcing that she is conducting anthropological research about sex work in Japan. She discloses her purpose as if it is the most ordinary endeavor, declaring simply, "We're *out* for information."[65] Theodosia's imperialist project, posing as academic study, reifies Edward Said's notion that in authorizing views of an Orientalized Asia as distinct from the West, the "Occident" creates a body of knowledge that becomes an "accepted grid for filtering through the Orient into Western consciousness."[66] As scholar Emily Goodell keenly observes, the cultural opposition reified in the play contradicts Eaton's original intent in the novel, which she gestures to in the title of chapter 5: "In Which the East and West Are United."[67] Furthermore, Theodosia, who is nonexistent in the novel, is a more fully developed character when juxtaposed with the limited, two-dimensional Yuki. While the book opens with all eyes, including those of the reader, focused on Yuki's entrance on page 5, in the drama, the entire opening sequence is filled with the back stories of the white folks and Theodosia's data-collecting exchanges. She scribbles discoveries in her notebook, evincing that geisha are "a bit slow . . . and common" and can be ordered "you know—just as you order tea."[68] Jack Bigelow, who knew nothing of Yuki in the beginning of the novel, is already smitten when the curtain rises. The script's white, Western positionality is undeniable.

Furthermore, Young's adaptation erases Eaton's interrogation of the subdominant discourse and the doubly liminal state of the hapa figure. Early in the novel, Eaton introduces these concepts through the owner of the tea house where

Yuki dances, and the proprietor's mistrust of Yuki concretizes her tenuous state as a half-caste woman. His primary function in the narrative is to establish her circumstances as someone who is not fully accepted in either Japanese or American society. In the play, however, this proprietor is none other than Yuki's childhood nurse, whom she has sought out at the tea house for guidance and protection. The presence of the nurse and Yuki's monoraciality signal an erasure of Eaton's deeper intervention and also lay the groundwork for a different narrative entirely in which Yuki is running from a potential husband forced on her by Young's invented stepmother—rather than trying to secure one of her own choosing.

Young's modification of the mother figure from Yuki's biological mother in the novel to a stepmother in the play alters the plot and puts it in line with a common Western construct. As Goodell argues, *A Japanese Nightingale* was marketed as a Cinderella story (or *Aschenputtel* in German) where a lowly common girl finds love with a wealthy gentleman of means. The *Aschenputtel* narrative has become a popular "rags-to-riches" story, and one that operates as a kind of intertextual shorthand for which a reader or a spectator can quickly understand the parameters of the main text.[69] *Aschenputtel* stories rely on the absence of a biological, benevolent mother and the presence of a deceitful, self-serving stepmother to supply the strife necessary for the story to function. Yuki's biological Japanese mother, a meek character by comparison to the bold Raku-San in the play, arrives only halfway through the novel and gives Yuki a reason to continue her marriage to Jack. By contrast, the stepmother of Young's Yuki, as in Charles Perrault's "Cinderella," appears at the top of the narrative, searching for Yuki in order to carry out her own ambitious plans.[70] She is accompanied by Nekko-San, to whom she has pledged Yuki in marriage. Nekko-San bears a striking resemblance to the character Yamadori in Belasco's *Madame Butterfly*, a member of the wealthy Japanese elite, who means to coerce the ingenue into marriage. Young, it seems, reimagined *A Japanese Nightingale*, putting together elements of successful, familiar narratives—one ingrained in the Western cultural consciousness and the other a current commercial success—in order to make the play more profitable and palpable for his audience.

Young also reversed the roles of Yuki and Jack in the play. In the novel, Eaton centers Yuki as an Asian woman, who engages a matchmaker and proposes marriage. Jack is the confused and unwilling party. He refuses to consider a marriage that is superficial, and the sheer artificiality of the meeting with Yuki prevents him from taking the interaction seriously. However, in the play, it is the reverse. Jack relentlessly pursues a tête-à-tête with the geisha, who continuously declines. It is Jack who insists on the nuptials, and Yuki who is afraid of a "Japan-only" marriage, underscoring the assumption that all women want to be in legal and long-standing unions. In the book, Jack cannot imagine entering the institution unless the love and connection are real, and the theatrical version of Yuki seems to express Jack's reluctance from the novel:

YUKI What would you of me? To be my friend—for a little day?

BIGELOW No! but to hold you fast, forever—in love, honor and respect—such
honor, as man may give to his own true wife.

YUKI Ah! You say . . . Wife! Not for Japan, only?—Not to go again, and forget?

BIGELOW Wife—by the laws of my own land—in any land—through life and
in death.

YUKI But why—Why?—*You have seen me, scarcely—once—twice. You know me not.*[71]

In Eaton's book, in a corresponding scene, it is Yuki who coaxes Jack into marrying her "for Japan, only" as her counterpart above contends:

> "I will be true, good wife to you forever," she said, and then swiftly corrected
> herself, as though frightened by her own words. "No, no, I make a ridiculous
> mistake—not forever—jus' for liddle bit while—as you desire, augustness!"
>
> "But I don't desire," he laughed nervously. "I don't want to get married.
> I won't be over a few months at most in Japan."
>
> "Oh, jus' for liddle bit while marry with me," she breathed,
> entreatingly—Please!"[72]

Jack hardly seems to want Yuki "through life and in death" in Eaton's version,
and furthermore, he is skeptical of the kind of marriage that she offers him, musing, "But why had she come to him asking him to marry her? He shook his head
at that; he didn't quite like it. . . . Marry her? He sat up straight. The idea was
absurd. It was absurd for him to think about marrying anyone."[73] This is significant because Yuki's desire for a temporary marriage and her bold, conscious
choice to pursue one overturns the spell of the Orientalized lotus blossom, a subservient, docile Asian woman who is at the mercy of a dominating, white, Western "husband." This stereotype is reified in the play. The powerless theatrical Yuki
is worried that hers is a provisional marriage, and she clutches her American marriage license to her chest (a "foreign" document that may be null and void in
Japan) trilling, "Never let it leave me!" whereas Eaton's Yuki has no need for what
a marriage might culturally or legally bestow on her.

While Eaton's novel deceptively upends Orientalist renderings of the lotus
blossom archetype, the play follows the novel's predecessors in the genre and
embodies the stereotype. In act 2 of the drama, Yuki waxes on thus: "I obey
Excellency—But you so fine when you say 'I command you.' That so good—of
you!"[74] Young's Asian ingenue values the authority of the West as exemplified
by her Western husband. By contrast, Eaton's Yuki toys with Jack and asserts
her dominance. In a similar scene, when she finally returns after being gone for
four days, Jack "sternly" ignores her to which Yuki responds, "You angery ad me
excellency? . . . You very *mad* ad me, augustness? . . . You very cross ad me, my
lord?"[75] After he upbraids her in a "contemptuous silence, she laughs and says,
"Hah! You very, very, very, very *affended*, Mister Bigelow? . . . Ah, tha's so nize. . . .

I thing you grown more nize-loogin."[76] She never once uses the word "obey" in the exchange. Rather, she seems delighted by his reaction and remarks that he is, in effect, "cute" when he's angry. In fact, when he threatens her and tells her not to return if she leaves again, she merely counters, "Whad you goin' do? Git you nudder wife?" After which Jack, confesses, "I have missed you terribly."[77] Yuki's performance as a lotus blossom is deliberate, designed to control Jack and the situation. Her confidence is evidenced in the continual, subsequent disappearances that Jack must unwittingly endure. Her agency further overturns the nature of the East/West dyad as she refuses to represent the imagined, feminized weakness of Asia, a vulnerability that Young's drama amplifies. By contrast, in the play, Jack repeatedly asserts that if he should fail her, "My country shall protect you—with all its power."[78] His authority and self-confidence as well as the strength of the West comfort the powerless Yuki.

Eaton frequently disrupts Orientalist expectations in her other literary work. Her protagonists knowingly and deceptively enact Orientalist performances, well aware of the power they hold over their spectators. As literary scholar Melissa Eriko Poulsen notes in her analysis of Eaton's short story "A Half Caste" (1899), the mixed-Japanese geisha Kiku emphasizes "the performative nature of this gendered American fantasy. Acting artless . . . is a part of her—and, by extension, of all geisha's—profession."[79] In framing her artlessness as labor, Eaton reinstates agency to the mixed-race geisha, which the spectator, Kiku's customer, Hilton, assumes she lacks.[80] Yuki exhibits the same deliberate tenacity as her predecessors in other Eaton stories.

The East/West dyad is further reified in Young's script through the transformation of Yuki's brother Taro into a malevolent, monoracial Japanese antagonist. While Young depicts Yuki as a damsel in distress with Jack as her white savior, Taro is repurposed as the villain of the play, completing the triad of melodrama. In the play, Taro has been sent to university in the United States by the emperor to learn "the wisdom of Westerners" in order to bring back this knowledge to Japan.[81] Not only does this dramatize the West as enlightened and civilized but it also eliminates Yuki's reason for marrying Jack, since Taro's expenses are being subsidized by the emperor. The core of the narrative, sacrifice for family in which mixedness is inextricably intertwined, is completely altered into a narrative about a white man's love of a monoracial Asian woman. His white American peers are benevolent and kind, and the Japanese figures, including Yuki's own family, are callous and deceptive.

In the playscript, Taro had left Yuki in the care of their stepmother with the intention that Yuki should become a priestess at their Buddhist temple. Their stepmother, Raku-san, however, arranged for Yuki to marry Nekko-san, a character who is nonexistent in Eaton's novel. Taro prefers this arrangement to his original plan for his sister. Yuki, of course, has thwarted his plans and married Jack, which enrages her brother. This is significant because in the novel Taro's distress stems primarily from his desire to protect his mixed-race sister because

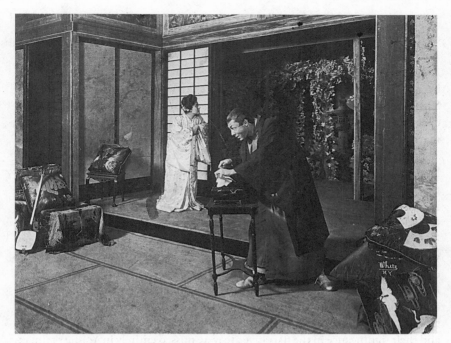

FIGURE 3.2 "The marriage certificate is stolen by Ido." *A Japanese Nightingale*, 1903. (Photo by White Studio ©Billy Rose Theatre Division, The New York Public Library for the Performing Arts.)

'of their traumatic childhoods. Taro's rage in the play emanates not from his fear for his sister, but rather from her betrayal. In the play, after Taro learns in horror, as he does in the novel, that his sister has married a white American, he leaves in a disgusted rage, seething, "My curse upon you—and upon her!"[82] Jack and Yuki are unable to produce their marriage certificate, conveniently stolen in the preceding scene by Ido under Taro's direction (see figure 3.2). Jack's acquaintance, the rational, even-keeled Harker, comments on Taro's hypocritical behavior in a subsequent scene, for while Taro professes to have Yuki's best interests "at heart," his contradictory treatment proves otherwise.[83]

By contrast, in the novel, Yuki's brother, Taro, recounts the ways in which he had "manfully and bitterly" fought monoracial Japanese children, who tormented the siblings for their half-caste status. Eaton asserts, "Their nationality [ethnicity] had to a large extent isolated them from other Japanese children, for the Japanese children had laughed at their hair and eyes.[84] Eaton's use of the word *nationality* as synonymous with ethnic background foregrounds how notions of race and nationality were conflated in 1900. Additionally, Eaton describes the siblings, resultantly, as having "a stronger bond of sympathy and comradeship . . . than is usual between brother and sister."[85] No doubt she was speaking from experience about her relationships with her own siblings.[86]

Young's missteps in the play adaption crystalize Eaton's central purpose in clarifying the mixed-race experience and illustrate, through the comparison, how Asian American critics have misinterpreted her work as aggrandizing Orientalism. Taro's "wrathful and contemptuous" behavior toward Yuki's supposed betrayal persists for the remainder of Young's drama.[87] Like Belasco's Cho-Cho-San, Yuki is not a subject but an object that men argue over, and her shallow characterization affords her little say in her future. Furthermore, the reason Yuki marries Jack in the novel is for the love of her brother, illustrating the bond the siblings share, highlighted by the fact that they are multiracial. When Bigelow learns that Yuki is Taro's sister, especially as he had promised Taro not to participate in a Japanese marriage out of respect for their friendship, Jack looks into his friend's face, which had "taken on the color of death," saying brokenly, "My God! Burton, forgive me. . . . We can remarry if you wish, and I swear to protect her with all the love and homage I would give to any woman who became my wife," to which Taro replies weakly and with half-comprehension, "Yes, you must do that."[88] This brother would never treat Yuki the way his counterpart treats her in the play. The bond between the siblings aside, the characters in the novel are autonomous and have equal agency, whereas Yuki, as depicted onstage, is at the mercy of men who direct her life, including her brother. These crucial details and their significance in the narrative arc were missed entirely in Young's reimagining of the novel, and the siblings' bond, strengthened due to their mixedness, was entirely erased in performance. Rather than this central focus, the play is a story about Bigelow, refashioning a white, male subjectivity as the lens through which to witness the narrative. Although a two-dimensional figure, at the very least, *Madame Butterfly* is a play about Cho-Cho-San and not about Pinkerton.

Young's drama upholds Western notions of patriarchy and masculinity inherent in the imperialist mindset. As in the novel, Yuki disappears for an extended period of time at the end of act 2, but for fear of her brother and her impending marriage with Nekko. At the beginning of act 4, Jack enlists his friend, Bobby Newcome, to help him search for her to the dismay of Theodosia's father, Harker, who also wants to join. Their responses toward the search belie their collective, imperialistic attitude as one of adventure and intrigue in exotic Japan. Metaphors of sport and of the "game," reminiscent of the colonial scramble for Africa and Asia by Western powers, undergird their task. Newcome, upon declaring his intention to accompany Jack, asserts, "I've just been dying for a lark," and Harker, their acquaintance, who must stay back to take care of his daughter, the amateur anthropologist, retorts, "And I'm not to have any hand in this game?"[89] Later when Bigelow thanks Newcome for putting himself in harm's way, Newcome counters, "Thank me—for what? Didn't I tell you I was just spoiling for excitement?"[90] They are Western men hunting for feminine Asian quarry in the wilds of Japan, on adventure in the exotic Orient.

By contrast, Western belief that the East is wayward and uncivilized is powerfully subverted in microresistances in the novel. On an autumn day, Jack comes home triumphant, bearing an invitation to the Mikado's birthday.[91] Jack contends that it "isn't a Japanese affair at all," but one taking place at a European hotel.[92] When he fails to convince Yuki to attend, he goes alone. Eaton describes the motley streets of Tokyo as full of "ramshackle" transportation, "small men, small women, small children and small dogs and cats."[93] She contrasts these "little bits of humanity" with the militaristic scene Jack encounters on the celebratory parade grounds, noting that there was "nothing Oriental in this brave display of the imperial army."[94] The military display that "dazzles" Bigelow, though described as synonymous with the "modern Western world," disentangles Japan from the Orientalist scenes that Bigelow encounters on the streets the page before.[95] As Eaton tells us, it seems as if Bigelow "had suddenly left Japan altogether," but, of course, he hasn't.[96] Eaton, working within the genre, cogently undermines the East/West Orientalist binary in microresistances such as these in the text.

Though the narrative seems to uphold and reify Orientalist renderings of Japanese culture, in reality, Eaton's novel elucidates the confluence of cultures present in the mixed-race experience. Furthermore, underneath the curated descriptions of ornate and elaborate Orientalized locales and events, Eaton is quick to point out the stereotyped dressing and fallacy of such scenes. When Yuki's brother Taro returns home to Japan, he is brought into a guest room in the family home that "was supposed to be entirely Japanese, and was in reality wholly American, despite the screens and mats and vases."[97] Eaton's purpose seems to be twofold here. Taro, who has been educated and living in the United States, certainly could have influenced the interior style of the house just as much as his European father. Eaton highlights the fact that this seemingly Japanese house is not entirely Japanese at all but an amalgamation of cultures, similar to Eaton's childhood homes growing up. That she could see this possibility and craft it in the middle of an "Orientalized" depiction is worth noting. She also seems to be revealing her own shape shifting performance within the novel. As she notes, Taro, the mixed-race hapa sojourner in the narrative, is "ushered" into a guest room, a liminal space, that is supposedly his childhood "home." However, the liminal space is the novel itself, one that "was supposed to be entirely Japanese, and was in reality wholly American, despite the screens and mats and vases."[98] Eaton clearly outlines both a liminal space in the novel and one that she occupies as a shape shifter, writing from a place of lived experience within the text.

Young's significant departures from the novel would be enough to explain the unsuccessful run of the production; however, negative press also tainted the show's opening. In 1902, Eaton found herself at the center of a devastating lawsuit. After she had retrieved her manuscripts for agent Elizabeth Marbury, Belasco announced the debut of *The Darling of the Gods*, a new Japanese-themed, full-length drama he had written in collaboration with John Luther Long, the author of the original "Madame Butterfly" short story.[99] Subsequently, Eaton traveled to Baltimore to see the production and was shocked to discover how closely it resembled *The Wooing of Wistaria* synopsis, a text that had been in Belasco's hands for months prior.

Eaton filed an injunction, accusing Belasco of stealing from both *A Japanese Nightingale* and *The Wooing of Wistaria*. According to Eaton, "The characters were almost identical," and she described for her lawyer the resemblances of scenes and plot points not only taken from *The Wooing of Wistaria* but also similar scenes from *A Japanese Nightingale*. Eaton argued that the "Japanese" aspects, such as the Orientalized bridges, were inauthentic fabrications—perhaps a similar concern she may have had with the Young production. As performance theorist Esther Kim Lee has similarly contended, Belasco was not interested in representing realistic portrayals of Japanese culture, but instead staged environments as "depicted in art works and fictional stories."[100] Crucially, this further indicates how spectacular Western interpretations of Japanese culture evolved on the professional stage and captured the imaginations of the American public. Since the majority of American spectators had not been to Japan, they relied on performances and depictions like these for their information and education.

Furthermore, Eaton questioned why *The Darling of the Gods* was spoken in the pidgin that she introduced in *Nightingale*, pointing out that its use did not follow the logic of Belasco's play. While Eaton was trying to capture the accent of an Asian speaking in a second language, this creative decision was bastardized under Belasco and, to Eaton, made no sense, considering that his characters were supposed to be speaking Japanese to each other. Eaton wrote "Belasco even had to introduce the dialect in Pigeon Japanese, common to my short stories in 'The Nightingale.' But why he does so is a mystery in view of the fact that his characters are supposed to be talking in Japanes[e]. Why then the dialect."[101] This is significant because this line of inquiry demonstrates that Eaton recognized that the Japanese characters would have understood each other in their first language. Consequently, the corresponding language on stage in New York would have been English. This convention, centering the culture of the onstage characters through the use of the primary language of the spectator, is a prevalent practice used today. Ahead of her time, Eaton's comment suggests that she would have done the same and centered the perspective of Japanese characters, rather than distance the audience from them. The use of the pidgin in her stories was a calculated move on Eaton's part that The Wizard did not understand. Eaton continued to lambast Belasco for the fantastical absurdities in his play, declaring, "No such thing could even have taken place in Japan; no prime minister of Japan ever presided within the last forty years or a hundred years for that matter over a Chamber of Horrors. Mr. Belasco shows his ignorance in this of things Japanese. The last two scenes are very much like the finale in Faust."[102] Belasco's use of pidgin in plays like *The Darling of the Gods* as well as his sinister imaginings of Japanese culture demonstrate how he assisted in the Orientalization of Asian theatrical representation in the early twentieth century.

Furthermore, Eaton was caught in a long-running feud between Belasco and her producers, Klaw and Erlanger, the latter of whom may have put Eaton up to publishing the damaging accusations without disclosing to her the full ramification of her actions.[103] Belasco retaliated and countersued Eaton for libel, and the New York Supreme court issued an order for her arrest. Belasco contended that Eaton "caused to be printed in a newspaper a statement to the effect that he had stolen his play . . . from the manuscript of *A Japanese Nightingale*, a story which she had submitted for his approval."[104] By February 6, 1903, Justice Leventritt, presiding over the complaint, had vacated the order for her arrest. Leventritt attested that though "there is no doubt that the publication was libelous . . . there was no proof that Mrs. Babcock was either the author or the instigator of it."[105] Belasco's attempt to net "$20,000 for alleged libel" had failed, but for Eaton, greater damage to her reputation was already done.[106]

Even with an all-star production team, the highly anticipated run of *A Japanese Nightingale*, which opened on November 19, 1903, suffered negative reviews that were not helped by Eaton's arrest and lawsuit. The Sunday before the Thursday night opening, the *New York Times* printed the cast list in full—in which Margaret Illington and Orrin Johnson were starring as Yuki and Jack Bigelow—along with an overview of the locales depicted in the play and emphasized that the production attempted to make "every detail true to Japanese life."[107] Nonetheless, on opening night, one reviewer found the production's "lack of native atmosphere" debilitating and asserted that "the actors worked gallantly, but without Japanese ozone, their efforts, while gallant, were fruitless."[108] Alan Dale from the *New York American* saw little to no representation of Japanese culture other than "a nice satin kimono and two streaks of make-up in her [Illington's] eyes."[109] To make matters worse, the *New York Daily Tribune* went so far as to suggest that production was an "inferior" copy of the staging conventions in *The Darling of the Gods* and contended that Belasco "did it first."[110] Abraham Erlanger accused the critics of bias and alleged that Belasco had monetarily lined their pockets in order to undermine the production.

Margaret Illington, a relative newcomer to Broadway, portrayed Yuki in yellowface as a mono-ethnically Japanese woman. In production photographs of Illington, her Yuki appears in the black eye makeup observed by Dale and in a black wig. Eaton's hapa character with her blue eyes and "rich bronze-black" hair cannot be detected.[111] In fact, though the *New York Times* found Illington to be at times "sweet, winning, and sympathetic," the review emphasized that "she is never Japanese or anything like it."[112] Additionally, the review noted that Illington's inconsistent gestures and speech in the performance vacillated between French and "plain everyday American," even though the photographs reveal Illington's hands held in an Orientalized manner (see figure 3.3). This is significant because Illington's yellowface performance was reviewed as being inauthentic.

The article also implied that Illington did not perform the role in the pidgin English characteristic of Eaton's novels, though often misused, according to

FIGURE 3.3 "Kayo-San and Yuki." *A Japanese Nightingale*, 1903. (Photo by White Studio ©Billy Rose Theatre Division, The New York Public Library for the Performing Arts.)

Eaton, in performance. Illington's lack of a pidgin accent seems to have disrupted the reception of Japaneseness for the spectators, as the reviewer clearly expected a racialized performance. Furthermore, in Young's script, Yuki does converse in an accent, dropping articles and transposing letters like *b* for *v* as in "lobe" for "love."[113] It appears, however, that May Buckley, who played Yuki's attendant Kayo-San, was more successful in performance.[114] The review praised Buckley as contributing "by far the most colorful and convincing picture."[115] The *New York Daily Tribune* review suggested that Illington was physically miscast, asserting that she was "hardly so *small* and Japanese in appearance as might have been desired."[116] Certainly, the spectators expected an Orientalized portrayal of Yuki—which was not delivered effectively by Illington—as an audience entrained to expect yellowface portrayals, such as those popularized from the depictions in *The Mikado* or in vaudeville melodramas, performed as early as 1854, or as seen in Belasco's Japanese productions.[117]

Reviews for Belasco's *Madame Butterfly* and *The Darling of the Gods*, which had opened in 1902, highlight successful productions that seem to effectively "represent" Japanese culture and customs. A 1900 review of Madame Butterfly called the play a "picturesque little tragedy of the deserted Japanese dancing girl, admirably and effectively performed in every particular."[118] *The Darling of the Gods*' production was described as rivaling "in artistic beauty anything ever seen on . . . stage. The costumes were rich and gorgeous in color, and the electrical effects unique. The musical setting . . . was heartily applauded."[119] Curiously, the mise en scène did not seem to be a problem for *A Japanese Nightingale*, either. On the contrary, the *New York Times* describes the show as having rich scenery and rich costumes. Music that is pleasing to the ear and dancing that is delightful to the eye."[120] The *New York Daily Tribune* equally echoed the *Times*, highlighting costumes that were "rich and lovely" and calling the music effectively "Eastern and odd." Furthermore, under Klaw and Erlanger's watchful eyes, the electrical effects were also not spared. Yuki was described as appearing in "Loie Fuller" light,[121] but, for all the detail outlined in the review, the *Times* followed up this description contending that Japanese dancing and music "do not constitute drama."[122]

The failure of the production seems to be the failure to effectively reproduce yellowface. In an interview in the *New York Times*, Blanche Bates, who played Cho-Cho-San in *Madame Butterfly*, described her pre-show makeup routine thus: "Mme. Butterfly takes a great deal of time, and while I ought to be getting into the spirit of the play I am dabbing on red and putting on eyebrows and tying on the funny little Japanese clothes. In making up for Mme. Butterfly, I have to be very careful for the real eyebrows have to be entirely obliterated and the others marked on."[123] Production images from *Madame Butterfly* and marketing materials for *The Darling of the Gods* reveal thin, winged eyebrows marked onto Bates's face and an exaggerated widow's peak drawn halfway down her forehead. When compared with Bates's makeup, Margaret Illington's theatrical countenance as Yuki looks relatively unchanged from her studio portrait except for the addition of a black wig. As cultural historian Mari Yoshihara affirms, "The American audience in the 1900s knew fully well that Cho-Cho-San was a white actress's impersonation of a Japanese woman," and the interpretation and mastery of the performance of race appealed to spectators. Certainly, critics and audience members saw Illington's inability to effectively craft a performance of Japaneseness as a reflection of her abilities as an actress.[124]

In many ways, Eaton's novel and its subsequent dramatic adaptation succeeded in sidestepping the victimization of its central Asian feminine figure and depicted a white, American husband who, in integrity and sincerity, kept his word to his Japanese wife. Young, to his credit, preserved Eaton's literary ending. In *A Japanese Nightingale*, Yuki and Jack are reunited and reconcile in bliss. This makes the adaptation even more bittersweet, because if the production had been well received, perhaps this ending would have had an impact on the evolution of the Butterfly narrative in the twentieth century. Perhaps it would have altered a now familiar plot line that concludes in bitter tragedy for its Asian heroine. In Puccini's operatic variation of the story, the plight of Butterfly is all the more tragic and offensive because Cho-Cho-San is a vulnerable fifteen-year-old adolescent who has been deceived, impregnated, and abandoned by an adult man. Perhaps, though, due to the Orientalist tendencies of *A Japanese Nightingale* production, it is providence that the play has faded into obscurity. It is certainly the reason the drama is often a footnote in Eaton scholarship. The novel is remembered, but often only recalled as an Orientalist, middlebrow best-seller, a kind of Japanese *Gone With the Wind*.[125] Additionally, many Eaton scholars believe that the play-script has been lost and because of its box office failure, have been glad to imagine it gone.

I suggest that Winnifred Eaton did not engage in the subjugation of Asians nor Asian Americans in the novel *A Japanese Nightingale*. Though "her" play is remembered as participating in the theatrical projects of the early twentieth century that contributed to the stereotypical renderings of Asians and Asian Americans, these theatrical narratives were written from a white male subjectivity, whose exertive authority imbricated white male fantasies over representations of the feminine Asian body. *A Japanese Nightingale*, along with stories like "A Half-Caste" and "A Father," were wholly unlike the comparable narratives of the period that William Young, in taking liberties, sought to emulate with his dramatic adaptation. A clipping announcing the closing week of Young's production asserts that the play hardly reflected "the delicate poetic charm of Onoto Watanna's book."[126] Even the critics knew that the play and the novel were hardly the same.

Hollywood and the Pre-Code Era

Eaton's continued success as a novelist and a short story author in the early twentieth century made Hollywood sit up and take notice. For all intents and purposes, the transnational Chinese English Canadian–turned American should never have become one of the most prominent Hollywood writers in the 1920s, yet her reputation as a successful wordsmith had preceded her arrival, and by 1925, her influence was felt across Hollywood both professionally and personally.[127]

Her career as a Hollywood scenario writer and screenwriter was filled with scripts of mixed-race characters and traces of interracial relationships. These subjects often made it into her treatments, such as in "A Savage in Silks" about Gloria, a mixed-race "gypsy," who asserts her claim to her white aristocratic father's fortune to the chagrin of her paternal relatives.[128] Eaton no doubt understood from previous experience, lived and literary, that taboos like interracial relationships and race-bending were intriguing for her white American audience.

In Hollywood, Eaton did not hide her ethnic background, but she certainly downplayed her Asian heritage. She abandoned the kimono she wore early in her writing career for mainstream Western business attire and went by her married name, Winnifred Reeve.[129] It seems that she shape shifted into whiteness in plain sight, and no one seemed to mind. This is significant considering that all "full-time professional screenwriters" of the 1920s were white.[130] Eaton once again shifted into the racial background that afforded her the most access to her career of choice.

Though prolific in her own right, it is no surprise that many of her films were adapted from plays or, like *A Japanese Nightingale*, from novels that became playscripts. Eaton worked uncredited on the script for *The Phantom of the Opera* (1925) and wrote the early synopsis for *Show Boat* for Universal Pictures in 1926 with Eleanor Fried.[131] She penned the scenario and dialogue for *Shanghai Lady* (1929) with Houston Branch and the adaptation of *East Is West* (1930) with Tom Reed, which featured a half-Asian, half-Latiné character.[132] Moreover, her treatments and film scripts often dealt with miscegenation like the aforementioned *A Savage in Silks* and *East Is West*, as well as *East of Borneo* (1931).[133]

The Motion Pictures, Producers, and Distributors Association content regulation group, also known as the Hays Office, encouraged studios to steer clear of representations that painted sin or crime in a sympathetic light. These included light fare, such as gambling and drinking, but depictions of homosexuality, abortion, and miscegenation were strictly off-limits.[134] These dictates were loosely adhered to, but by 1934, the Hays Office had been reestablished as the Production Code Administration (PCA). The Hays Code emerged with complete governance over film production in the mid-1930s and remained in effect until the early 1950s.

The absence of multiracial characters was due partly to these restrictions placed on references to miscegenation by the PCA, which banned depictions of mixedness in early films. Race scholar Ralina L. Joseph astutely refers to these bans as "Hollywood's own version of an anti-miscegenation law."[135] It is not surprising that the PCA's Code was put into effect during the period from 1924 to 1965, when immigration from Northern (white) Europe grew due to the national quota system of the Immigration Act of 1924 in an effort to engineer a population with a white majority. Intermarriage and miscegenation would have been detrimental and highly discouraged. Hollywood either avoided topics of race or relied on the persistent, yet familiar, racial stereotypes that had dominated the vaudeville stage. Eaton was often assigned to Asian-themed or "ethnic" projects, though she was straitjacketed by the studios' demands under the Hays guidelines, and her contributions to films like *Barbary Coast* (1935) were silenced at MGM.[136] The portrayals of mixedness seen in the pre-code era eventually vanished. Frustrated and fully aware that the removal of miscegenation fundamentally changed her story lines, among other reasons, Eaton left her position as scenario editor-in-chief at Universal for Canada in 1931, where she remained until her death in 1954 (see figure 3.4). In Canada, Eaton cofounded the Calgary Little Theatre Association and continued to pen dramas through the 1940s. Her plays, including *A Japanese Nightingale*, received productions in Calgary and Winnipeg into the mid-twentieth century. Eaton's impressive theatrical legacy lives on in the Reeve Theatre on the University of Calgary campus, which was dedicated in 1981.[137]

Malaise in the Monoracial Midcentury

Even though the PCA overtly limited the depictions of multiracial bodies in film in the twentieth century, sometimes mixed-race characters appeared on

FIGURE 3.4 Winnifred Eaton in Calgary. (Photo courtesy of Elizabeth Rooney and Diana Birchall.)

celluloid already under a veil of monoraciality, though these narratives produced different interpretations of mixed-race people. Such is the case with Anna Leonowens, who hid her multiethnic heritage from the public and chose to shape shift into whiteness, which became her known identity in subsequent character portrayals. Leonowens has been featured in various film adaptations as well as in the 1951 stage musical *The King and I*. All of these characterizations were based on the 1944 novel *Anna and the King of Siam* by American author Margaret Landon. Landon detailed, and sometimes fictionalized, the events of Leonowens's life as the governess of King Mongkut in Siam (modern-day Thailand) in 1860.[138] Leonowens had been born in India in 1831 to Englishman Thomas Edwards and Mary Anne Glascott, a woman whose ethnic parentage was not fully known. Glascott's parents, Leonowens's maternal grandparents, were William Glascott, an officer in the British army and a "lady not entirely white."[139] Leonowens's biographer Susan Morgan affirms that William Glascott's wife was a "local woman" whose name and presence remain lost to history, save for traces of her existence as the Glascott matriarch. Her omission from the ledger of marriages by the civil servants of the East India Company suggests that she was not European but most likely Eurasian (mixed-race "Anglo-Indian"). Leonowens herself kept the ethnic background of her grandmother and mother hidden and instead presented, even to her nuclear family, a version of herself that she invented.[140] She chose to shape shift completely into British whiteness. In the *Anna and the King* novel, Margaret Landon refashioned many details of Leonowens's life, including her ethnic background, partly because Leonowens kept these details in obscurity. Morgan asserts, however, that Leonowens "would have been delighted with her resurrection as the well-born and gently bred English lady of Margaret Landon's book. Landon's Anna was the very gentlewoman whom Anna, so long ago in Singapore, had envisioned and then declared herself to be."[141] By the time Leonowens appeared as a character in the musical production of *The King and I* in 1951, the reality of her mixed-race body had vanished altogether in the portrayal by white English actress Gertrude Lawrence.[142]

In theater, depictions of mixed-race Asian characters also appeared in the dramas of monoracial Asian American playwrights, especially in response to the pan-Asian movement of the late 1960s. For example, *The Chickencoop Chinaman* by first-wave Asian American playwright Frank Chin was the first professionally produced Asian American play in New York at American Place Theatre in 1972. The play expresses protagonist Tam Lum's deep desire for masculine Asian and Asian American role models and challenges the emasculation of the Asian male in popular discourse. However, the play surreptitiously includes two mixed-race characters. Lee and her son, Robbie, live with Tam's best friend, Kenji. Rarely discussed in the criticism of Chin's plays, Lee is described as a "possible Eurasian or Chinese American passing for white," which conflates two very different racial identities into the same subjectivity.[143] Robbie, whom Chin simply describes as her "weird" son, represents a further dilution of racial mixedness (read: not "real") and a loss of Asian masculinity.[144]

Like Anna Leonowens in the stage production *The King and I*, Lee was portrayed in the original production of *Chickencoop Chinaman* by a white actress—in this case, Sally Kirkland.[145] This is all the more curious given that lines from the play clearly mark her as mixed-race. Protagonist Tam Lum confronts Lee's Chinese American ex-husband, Tom, who refuses to recognize her Chinese heritage.

TAM You wanted to be "accepted" by whites so much, you *created one* to accept
     you. You didn't know Lee's got a bucket of Chinese blood in her? At least a
     bucket?[146]

Tam seems to subscribe to the rule of hypodescent in the aforementioned assertion. He implies that Lee's white identity is a fabrication since her "bucket of Chinese blood" disqualifies her from claiming her whiteness, yet Lee was portrayed by an actor who was white.

Unlike Leonowens, whose desire to shape shift resulted in a persona that was, in many ways, a "transformed descendent of the version" she created, the character of Lee provides evidence of the subdominant discourse that Chin inadvertently highlights in his play.[147] The drama unintentionally reveals a bias against hapa subjects who choose to shape shift, a phenomenon Eaton's character Yuki had encountered seventy years earlier. Chin characterizes Lee as a Eurasian *or* as an Asian American passing for white. While it may seem that Chin highlights the ambiguity of Lee's social position, the parallel assumes that mixed-Asian subjects prefer to identify as white people or that this claim to whiteness would, in fact, be a fallacy and a betrayal. This is particularly significant because it demonstrates how the subdominant discourse views a mixed-race Asian body as not fully Asian, while the dominant discourse would view the body, contrastingly, as a monoracial Asian American. This example of the subdominant discourse in drama emerges, perhaps ironically, at the confluence of the equal rights movements in the late 1960s and early 1970s when pan-Asian identity signaled a show of solidarity among those of Asian descent. Performance scholar Karen Shimakawa argues that Tom's inability to perceive Lee's Chinese ancestry is the dilation of his abjection of his own ethnic Asianness.[148] In other words, Lee's mixed-Asian body is co-opted to support a unified monoracial Asian American desire for personhood. Tam recognizes Lee's "Asianness" and demonizes her for not identifying with her Chinese background, but the play proceeds to mark her as white in the minds of other Asian American characters in the text and on stage physically in the original production. The result dismisses her mixed-race identity—which equally encompasses both ethnic backgrounds—and erases her multiracial body from view in casting a white actress to portray her.

This is no different than the 1989 production of *Miss Saigon* in which producers cast white Welsh performer Jonathan Pryce to play the Eurasian character known simply as The Engineer. Mixed-race scholar Cynthia L. Nakashima notes that The Engineer was originally a Vietnamese character that was later changed to Eurasian so that Pryce could embody the role.[149] The assumption that the revision of The Engineer as a mixed-race persona would permit the use of a white actor reveals a gross ignorance of mixed-race subjectivity. Even when Asian American theater makers decried the casting and demanded that an actor of Asian descent fill the role, they dismissed multiracial Asian scholars Velina Hasu Houston and Teresa Williams-León, who asserted that a mixed-race actor should have been cast. Asian American artists, a minoritized group of color, were also guilty of an erasure in their demands for the recasting of Pryce. In these examples of Lee and The Engineer, mixed-race bodies were co-opted to serve a specific purpose in the larger narratives in which they appear. Monoracial artists and theater makers in Asian and white America have failed to recognize the unique subjectivity of the multiracial characters present in their productions.[150]

As Caroline A. Streeter asserts, stories about the ways in which upward mobility can be achieved through passing and the corresponding betrayal of one's mixed heritage dominate narratives that depict mixed-race identity. Successfully passing as monoracially white can liberate the tragic mulatto/a figure from the racial signifiers and social confines of Blackness, even though it heralds a racial fraud. According to Streeter, however, in passing narratives, mixed blood specifically jeopardizes the tragic mulatta's chances for respectability by biologically cursing her with impure sexual tendencies and loose morals. This is certainly true for the divorcee Lee, who, as a similarly tragic Eurasian, is described by Chin as having "borne several kids in several racial combinations, but mothers only one."[151] Additionally, it is through the trope of passing that the mulatta figure can gain access to a protective, respectable heterosexual lifestyle vis-à-vis marriage to a white husband, even though she runs the risk of being exposed by her own mixed blood. This ability to pass and procure a proposal raised the mixed woman's social status and redeemed her tenuous state.[152] However, the subsequent cost of miscegenation is interpreted as a "double loss" for the Black community: the potentially permanent loss of the mixed woman's Blackness and the loss of her ability to produce offspring.[153]

Chickencoop Chinaman belies a deeper discursive erasure in the representation of a mixed-race figure. Tam's best friend, Kenji, who lives with Lee, announces that he and Lee are having a baby at the play's end. The assertion, apparently a desire that Kenji has been entertaining in secret, surprises even Lee. Like the tragic mulatta figure whose "lost" Blackness also means the loss of Black children, Kenji marks Lee as a tragic Eurasian in need of saving. His announcement of the future pregnancy serves as a reclamation of Lee's body and an opportunity to achieve redemption through the birth of an almost fully Asian child.

As Parikh astutely observes, the presence/absence of the women in *Chickencoop Chinaman* like Lee—an "incomplete" Chinese woman for whom Kenji is allowed to speak—amplifies the Progressive Era anti-immigration policies that limited the population of Asian women and the subsequent cultural discourse that recycled the tropes of the tragic.[154] Lee's absence, physicalized in the embodiment of a white (and white-washed) body onstage, points to the ways in which Asian women, and mixed-race women in my assessment, have been regulated to the "parenthetical margins of national belonging."[155] While the figure of the Asian feminine is repressed in the narrative more broadly—a move for which Chin has been continually upbraided—Parikh asserts that the play fearlessly acknowledges the possibilities that this figure harbors for the future. Despite his bravado, Tam must reconcile her varied histories of erasure in order to fully claim an (Asian) American selfhood.[156] While Parikh's analysis does not examine the conflation of a mixed-race body with a monoracial corporeality, it does expose how Chin's mishap in his construction of the character of Lee reveals a valuable rupture in Asian American discourse that must reclaim not only Asian American women but also multiracial Asians. This intervention begins to open the possibility for rightly positioning the hapa figure within multiple histories.

In this light, then, it is perhaps easy to see why Chin did not include Winnifred Eaton in the seminal Asian American literary anthology *Aiiieeeee!: An Anthology of Asian-American Writers* (1974) and why he, along with other Asian American writers and scholars, considered Eaton to be a racial traitor, as they also subscribed to the hegemonic monumental.[157] Eaton's willingness to explore the doubly liminal identity in her work and her refusal to subscribe to easy categorization and stagnant, monoracial malaise serve as the performative remains from which mixed-race Asian writers in the latter half of the twentieth century would begin.

4

Cosmopolitan Identity in
Mixed Dramatic Forms

• • • • • • • • • • • • • • • • • • • •

He sits on the porch, dejected. His forearms rest on his thighs, hands hanging limply from his wrists. In a khaki shirt and pants, Joseph is clean-shaven with short brown hair. The edge of a white T-shirt peaks out from the collar of his button-down shirt. Though he is a farmer, Joseph's attire in the 1986 Asian American Theater Company's production of *Thirst* (1985), makes him look more like Christopher Scott, the GI protagonist from *Miss Saigon* (1989), who would not appear onstage for four more years. Joseph's physical form conveys his disillusionment following the rejection of his former lover, his half-Japanese neighbor, Plinka. In contrast, the self-assured Plinka is not interested in reconciling. She sits on the porch step next to him, her eyes contemplating the ground at their feet. He wrings his hands slowly. She puts her hand on his shoulder and encourages him to cry.

Plinka, the mixed-race Japanese protagonist of Velina Hasu Houston's play, *Thirst*, emerges from the Asian American theatrical canon as a formidable force, an early voice in the mixed-race social movement of the late twentieth century. Plinka, the main character, is not a political activist, but her mere presence onstage in the mid-1980s marks an early rupture in the contemporary racial discourse about the mixed-race individual's place in a monoracial hierarchy.[1] This is because she lends credence to the notion that a half-Asian subject is, in fact, wholly Asian. Furthermore, Plinka's mixed-race positionality arms her with an agency that, like her predecessor Yuki in the 1901 novel *A Japanese Nightingale*, subverts the Asian femme fatale lotus blossom trope that reemerges in the 1980s with the popularity of the musical *Miss Saigon*.[2] Plinka is not like Christopher Scott's lover, Kim—an analogue for Cho-Cho-San from *Madame Butterfly*—who is in need of a white man's affection and salvation.[3] Rather, Plinka is the jilter, and Joseph, her white male lover, is the jilted. *Thirst* displays Houston's bold portrayals of mixed-race identity and the empowered feminist critique of society that is characteristic of her theatrical oeuvre.

In this chapter, I argue that the plays of internationally acclaimed, Japanese African American playwright Velina Hasu Houston dramatize mixedness not only in the content and the embodiment of characters but also in the theatrical form of her work. Houston's plays differ from the dramas of other mixed-race playwrights of the 1980s and 1990s in that they do not merely explore mixed identity as a circumstance to be understood, the reconciliation of two "halves," nor as a vehicle for self-expression. Rather, Houston depicts the hapa figure as an integrated subject who has seamlessly blended a myriad of social, cultural, and political experiences into one whole identity. This is significant, as mixed-race identity had been transformed into an anomaly in a monoracial society emerging from the equal rights movements of the late 1960s and 1970s. "Minority" groups, in asserting their solidarity, were galvanizing their identities as cohesive populations of color. Mixed race scholar Maria P. P. Root also notes that the oppressed groups' "insistence on singular ethnic or racial loyalties" stemmed from an internalization of the hegemonic racial system.[4] The mixed-race subject presented a conundrum and a threat in this landscape as a figure who could lay claim to multiple ethnic backgrounds. Furthermore, public discourse had wavered little in its attitude since the early twentieth century, when the mixed-race figure was viewed as a tragic outsider. The representation of the mixed-race Asian body was simultaneously whitewashed and erased from public viewing during the midcentury.[5] Houston's work marks the beginning of a shift in the political visibility of the mixed-race hapa figure, which begins to embrace multiracial Asian characters in late twentieth-century performance.

The work of Velina Hasu Houston examines shifting cultural boundaries, feminist perspectives, and histories of transnational migration. She is most widely known for her 1985 drama, *Tea*, which illuminates the struggles of Japanese war brides transplanted in the American Midwest after World War II.[6] Of mixed heritage, Houston is herself a product of the postwar migration. The daughters of a Japanese international bride and an African American–Native American serviceman, Houston and her sister grew up in a small Kansas town, listening to the rich, cultural stories of her mother's life. These early experiences helped to shape a cosmopolitan sensibility through which Houston writes about the Asian American and mixed-race experiences in her plays. This double lens, coupled with a predominantly Japanese cultural upbringing, caused Houston to turn to literature and drama to escape the "alienating monoracial perspective of the U.S. society" and to find worlds that more closely matched her own spaces, where Japanese and American cultures seamlessly coexisted the way they did in her childhood home.[7] As Houston recounts, "Initially, I believed that becoming involved in the theater would allow me to create a public space that could be parallel to that private space—a sphere in which I could navigate, at least in certain ways and at certain times, without thought to race or gender."[8] Houston's theater not only explores questions of cultural identity and conflict but, through her own unique lens as a mixed-race "cosmopolite," she also creates theater that fuses different theatrical traditions. Her manipulation of dramatic forms and conventions reflects this sensibility, blending her "own unique brand of magic realism," with Western realism and Japanese Noh drama.[9] The importance of this study of her work through the lens of double liminality is then twofold; the plays emphasize the promise of a mixed-race identity moving forward, and Houston advances this idea by combining multiple approaches to create a new vision of theater.

bell hooks notes that for oppressed people of color, living at the margins is, in reality, living in centralized space. For the oppressed, this "center" serves as a "site of resistance."[10] Anurima Banerji further articulates this as "paratopic space" that comes into being through the act of performance—in this case, the performance of self.[11] Taking hooks's and Banerji's cues, I apply their observations to the mixed-Asian experience and extend the "centered" marginality or paratopic space to include the integration of two cultural and racial "centers" from which the hapa subject operates, a locus I call double liminality. Though not the first hapa playwright to claim this centralized, integrated space, Houston is perhaps one of the first to dramatize it in contemporary theater. In her plays, she demonstrates how two racialized states of being give way to each other, continuously calling on the multiracial subject to culturally code-switch in different social contexts. By carving out theatrical space for the mixed-race subject in the 1980s, Houston has evoked a need for the theatrical landscape to *recast* its perception of mixed-race persons and to reconsider the future performers who would fill these roles. Performance theorist Christina S. McMahon reminds us that recasting denotes multiple meanings. The term signifies both a transformation and an interruption of grand narratives, where old notions can be *cast again* and reforged in a new way.[12] Recasting in theater also denotes changing the living, breathing performer who will be hired to portray a role. As McMahon keenly elucidates, if a particular actor no longer serves a performance or if the needs of the production change, the performing body may need to be recast.[13] In this way, Houston's work recasts the persistent nineteenth-century assumption that multiracial people have splintered identities due to incompatible mixed blood.[14] Her insistence on reformulating hapa characters as wholly integrated subjects demands that the theater community reconsider casting monoracial actors in mixed-race roles. As the visibility of hapa figures continues to rise, due in part, I argue, to Houston's early contributions in theater, monoracial actors no longer serve these narratives.

While Houston's plays increase the visibility of mixed-race Asian portrayals, she also combines a variety of theatrical traditions into the architecture of her plays to create a hybrid dramatic form. Like her mixed-race predecessor of an earlier era, writer Winnifred Eaton, Houston is a transnational artist and culturally ambidextrous, having been raised with Asian and Western worldviews.[15] Like Eaton and mixed-Japanese playwright Sadakichi Hartmann, Houston seems to employ literature and theater as a tactic, which Michel de Certeau defines as a means to navigate society's dominant myths and structures of power, including racial hierarchy.[16] However, Houston does this not to process the angst created by abandonment and misunderstood multiraciality as Eaton and Hartmann do. Rather, she builds on their early literary and dramatic work and transforms theater through a fully acculturated sense of vision and self. In her plays, her mixed-race characters have the liberty to embrace all of their racial and cultural backgrounds, which, I argue, is informed by Houston's own integrated hapa identity.[17]

The groundbreaking play *Thirst* also exposes the existence of the subdominant discourse, or the discrimination that multiracials encounter from other monoracially identified groups of color.[18] In the play, Houston rejects the notion that a mixed-race person is a fragmented, half-racial self, and, therefore, inadmissible in a world of monoracial categories. Nineteenth-century notions of the mixed-race figure as biologically impure and mentally unstable have persisted into twentieth-century subdominant discourses and led to intraracial discrimination against mixed-race subjects, such as the separation that occurs between main characters Plinka and her "full" sisters in *Thirst*.[19] Houston elucidates this phenomenon not only in the journeys of her characters but also in the dramatic form itself, creating works that are inherently and inextricably intercultural and multiethnic. In short, she creates plays that are themselves "hapa." Her plays explore mixed-race hapa identity and themes, even while her hapa subjectivity reveals itself in the dramatic form. They create what Julia Kristeva has called a "laboratory of new discourse," which Houston achieves by blending a myriad of conventions and texts that are representative of different traditions into her plays.[20] That she does this in the context of America means that she creates her own brand of Asian American drama, shedding light on a unique, and continually emerging, corpus of Asian American plays, those of the Asian American hapa experience.

Houston invokes classical Japanese drama in her work in addition to weaving Western plot structures and characters into other plays, thus revealing her ability to work seamlessly in both genres. This is perhaps indicative of her transnational ability to work easily in both cultural traditions, demonstrating that she does not favor one over the other. That she is, in fact, both.[21] In *Thirst*, Houston pens a drama about an Asian American family of farmers coming to grips with the death of a matriarch and the loss of their land within a Chekhovian framework. The Japanese American cultural narrative unfolds inside the familiar, iconic plot patterns of Anton Chekhov's *Three Sisters* (1900) and *The Cherry Orchard* (1903). In the 1994 play *Kokoro (True Heart),* Houston depicts a

Japanese *shin-issei* family desperately trying to acculturate to American life.[22] Houston mixes their desires to navigate life in America with elements from Noh theater, flipping her source material from the Western canon to classical Japanese drama. By not privileging one canon over the other, Houston enables us to see how, in theater, she effortlessly moves from one parent culture to another. This is significant because, unlike Sadakichi Hartmann and Winnifred Eaton, who wrote within Western influences, Houston's transnational sensibility enables her to draw on both Japanese and Western drama to build a theatrical canon that reflects her own unique multicultural, multiracial, and transnational voice.

Both *Thirst* and *Kokoro (True Heart)* are important as early dramatic works that foreground mixedness at the beginning of the multiracial movement in the late twentieth century. Beginning in the mid-1980s, the American cultural current saw an emergence of mixed-race or interracial community organizations, print media, and political activism in public discourse and academia.[23] Houston's plays, developed during the height of the multicultural education movement, pushed the zeitgeist to embrace multiraciality as an extension of multiculturalism by chronicling the mixed-race experience and depicting it in theater.[24] Beliefs in mental and physical multiracial impurity, splintered mixed-race identity, the naturalization of hypodescent, and the mixed-race body as novel are all explored in these dramas. Houston's work in theater paralleled that of seminal mixed race scholars like Maria P. P. Root, who had just begun to write about the notion of mixed-race subjectivity in the 1980s. Together, these early interventions paved the way for the grassroots multiracial movement to eventually change the racial categorization and enumeration on the U.S. census in 2000 and to open up the consciousness of most of the public.[25] Specifically, Houston's dramas opened the doors for playwrights in the new millennium to carve out space in the theatrical landscape for a new kind of racial discourse.

The Desire for Wholeness in *Thirst*

Although critic Bernard Weiner characterized Houston's 1985 play *Thirst* as an Asian American story, he also equated her narrative with the work of Russian dramatist Anton Chekhov, whose principles revolutionized the drama and the short story at the beginning of the twentieth century.[26] While other American writers have also emulated Chekhov's oeuvre,[27] Houston's canon is not limited to adaptations or likenesses, which revise narratives in contemporary settings. Rather, she pens "mutations" of Chekhov's work, thus creating new forms through her use of intertextuality. French theorist Julia Kristeva observes "that the literary avant-garde experience, by virtue of its very characteristics, is slated to become the laboratory of a new discourse . . . thus bringing about a mutation."[28] In her dramatic work, Houston contributes to the "literary avant-garde" both in the transformation of the Chekhovian text and through direct references to Chekhov's plays within her own, thus creating a variant form of neo-Chekhovian Asian American work. However, rather than a "mutation," as Kristeva asserts, I offer instead Houston's theatrical work as a "literary metamorphosis," one that points to Houston's hapa sensibility at the core of its dramatic structure. This amalgamation on the architectural level of the plays assists Houston in recasting how a reader or spectator might perceive hapa characters. Additionally, mixed-race or monoracially Asian characters "recast" in familiar Chekhovian roles serve as an underwriting that gives the observer an accessible frame for receiving a new narrative. Houston's use of Anton Chekhov on a personal level is perhaps no surprise, as he was the first Western playwright she read as a girl in Kansas, and his work left an indelible impression on her. As she told me, she did not set out to follow the plot of *Three Sisters*, per se, but was drawn to the chemistry of the three siblings.[29] Furthermore, her own experiences as a mixed-race subject have led her to explore issues of mixedness and feminism in many of her plays: "As a hapa—the daughter of a Japanese immigrant and an African American and Blackfoot Indian father—the very nature of my earlier work was informed by my background, as has been the case with many playwrights."[30] Houston's intertextual references to the Russian dramatist coupled with her own cosmopolitan vision as a mixed-race subject have coalesced to create a new literary metamorphosis in drama.

Through this amalgamation, Houston is able to illuminate the experiences of the mixed-race subject to interrogate rigid racial codes and challenge subdominant and dominant discourses. The linear, chronological narrative of *Thirst* revolves around the Tada family children, now adults, who gather in their mother's home following her death. In attendance are daughters Plinka, Calista, and Marina; Calista's husband, Jimmy; and their mother's neighbors, siblings Samantha and Joseph McBride, with whom the Tada sisters grew up.[31] Their Japanese mother, portrayed by a disembodied voice, speaks over the world of the play at the beginning and the end, bookending the narrative. Oldest sister Plinka is mixed-race, specifically half-white and half-Japanese, having been fathered by a white American soldier during the American occupation in Japan. Her half-sisters, Marina and Calista, share a different father, who was of Japanese American descent (see figure 4.1).[32] The dramatic action opens as the sisters attempt to settle their mother's estate in the days following her funeral. The refined Plinka and her loose-talking brother-in-law, Jimmy, are at odds over what to do with the property. Plinka longs to sell the farm and return to Tokyo. Jimmy wants to take possession of the estate and move in with Calista until he learns that half of the land does not belong to the Tada women. It is owned by the McBrides, whose father loaned the Tada patriarch the money to buy the land before the Second World War.[33]

Perhaps the most noteworthy element of *Thirst* is Houston's use of *Three Sisters* to dramatize a story that foregrounds the hapa experience. This is

FIGURE 4.1 "The three Tada sisters: (from left to right) Marina, Calista, and Plinka." (Photo by Bob Hsiang.)

especially significant, considering that the drama is one of the earliest plays in the twentieth-century multiracial movement to depict hapa identity and subjectivity. Houston utilizes the differences in the beliefs and lifestyles of the two older Prozorov women to juxtapose the Tada sisters' varying relationships with their Japanese culture. The philosophical debates that the Russians engage in about truth, freedom, and the future transform into Plinka's culturally Japanese outlook on life in *Thirst*. Her Japanese-centric view seems useless to the other Asian characters, who seek to shed their maternal culture. It is also significant that Plinka, who would be considered "half" Japanese in a monoracial framework, is more culturally Japanese than her supposedly "full" sisters.

Through Plinka, Houston challenges the notion that Hapas are less Asian (read: not "real") because of their mixed-race identity. Plinka's sisters, who struggle to assert their Americanness, repeatedly question the need to keep their Japanese ancestry alive. In fact, all of the Japanese characters in the play find fault in Plinka's whiteness and continuously refer to her as a "half-breed," even as they simultaneously attempt to shed their Japanese identity and assert their claim as Americans. Yet "half-breed" Plinka, who proudly claims her white parentage, culturally identifies as Japanese, while her sisters, in reality, are the ones fragmented by their "half-Japanese" selves.

The family's disdain for Plinka's multiethnic identity also underscores the nineteenth-century belief in degeneracy as a characteristic of miscegenation.

Calista suggests that Plinka's mental activities are impractical, while Jimmy conflates Plinka's mixed-race body with abnormality.

JIMMY Your sister.
CALISTA Which one?
JIMMY The half-breed.
CALISTA She's different than us . . . always dreaming and all the time thinking.
JIMMY Hey, ain't normal.[34]

Calista and Jimmy's exchange is reminiscent of the popular suspicion that the mixed blood of the "biologically impure" mixed-race subject produced a mentally unstable personality, and their commiseration indicates that this idea has persisted until the end of the twentieth century. Later in the play, even middle sister Marina admits, "I don't love you anymore, Pinky. You're too *strange*. . . . I won't be your sister."[35] In the same way that Caryl Churchill's play *Cloud Nine* (1979) interrogates the Victorian ideals of gender that still linger in the late twentieth century, so, too, Houston's play dilates and interrogates enduring nineteenth-century beliefs about mixed-race people as mentally weak and impaired.[36] Cynthia L. Nakashima refers to these notions collectively as the theory of "hybrid degeneracy," which contends that mixed-race offspring are genetically inferior specimens—prone to strange and deviant behavior. Nakashima maintains that the theory of hybrid degeneracy undergirds the othering that characterizes mixed-race people as "mythological multiracial monster[s]."[37] Hybrid degeneracy as a concept took root in popular culture toward the end of the Civil War and continued through the first few decades of the twentieth century, where, I suggest, traces of its potency still circulated in cultural discourse till the end of the millennium.

Thirst also questions the cultural attachment to naturalized hypodescent, further demonstrating how the white dominant discourse marginalizes mixed-race people through the application of the one-drop rule. Plinka's white neighbor Samantha contends that she sees Plinka "as whole. . . . They see you as fragmented—half-breed, half-sister. They've always resented you."[38] (See figure 4.2.) Even though Samantha identifies Plinka as a "whole" Japanese, this assertion could also convey her inability to recognize Plinka's whiteness, reifying the dominant Western belief in hypodescent.[39] In the text, Samantha does not seem to make this distinction, but her brother, who is also Plinka's former lover, does, referencing the trope of the tragic that assumes all mixed-race persons struggle with warring half selves.[40] In act 2, he cites her mixedness as the reason for their breakup.

JOSEPH I mean, I never quite got the gist of why you left me. I figured it was because I was white, right? And I reminded you of *what you didn't want to be*?
PLINKA I like being Japanese and I like being white.[41]

FIGURE 4.2 "Samantha and Plinka." (Photo by Bob Hsiang.)

In the 1986 production, this scene is a moment of confrontation between Plinka and Joseph. The performers Nadja Kennedy and Michael O'Brien are staged opposite each other on the farthest edges of the proscenium in a distance that garners a palpable tension between them. As O'Brien delivers the accusation, "I figured it was because I was white," he vocally punches the word "white" for emphasis. Kennedy coolly levels her response at him. It is in this blocking that she proclaims to O'Brien's Joseph, "I like being Japanese and I like being white." It is not a challenge, but a confident assertion that comes from the actor's core. Plinka does not differentiate between being half-Japanese nor half-white. In Kennedy's performance, Plinka is neither confused nor fragmented, and she certainly does not need this white man to understand her or her motivations. She asserts a wholeness that encompasses both a white and an Asian subjectivity. That her assertion of identity is made, as Houston describes in the play's setting, "too late in the 1980s," is nothing short of revolutionary, considering the play predates the beginning of the multiracial movement.[42] Houston seems to suggest that this declaration of mixedness and its public acceptance are long overdue.

Perhaps the most striking theatrical intervention accomplished by the *Thirst* production is the way it demonstrates Plinka's ability to shape shift physically onstage before spectators. Visually, the hapa actress, Kennedy, becomes phenotypically white when she is in the presence of her "full" Asian American sisters and then transforms into an Asian body when she is with her white lover, Joseph. Her racially ambiguous face shape shifts into its white European visage again when her sisters return to the stage, because when she is next to her "full" Japanese sisters, one can see that she is mixed Asian. The transformation is arresting and undeniable. Her ambiguity enables her to shape shift before the spectators' eyes. The vision of hapa corporeality contrasted with monoracial bodies is immediate. Monoracial audience members may tend to assign mixed-race bodies to fixed racial categories. However, when the mixed-race body is juxtaposed with monoracial figures, in this case with performers of Asian American or white descent, it prevents easy classification and challenges notions of racial categorization as immutable and accomplished through the perception of visual markers.

The use of staging in the production also emphasizes Plinka's othered status as a mixed-race figure. In act 2, the three sisters sit on the porch steps, grappling over what to do with their mother's things. When Plinka and Calista accuse Marina of flippantly disrespecting their mother's memory, Marina justifies her actions by jealously retorting that their mother "loved Plinka first."[43] Sharon Iwai's Marina sits on the top step, and Fay Kawabata, who plays Calista, pauses on the second step. Nadja Kennedy perches uncomfortably on the *bottom* step, which seems to be symbolic of her precarious status in the family as the half-breed, half-sister. Furthermore, even though Kennedy is situated in the lowest position of the three bodies, this moment is one of the few times that the sisters are placed physically close together. In most tableaux, Marina and Calista are staged in close proximity to each other while Plinka maintains a recognizable distance from them, no matter how small. The blocking seems to reinforce Marina's belief that they are "always divided. Calista, me and Papa on one side, and Mama and Plinka on the other. America versus Japan."[44] Kennedy's Plinka is often placed on the porch steps opposite her sisters while they lean on each other, or she is sent to the bench in the yard at the opposite end of the stage.

Like Plinka, Houston also felt racially distanced from the rest of the production team during the rehearsals for *Thirst*. As she recounted to Asian American performance scholar Esther Kim Lee and to me in two different interviews, her status as a "half" Asian artist seemed to diminish the value of her artistic voice during the process.[45] Furthermore, the Asian American Theater Company never paid her royalty fees for the production of the play. Though she wrote multiple letters asking for payment, her status not only as an Asian American woman but also as a mixed-race Afro-Asian playwright, seemed to push her to the bottom of the intraracial hierarchy in an organization that appeared to privilege gender and monoraciality. This meant, in the end, that Houston did not get paid at all. Lee contends that "the discrimination against her [Houston] was obvious," although Lee also notes that 1986 was a difficult year for the company, whose management was in transition, which also may have contributed to their failure to compensate the dramatist.[46] Nevertheless, Houston reasons that the discrimination she felt extended into rehearsals, where she was treated as if she were both artistically and racially inferior. The lack of value placed on her contributions as the playwright and as an artist was, Houston contends, due to a "deep-seated anti-Blackness" she uncovered that dominated her encounters with the production team, including in rehearsals. The director and production staff treated her as if she were a racially "inferior creature."[47] According to Houston, the staging of Plinka was not so much a statement about her sisters treating her as their subordinate, but about the director revealing her attitudes toward mixedness in the character's blocking. However, perhaps without intending to, the director's staging also illuminated the social discrimination Plinka was forced to confront and endure in her own Asian American "family."

Houston has been critical of this lack of acceptance specifically within the Asian American theater community. The mistreatment and skepticism made physical in the blocking in *Thirst* were not uncommon to her, and she, too, has contended with the same "issues troubling that character."[48] Houston asserts that Asian American theater companies "must be as equitable as they want the white community to be" and must recognize the "diversity within their [own] community."[49] Lee observes that Houston's successes as a produced playwright have often come from mainstream regional companies, rather than ethnic theaters, which might affirm the lack of acceptance Houston felt from Asian American companies as a mixed-race playwright in the 1980s and 1990s.[50]

At the end of *Thirst*, youngest sister Calista loses her baby in a late-term miscarriage. As Plinka tells Jimmy, the tragic death of the child becomes symbolic of the family's cultural loss. In the 1990 revision of the play, Plinka intones, "I think we're all hemorrhaging. Some things are gone and we can't ever get them back. Like Mama. Like our culture, whatever that means to any of us anymore."[51] Plinka, though half-white, is the most connected to the family's Japanese heritage, and her recognition of a collective bleeding perhaps underscores the understanding that the family's cultural identification has begun to fracture. In the 1985 draft of the script, the version used for the 1986 production, Plinka continues, "It may never rain here until winter. Maybe come December a few drops will fall. But we'll be gone."[52] Earlier in the play, Marina also expresses this same resignation and finality to Plinka:

MARINA It's gone. Everything that defined us is gone.
PLINKA Really, so who are we then? Maybe we really aren't Japanese. Anymore.
MARINA We're Americans.
PLINKA Is that all? It's sad.
MARINA It's inevitable. Fight or die.[53]

Plinka's distress and fear that the women's cultural identities will disappear sounds similar to Olga's lamentations at the end of *Three Sisters*. In Chekhov's play, Olga contends, "The day will come when we'll go away forever, too. People will forget all about us, they'll forget what we looked like and how many of us there were."[54] Yet as Verna A. Foster has astutely noted, future theatergoers have not forgotten that there are three Chekhovian sisters, no matter what their future names have become.[55] Houston's insightful choice to tap into the powerful image of three sisters, orphaned as adults who struggle with uncertain futures, becomes a powerful vehicle through which to explore bicultural and multiracial identity and to question the assumptions of monoracial cultural logic. A classical drama from Chekhov's canon seems perhaps an unlikely place to explore themes of mixedness and acculturation, but Houston's mixed-race subjectivity, grounded firmly in two theatrical traditions, easily constructs a theatrically intercultural play that utilizes a Chekhovian process plot to explore mixed-race identity in the late twentieth century.[56] Moreover, Houston's use of intertextuality in direct and indirect references to various Chekhovian plays creates a literary metamorphosis of *Three Sisters* reimagined in contemporary Asian America.

Houston's use of intertextuality allows the audience to engage more fully with the dramatic narrative, making meaning through the recognition of familiar elements while also being surprised by their differences. This use of intertextuality enacts what J. Douglas Clayton and Yana Meerzon call a "dramatic palimpsest" that enables an audience to experience two dramatic texts at once.[57] Much like a literal palimpsest, in which the original material bleeds through a new image on reused parchment, the use of Chekhov's dramas becomes a kind of underwriting for Houston's play. This double reception brings the memory of the first text to the second and creates a richer experience where the mood and tone of *Three Sisters* enhances *Thirst*, fully fleshing out each nuance as the story unfolds. It also provides the spectator or reader with a familiar backdrop against which to encounter the mixed-race subject. Houston's drama is an ideal site to explore the cultural intervention conducted in this literary metamorphosis, especially when considered through the lens of Chekhov's plays *Three Sisters* and *The Cherry Orchard*.

Thirst bears striking similarities to *Three Sisters*, in which the siblings pine for a better life as they grapple with a relative's disruption in their home. In *Three Sisters*, the Prozorov sisters Olga and Irina share their provincial domicile with their brother, Andrei, and welcome frequent visits from married, middle sister Masha, and the army doctor, Chebutykin, who is an uncle-figure to the siblings. The dramatic action opens with Olga recounting their father's death the prior year. During the course of the narrative, Andrei marries the sharp-tongued Natasha, who moves into the home and eventually strips the responsibilities of the household away from Olga. Rebellious Masha begins an affair, and Irina's jealous suitors, the Baron and Solyony, fight in a duel, leaving the Baron dead.

Thirst is also reminiscent of *The Cherry Orchard*, where a family struggles with the loss of their family estate and squabbles with a family friend over the stewardship of the land in the face of mounting debt. While famous cherry orchards dot the landscape of the Gaev estate in *The Cherry Orchard*, orchards of almonds and peaches populate the Tadas's farm. The Japanese American estate is also inspired by the persimmon orchards owned by Houston's maternal grandfather in Japan, a place that was also a site of contention in her mother's family.[58] The process of selling a family estate in *The Cherry Orchard* or in *Thirst*, serves as a backdrop against which the spectator may witness the characters' underlying subtexts, which are revealed in their actions and reactions.

Houston succeeds in deconstructing the familial relationships and patterns in the Chekhov dramas and recasts the Prozorovs as an Asian American family in California in the 1980s. The play *Three Sisters*, like The *Cherry Orchard*, begins with an arrival. After recounting their father's death, or, in the case of *Thirst*, after the actual death of the mother, guests begin to arrive. In *Three Sisters*, the siblings welcome visitors for a dinner party to celebrate Irina's name day; in *Thirst*, the "guests" are the siblings themselves—who arrive from various cities—as well as the local neighbors. All convene in the Tada farmhouse in Central California for their mother's funeral and to celebrate O-bon festival, the Japanese festival of the dead.[59] At the opening of *Thirst*, oldest sister Plinka, a teacher, writes in her journal, and the image mirrors that of the oldest Russian sister, Olga, who begins *Three Sisters* bent over schoolwork, grading papers. While the Prozorov sisters long to return to the city, Moscow, in *Thirst*, some of the Tada children have already "arrived." Marina and Calista have traveled from urban centers like Manhattan and San Francisco to return home to rural California. The new life they hoped to find, as their Chekhovian counterparts hope they themselves will, is rife with the same alienation and unhappy fate they experienced before. As youngest sister Calista remarks to middle sister Marina, "Since you've been living in New York, it's like someone rubbed your tongue with pumice."[60] In Marina's case, she is perhaps more acerbic than when she first left.

In *Thirst*, Plinka's cultural connection to Japan is contrasted by her sisters' desires to return to the urban centers they now call home. The sisters' preferences for American city life differ from Plinka's need to return to Japan, since she has not yet experienced an escape from the country. Like her Russian alter ego, Olga, who pines for Moscow, Plinka dreams about traveling to Tokyo where she once lived as a child. Plinka tells her neighbor, Samantha, "Growing up in Tokyo was the favorite time of my life," and she later reiterates her desire to return to Tokyo, asserting, "Maybe we would have gone back . . . to the house in Shinagawa, instead of staying here."[61] Plinka expresses her desire to sell the farm, take the money, and move back, which precisely mirrors the Prozorov sisters' nostalgia and intentions to sell their provincial home and return to Moscow in act 1.[62]

Houston's narrative reflects the contemporary period in which it was written by altering the parent whom the siblings mourn in *Thirst*. The Tada sisters constantly talk about their mother, the way the Russians talk about their deceased father. While Houston, like Plinka, also feels intimately connected to her own Japanese mother, this change in the gender of the parent as the backbone of the narrative is also reflective of the mid-1980s. Not only does Houston write about mixed race during the advent of multiculturalism in the United States, but, as playwright David Edgar observes, "Many female playwrights who emerged in the 1980s wrote about what they saw as the invisible relationship of mother and daughter," where the daughter attempts not to fall prey to the mistakes of an earlier generation.[63] This is certainly the case with Houston's earlier play, *Tea* (1985), during which a group of Japanese war-bride mothers performatively embody each of their daughters, who are otherwise absent from the play. Physically "invisible" except in this embodied moment, the daughters question their mothers' decisions and motivations in American life and express a desire to behave differently than they do.[64] In *Thirst*, the same is true for the daughters, whose former relationships with their deceased mother exist only in their recollections. Like the daughters in *Tea*, the sisters struggle to find reasons to keep their mother's culture alive and question the ways that Japanese culture might serve them in adulthood, if at all.

Consequently, Houston reimagines *Three Sisters* in a contemporary American cultural landscape. Unlike Chekhov's drama, *Thirst* is unencumbered by the limitations of early twentieth-century propriety. Houston makes the Russian characters' subtexts apparent in *Thirst* through her characters' bold choices and behaviors, whereas these desires are only suggested in the character exchanges in *Three Sisters*. The relationship between the Tada sisters and Calista's husband, Jimmy, parallels the strife present between the Prozorov sisters and their brother, Andrei, and his wife, Natasha.

Houston transforms the early twentieth-century relationship between sisters and sister-in-law into a plausible modern-day equivalent to further illustrate the separation Plinka feels from her family as a mixed-race subject. In *Three Sisters*, Andrei marries Natasha, a woman deemed beneath his station, who moves into the Prozorov house and, to his sisters' disgust, gradually begins to dictate the daily operations of the home. She wields her power through her control of Andrei. In *Thirst*, Tada sisters Plinka and Marina detest their sibling's spouse and openly declare the disgust that their Russian counterparts silently imply. Youngest sister Calista, who serves as a composite of Andrei and the last Prozorov sister, Irina, is married to the crude, working-class Jimmy, who, like Natasha, uses his influence over Calista to push his own agenda. Just as Natasha begins to take control of the household, so too Jimmy exercises this same influence. In a twist on Chekhov's rendering of lowly born Natasha, her modern-day equivalent, Jimmy, emerges onstage as a common, blue-collar farmer. In the stage directions, Houston describes Jimmy as having "been working on the farm all day in the heat" and looking it.[65] Echoing Natasha's class and "country" origins, Jimmy, like Natasha, detests the way the sisters look down on him. As he explains to the neighbor, Joseph, "Don't you see? I didn't marry Calista. The Tada family "allowed" me to become one of them, like it was some kind of fucking honor."[66] Jimmy's disdain for Plinka seems particularly acute. He continuously refers to her as both a "half-breed" and a "princess," reifying the confusion and jealousy that Calista and Marina already feel for their older sister.

Houston also explores the physical and emotional loss of land as a metaphor for family memory in Chekhov. Like Natasha, Jimmy announces his plans to take over the familial house and to dictate the fate of its contents. For Plinka, this begins the act of cultural hemorrhaging that culminates with the loss of Calista's child at the end of the play. In act four of *Three Sisters*, Natasha surveys the family property and declares, "First thing I'm going to do is have them cut down all the old trees, especially that dead one. . . . And then I'm going to have them plant lots and lots of flowers, all over the place, so it'll smell nice and pretty."[67] Likewise, Jimmy reiterates her sentiments: "I'm going to get a few other things out. We can move some of your Mama's Japanese crap into the cellar. We don't have any need for all those fancy dishes and chopsticks."[68] However, Jimmy continues by voicing what seem to be Natasha's unspoken thoughts to Andrei: "You gotta plant a stake, Calista, or your sisters are going to take everything. Is that what you want?"[69] By contrast, while Natasha only alludes to "planting" her stake, Jimmy directly articulates his intentions. His desire to move into the family farmhouse and strip it of its Japanese cultural artifacts, represented by their mother's things, is reminiscent of Natasha's plans to erase the Prozorovs' particular cultural aesthetic from the home.

In Houston's drama, the hapa character is not mentally weak but, in fact, possesses the most resolve in the family. Plinka confronts Calista about Jimmy's desire to keep the farm, since she, like Chekhov's Olga, wants to sell the house and return to the city of her childhood.

PLINKA Callie, you know Jimmy wants to keep the farm, don't you?

CALISTA So? Don't you think we have a right to it? If he wants to stay here, we'll stay here, even if we have to build a new house on whatever part of the farm I own.

PLINKA Why don't *you* decide what you want to do, Calista? Why don't you make it your decision? You've never made a decision about anything. Even being pregnant. That's why sometimes I look at you funny. It's not because I think you're stupid. I just want you to be brave. Because I love you, don't you understand?[70]

Houston repurposes Olga's distress over her brother's lack of courage as an opportunity to demonstrate Plinka's mental and emotional fortitude. In this way, Plinka expresses Olga's frustration regarding Andrei's inability to stand up to Natasha, further explaining Olga's treatment of her brother. Andrei insists that he loves and respects Natasha and wants his sisters to respect her as well. He berates his siblings for their attitude toward his wife and refers to her as "lovely," "honest," and "good." In similar scenes in *Thirst*, Calista defends Jimmy to her sisters. In the same way that Andrei paints a picture of Natasha as being honest and kind, so, too, Calista claims that Jimmy has a sensitive side that only she understands or, like Andrei, at least clings to in order to make the marriage work.[71] Because Calista is a composite character, she retains the hope Irina has about her life and her future. But Plinka articulates Olga's dissatisfaction with Andrei's despondency and its consequences for the family and their future relationships. The exchange galvanizes Plinka's moral fiber and mettle.

Like Chekhov's *Three Sisters* and *The Cherry Orchard*, *Thirst* ends with the dissolution of the family home. The Tada family knows that they must ultimately decide how to divide their mother's possessions. Both *Three Sisters* and *Thirst* are structured around untimely deaths and culminate with a departure at the summer's end, leaving the sisters to contemplate their fates in a provincial home. In *Three Sisters*, the women mournfully watch the army leave their post in town, marching toward a new life while a military band plays. In *Thirst*, the women watch their lanterns lead the dead, their mother among them, back to heaven, marking the end of Obon festival. According to Japanese Buddhist tradition, Obon festival is the one time of the year when the dead return to the earthly plane to be reunited with their families.[72] Like the military officers that attended Irina's name-day celebration at the beginning of *Three Sisters*, the dead relatives, along with the Tada mother, celebrate Obon festival at the beginning of *Thirst*.[73] This extended family leaves the three sisters at the end, as they similarly do in Chekhov's play, to figure out how to continue on in an uncertain future, especially the mixed-race Plinka, who must defend her mixed-Asian American identity. In *Thirst*, the sisters must also make sense of the shifting monoracial landscape in America as it approaches the end of the century. For them, this means confronting the expanding notion of Asian American to include multiracial Asianness. Additional parallels run throughout the play, referencing *Three Sisters*: character occupations, similar familial relationships, and an overwhelming desire to return to city life, all elements displaced and reassembled into landscapes tonally Chekhovian, but penned in Houston's unique dramatic voice.

Kokoro (True Heart): Presence and Absence in the Mixed-Race Dilemma

In 1997, the U.S. Census Bureau changed its racial categorization policy, allowing U.S. residents to identify with more than one racial box on the 2000 census. Simultaneously, theater saw an emergence of mixed-race playwrights in the 1990s whose work challenged the fixity of race and the ever-shifting boundaries of cultural identity.[74] These narratives capture the evolving political landscape in which they were written as their characters explore questions about multiraciality and authenticity in a culture that was and perhaps continues to be dominated by the one-drop rule. However, the casting of these dramas also reflects the dominant racial associations still held by many Americans in the new millennium. This is evident in productions of Velina Hasu Houston's 1997 drama, *Kokoro (True Heart)*, which depicts a Japanese woman's choice to commit *oyako-shinju* or parent–child suicide—a Japanese cultural practice that saw a recurrence in the context of the immigration of the shin-issei population in the postwar era—and the mixed-race neighbor who ultimately convinces her to choose life without her daughter. Productions of *Kokoro (True Heart)* explore a shift in the social acceptance of multiracial individuals. At the same time, the casting of mixed-race people in productions of the play concretizes the racial assumptions embedded in the word *American*. Like *Thirst*, *Kokoro (True Heart)* also highlights hapa subjectivity in a dramatic narrative that blends two different theatrical forms together in one mise en scène. In *Kokoro*, Houston foregrounds elements of classical Japanese Noh drama with Western realism in a play about an isolated Japanese national who has failed to acculturate to American society. The amalgamation of Noh and Western realism produces another example of Houston's brand of magical realism and creates, as in *Thirst*, a mixed dramatic form, demonstrating a hapa sensibility in the structure of the play and in its content.

Kokoro (True Heart) was written initially in 1994. The two-act, nonillusionistic play follows protagonist Yasako Yamashita, a Japanese woman living in San Diego with her restaurateur husband, Hiro, and their seven-year-old daughter, Kuniko. Isolated and unable to acculturate, Yasako wades into the Pacific Ocean and attempts *oyako-shinju* after discovering that Hiro is having an affair. Yasako succeeds in drowning her daughter before she is pulled from the surf and rescued. Though Yasako's cultural beliefs dictate that the "honorable" decision to commit parent–child suicide would have saved her daughter from a lifetime of shame as an orphan, she nonetheless finds herself charged with one count of first-degree murder in act 2.

Houston is able to communicate the complexity of *oyako-shinju* by blending theatrical elements of Japanese Noh in a text grounded in Western psychological realism. Through her use of the *shite* as a madwoman and the mixing of phantasmal and actual Noh from the form's fourth category,[75] Houston can examine the dichotomy between presence and absence and the *real* and the *unreal* in the drama. *Kokoro*, which translates as "inside of the heart" or "mind, heart, spirit,"[76] explores the realms of the living and the dead more overtly than in *Thirst*. Through the contrast between presence and absence, Houston depicts the mental and emotional plight of the main character, Yasako Yamashita, who functions as the *shite* in the neo-Noh play.

The examination of the real and the unreal also serves to explore authenticity in mixed-race identity. As Houston has observed, "Although I am comfortable with and confident about my hapa identity, perhaps the world has such strict definitions of what is a Real Something (a real playwright, a real African American, a real Asian, etc.) that, in the perceptions of others in society . . . I am never seen as a Real anything."[77] Through an exploration of the real/unreal dichotomy in Noh, Houston interrogates monoracial cultural logic and also champions hapa subjectivity as a whole authentic self rather than an unreal, fragmented identity in *Kokoro*.

Houston synthesizes characteristics and plot points from classical Noh drama with elements of Western dramatic structure in *Kokoro*. Noh drama finds its origins in Shinto rituals. In these religious ceremonies, the *shite*, or "possessed medium," historically reenacted stories of the gods and communicated with a *waki*, or the representative of the community. This same terminology is used in Noh drama, where the central character is known as the *shite* and the *waki*, who is often staged to the side of the playing space, narrates the drama for the audience.[78] By the fourteenth century, under the influence of Noh pioneers Kan'ami (1333–1384) and his son, Zeami (1363–1443), the drama became codified as the theatrical form witnessed today.

According to Noh scholar, Zvika Serper, Japanese Noh seeks to bring together elements that appear contradictory into a unified whole.[79] This theatrical form, therefore, seems to be an ideal medium through which Houston can explore hapa consciousness. The concept of the harmonious whole originates in Chinese philosophy and is often expressed through the contrasting poles of yin and yang or *in* and *yo* in Japanese. Similarly, Noh functions through and investigates a myriad of dichotomies, most notably *kyo*, or that which is fiction, emptiness, absence, and *jitsu*, or reality, fullness, and presence.[80] As Serper notes, "Kyo and jitsu form the basis of the theatrical medium—the coexistence and dynamic interaction of two alternate worlds."[81] This exploration of the essence of the real and unreal is reflected in Noh's two major categories of plays: *mugen no* (phantasmal Noh) and *genzai no* (actual Noh). Typically, the phantasmal Noh play comprises two acts, and the *shite* is an apparition who is revealed as a dead spirit in act 2. Time is fluid, and the main action often takes place in a dream. In the actual Noh play, time moves chronologically, and the main character is a live human being. Comprising only one act, actual Noh plays focus on the inhabitants of the real world rather than those who occupy realms of the dead. These two separate categories of plays together serve as their own dichotomy, the representation of *kyo* and *jitsu*, or the harmonious presence/absence in Noh.[82]

Noh can be further divided into five categories that are based on the persona of the *shite*. These include gods, ghosts, and women in love, which make up the first through third categories and demons, who occupy the fifth. I focus on the miscellaneous characters of the fourth category. These characters range from priests and goddesses to madmen and madwomen, the last often driven to insanity because of the loss of a child. Plays of this grouping belong primarily to the actual Noh category, although phantasmal beings often make an appearance in these narratives.

Houston summons Noh spirits into the space-time of performance in *Kokoro (True Heart)* and blends a fourth-category *shite* with actual events (*genzai no*) and fictional elements (*mugen no*). Houston affirms that *Kokoro* is not based on any single incident, but the play has an uncanny resemblance to the true-life events of Fumiko Kimura, who in 1985 drowned her two young children before she was rescued from death by suicide from drowning. A Japanese *shin-issei* woman, Kimura was resentful of the rescuers who pulled her from the water, saying, "They must have been Caucasians. . . . Otherwise, they would have let me die."[83] In the 1985 case of the *People v. Fumiko Kimura*, the defendant admitted that she waded into the Pacific Ocean in Santa Monica, California, and drowned her children, ages four and six months, after learning that her restaurateur husband had been having an affair for three years. She was unsuccessful in her attempt to drown herself.[84]

The play explores the plight of different types of marginalized Asian subjects, including mixed-race identities. As Houston asserts, "I'm always fascinated with the state of 'otherness,' not fitting in, being in a strange place or emotional situation."[85] In *Kokoro (True Heart)*, the Yamashita family are *shin-issei* or the "new first generation" to immigrate to the United States following World War II. Like Fumiko Kimura, Yasako maintains a traditional Japanese household and longs to return to Japan. Yasako's husband, Hiro, disappears to American life outside the home, and their daughter, seven-year-old Kuniko, attends school and balances American culture with her Japanese life in domestic space. Yasako entertains only one frequent visitor, the ghost of her dead mother, Fuyo, who, through her visits, keeps Yasako's connection with Japan alive.

America is an unseen place that exists beyond the boundaries of Yasako's sheltered life. In the play's opening, she recounts a typical day.

YASAKO August third. Seven to eight: make breakfast. Eight to nine: wash
    Kuniko's clothing. Nine to ten: piano. My world. America is outside, a place to
    visit when I take Kuniko to school. My husband buys the groceries, pays the
    bills. Once I had to take Kuniko to the doctor. That was hard. (Puts book away
    and calls out.) Kuniko! Kuniko-chan! Come, my child. Time for music. (Reacts
    as if a child has run in. . . . The child's entrance is always marked by wind chimes
    or the tinkling of bells.)[86]

Ironically, her own child is physically absent as the role is not portrayed by an actor onstage but only indicated by lights, sound, and in the mother's reactions in performance. In a voiceover, the unseen child participates with Yasako in the dialogue. The theatrical conventions employed in the place of the child's body onstage foreground Yasako's unwillingness to see the American influence already present in her home and in her life. This plot point and the theatrical conventions employed to indicate the child's presence assist Houston in crafting a *shite* that treads between the phantasmal and actual realms of Noh drama. Consequently, she begins the construction of a mixed dramatic form that will be fully illuminated in act 2.

Paradoxically, it is her mother's ghost, Fuyo, who materializes. Physically "real" to both Yasako and the audience, Fuyo is portrayed by an actor onstage. Though dead, her ghost is an embodied presence, and though she never speaks, her influence has a direct impact on Yasako's decision making.

Within this framework, these circumstances reveal Yasako as the madwoman *shite* from Noh. In the absence of a child present and the presence of a deceased mother, we see Yasako's confusion and her entrapment between two worlds: the real and the unreal. In the juxtaposition between living absence and dead presence, Yasako finds herself in the present in a foreign land with an absent husband and no extended family (see figure 4.3). As a result, her mental state becomes compromised. Her need for stability strengthens Yasako's dependence on the child and makes the family system more vulnerable to the *oyako-shinju* practice.

Houston transforms Yasako into a phantasm from the fourth Noh category by blending actual Noh and phantasmal Noh into one dramatic narrative, which serves as a larger metaphor for cultural mixing within the play. When Yasako learns that Hiro, her husband, has been having an affair for the past three years, her world begins to unravel. Remarking on her inability to sleep, Hiro asks, "What's bothering you every single night, walking the floors like a ghost."[87] Houston's *shite* is a spirit present, but moving outside reality. By blending characteristics from different categories of Noh plays, Houston constructs a play with "mixed" dramatic elements even within a Japanese theatrical sensibility.

Furthermore, fourth category Noh plays contain a specific group of dramas that depict deranged parents grieving over their lost children. Most end happily. However, one play, *Sumidagawa* (The Sumida River), most closely resembles the tragedy in *Kokoro*.[88] In *Sumidagawa*, a mother, known only as Madwoman, learns of the death of her kidnapped son after having searched for him for a year. While she is praying over his grave, the boy's ghost appears to her, but he slips from her grasp as she tries to embrace him. *Sumidagawa* was written in the fifteenth century by Zeami's son Kanze Jūrō Motomasa, who maintained that the play would not be effective without the physical appearance of the child's ghost. He insisted on the use of a *kokata* or "juvenile actor" to portray the boy onstage. Zeami, on the other hand, believed that the ghost should be portrayed as a voice and through the reaction of the mother alone. Though there were two different sets of stage directions in their time, one which used a *kokata* and one that did not, today the role is performed by a child actor.

The portrayal of the child in voiceover serves two functions in *Kokoro*. While it fulfills Zeami's original direction in *Sumidagawa*, it also prevents a young actor from having to perform the act of being drowned. In *Kokoro*, the shame felt by Yasako's failure as a wife far outweighs her husband's infidelity. But, for Yasako, divorce is not an option. Instead, she seeks death by suicide in order to join her mother, her only connection to Japan, via the netherworld. Rather than cursing her child to a life with only one parent or burdening relatives with Kuniko's upbringing, Yasako sees no other honorable choice but to "take her child with her" by drowning her.[89] In this way, *oyako-shinju*, which is scripted stylistically in the play's text, is meant to release the entire family of shame.

The traditional practice of parent–child suicide, though illegal in Japan, is rarely prosecuted because of strong cultural beliefs in honorable suicide and the parent–child bond embedded in Japanese culture, a tradition that reaches as far

FIGURE 4.3 "America exists beyond the boundaries of Yasako's sheltered life." (Photo by Michael Rueter/Capture Imaging for USC School of Dramatic Arts.)

back as the Tokugawa shogunate. The Confucian notion that children and their parents are inextricably conjoined has persisted in the Japanese cultural consciousness into modernity.[90] Known as *bun-shin*, the belief implies that until a certain age mother and child are inseparable.[91] So engrained is this mindset that it can manifest in modern society as *oyako-shinju* if the parent chooses suicide as a solution to trauma.

Failed *oyako-shinju*, in which the child dies but the parent lives, results in a "half-death" as the mother only successfully kills part of herself. At the end of act 1, following Fuyo's bidding, Yasako wades into the Pacific Ocean, drowning seven-year-old Kuniko before she herself is pulled from the surf and rescued by onlookers. She finds herself charged with one count of first-degree murder in act 2. Yasako is not interested in living and only desires to follow the daughter whom she has essentially sent to the netherworld without her. Already emotionally dead, Yasako is a ghost. As she explains to her attorney in act 2,

YASAKO *Bun-shin* is like a tree. The child is the branch that needs to stay connected to grow. So, if you—the tree—dies, the branch dies.

ANGELA But if the branch dies, can't the tree continue to live, grow new branches and leaves?

YASAKO (Without self-pity) Who cares about the tree? No one needs the tree.[92]

Likewise, this cultural sentiment is also iterated in the *Sumidagawa*. In the play, the chorus observes that while the "child's meaningful life was quickly ended . . . the *worthless life* of his mother still goes on."[93] This further illustrates the lesser cultural status of the mother in the wake of a child's death.

Houston's blending of Western and Noh dramatic structure is most apparent in the transition from the first to the second act. She employs the pattern of phantasmal Noh by revealing her dead *shite* in act 2, but by this midpoint, the play shifts from the nonlinear, space-time of Noh to more closely resemble a procedural drama in act 2. Yasako awakens in jail and is confronted with a series of visits from her defense attorney, her husband, and her neighbor, Evelyn. When Hiro visits Yasako, he begs for forgiveness and reconciliation. He expresses his remorse as well as his gratitude and relief for having not lost her, but Yasako only responds, "You did lose me, Hiro. I disappeared that day at the beach and I'm not coming back . . . you are looking at a ghost."[94] Yasako's presence as a living ghost foregrounds her utter sense of abandonment, her inability to read American cultural cues, her loss of homeland and culture, and her sense of self. This is her true heart. Her presence is merely absence.

In the play's final moments, Yasako has another chance at death, having obtained a special tea, which will allow her to "travel" to the spirit world through suicide. The tea is brought surreptitiously to the prison by her former neighbor, Evelyn Lauderdale. Fuyo, her mother's spirit, hovers near as Yasako contemplates death over life without Kuniko. Then the child appears, this time as a ghost, but she is only heard, not seen, reinstating Zeami's original direction in this fourth category play.

KUNIKO Mommy?

YASAKO Kuniko?

KUNIKO Where's Papa? Make him walk on the beach with you, Mommy. Make him sing like this: Down the river, oh down the river, oh down the river we go-o-o! Come on, Mommy, you can do it. Bye, Mommy![95]

Upon hearing her child, Yasako makes a herculean effort to put down the teacup and bows to her mother, sending the ghost away. With Kuniko's permission, she wants to live.

This exploration of the contrast between *kyo* (presence and realness) and *jitsu* (absence and the unreal) in *Kokoro* provides Houston a powerful vehicle for illustrating the complexity of Yasako's dilemma. Kuniko, though "real," also represents a culture that is, in many ways, absent to Yasako, while her own mother's culture is kept very much alive. Assisted by apparitions, traditions still linger like ghosts. In this way, we see how the blending of cultures is investigated not only in content but also in the theatrical form.

While the play explores mixedness in its dramatic architecture, it also follows the journey of hapa subjectivity through a mixed-race character, Evelyn Lauderdale. Early in the play, comfort for Yasako comes from Evelyn, a half-Japanese mixed-race neighbor, who befriends Yasako and her daughter prior to the suicide attempt. Evelyn bakes peach cobbler, babysits Kuniko, and shows Yasako how to take the bus. Though friendly, Evelyn never reveals her cultural background to Yasako, and her ethnicity is nebulous. When Evelyn, described only as "faintly exotic looking, warm," and "tomboyish,"[96] finally discloses her mixed-race Japanese heritage to Yasako in act 2, she confides, "My father was American, but my mother was from Japan."[97] Evelyn's racial illegibility prevents Yasako from detecting her mixed-race background and enables Evelyn to shape shift away from her Asianness.

In the exchanges between Yasako and Evelyn, Houston reveals how people of color also fail to recognize mixed-race subjects, which illuminates a dependence on monoracial categorization. Yasako's surprised and admonishing response, "You never told me," conveys her inability to perceive Evelyn's ethnic background.[98] Later in the act, when Yasako seeks Evelyn's empathy regarding her suicide and reminds her that she is Japanese, Evelyn reiterates her shape shifting ethnic ambiguity, asserting, "But I don't look Japanese, so it's easier for me. Sometimes."[99] Evelyn's response acknowledges a particular racialized reality that she may sometimes sidestep, but ultimately must confront, as must Yasako as a minoritized monoracial subject.

Though Evelyn is part Japanese, the specificity of her "American" heritage remains vague. It is highly possible that Evelyn could be a myriad of other ethnic backgrounds. At the very least, there is no overt reason to suspect that Evelyn is half-white, as is precisely stated in the character descriptions in Houston's earlier play *Thirst*. Furthermore, in her other work, Houston clearly delineates the ethnic backgrounds of her other mixed-race and monoracial characters. In the drama, *As Sometimes in a Dead Man's Face* (1994), about the relationship between a half-Japanese and half-Black woman and her adopted brother, the character's racial parentage is specifically stated. *Tea*, based on Houston's mother's life, is part of a trilogy that includes *American Dreams* (1984) and *Asa Ga Kimashita* (1981) and follows the interracial marriage of an African-Native American solider and his Japanese wife as they confront the disapproval of their respective families and communities. Houston's 2008 play *Calligraphy* is also semiautobiographical, inspired by her mother, who, in the play, imagines that her African American husband visits her from beyond the grave. Also written in 2008, the play, *A Spot of Bother*, specifies that the protagonist, Maya, is English and South Asian.[100]

In light of this body of work, it seems plausible that Houston intended for Evelyn's mixed-race heritage to be as diverse as possible to open up casting opportunities for the character. This seems especially true since her other mixed-race characters are of a multiplicity of ethnic backgrounds, and Houston herself is Asian, African American, and Native American Indian. However, as of yet, only monoracial or half-Asian and half-white actors have played the role, including in my own 2003 production of the play.[101] To my knowledge, an Afro-Asian (or other ethnic combination) actor has never portrayed Evelyn in performance. In its over twenty-year production history, from the 1994 world premiere to its most recent production in 2020, the mixed-race actors playing Evelyn have all been Japanese and white.[102] This decision to continuously cast Evelyn as a half-Japanese and half-white woman demonstrates a prevalent assumption that marks the word *American* as white, revealing a nation-based concept of race embedded in the term. As sociologists Michael Omi and Howard Winant point out, "Since the imperial dawn, the ideas of race and nation have been deeply connected through concepts of *peoplehood*. Both as North American colonies of European empires, and then as a nation-state of its own, the United States identified as white. This identification as a white nation remains visible in the associations with whiteness that are visible . . . in such concepts as "the American people."[103] Thus Evelyn's self-identifying term *American* has been interpreted by directors and casting directors, including myself, as white. Though it can clearly refer to American citizens of all races, the term is imbricated with whiteness, as elucidated by the embodiment of the role by half-white women, which erases all other ethnic possibilities from view.

In his article on mixed-race representation in literature, Sheng-mei Ma also differentiates not between Asianness and whiteness but between Asianness and "Americanness." Ma, who criticized Houston's portrayal of mixedness in her drama *As Sometimes in a Dead Man's Face* as reifying the trope of the tragic, monstrous Eurasian,[104] repeatedly points (perhaps correctly) to the instability and impossibility of a mixed-race category where the multiracial subject is immediately "converted" by an observer into a stable "American" or "Asian" monoracial designation. The nebulous use of the term *American*, which denotes citizenship, in a false comparison with the word *Asian*, which denotes race, exposes Ma's assumptions about the word that recall the nineteenth-century belief in the naturalized consolidation of race, culture, and nationality. As Ma conflates citizenship with race, the notion of American becomes tantamount to whiteness. Ma goes so far as to hypothetically interrogate a mixed-Asian person's facial features, noting, for instance, the "*Americanness* of the nose and skin tone."[105] It seems improbable that Ma means anything but American as interchangeable with whiteness here, especially since he differentiates between Asians and Caucasians, or minoritized people and white people, in plays that deal specifically with American citizens (with the exception of *Kokoro*). It feels doubtful that he means to discuss the "Americanness" of a subject who is both African American and Asian American, thus foreclosing the term *American* to other ethnic groups.

The only mixed-race portrayal Ma does mention favorably is that of Evelyn in *Kokoro*.[106] Ma still finds the depiction problematic, however, because Evelyn passes as non-Asian in the play. For Ma, her passing indicates her inability to truly be mixed because she can be assigned to a monoracial category. However, Ma fails to recognize that the assignment to a monoracial category does not erase her mixedness but illuminates the systemic need to classify and contain bodies vis-à-vis race. Furthermore, Ma's superficial analysis of the character overlooks Evelyn as an agent with the ability to self-identify. Rather than being forced to pass, Evelyn enacts what Maria P. P. Root calls "situational ethnicity," in which a multiracial subject will disclose as little or as much of her ethnic background as she feels the situation warrants.[107] Evelyn deploys situational identity to facilitate and eventually complete the shape shifting process because she will control how her observer racializes her. Ma asserts that "the mixed race is elusive and intangible" and that the "occasional and problematic 'sightings' on stage" cannot actualize the theoretical picture of resilient mixed-race subjects who can exist outside monoracial culture logic and categorization.[108] However, the portrayal of Evelyn's ability to shape shift between racial designations illustrates a resilience that defies categorization and serves her in different contexts in the play, especially when she serves as a cultural translator for Yasako and her defense attorney, Angela Rossetti.

This desire to cast a "half-American" as a half-white subject also illustrates what Angela C. Pao refers to as the "regime of verisimilitude." This belief in a logical match between the character's biological ancestry and the actor's phenotype continues to dominate casting in American realism.[109] The concept specifically reveals assumptions about what has been accepted as historically and culturally accurate about people of color in theater. Evelyn continues to be portrayed by a half-white actor because *American* is popularly synonymous with *whiteness*. This casting choice props up an "illusion of reality," which galvanizes the public misconception that Americans are predominantly white. As performance scholar Antonia Nakano Glenn asserts, "Casting as a communal process of authorizing and authenticating the performative act is politicized by the desire to reinforce (or alternately disrupt) *unequal power dynamics*. Casting is an act of social control."[110] Thus the interpretation of an unspecified mixed-Asian "American" character as half-white, in effect, reifies a racial hierarchy that privileges whiteness and keeps multiethnic people of color in marginalized states of invisibility.

The role's casting history also demonstrates a failure to fully recognize that the play grapples with the differences between cultures, not races. Evelyn's admission about her ethnic background is in response to Yasako's surprise upon receiving Evelyn's gift of homemade *o-manju* or Japanese red bean cake. Their subsequent conversation is about culture, nationality, and ethnicity.

YASAKO You made this o-manju? I have never known Americans to even eat these.
EVELYN My father was American, but my mother was from Japan.
YASAKO You never told me.
EVELYN I never told you she was Japanese because, well, it seemed unnecessary to point it out. Unless you had asked.[111]

In the foregoing dialogue, taken from a 1997 version of the script, Evelyn's refusal to divulge her cultural background illustrates what multiethnic writer Heidi Durrow calls "mulatto fatigue," an exhaustion or state of disillusionment, which stems from continuously having to explain and advocate for one's ethnic makeup.[112] As sociologist Kimberly McClain DaCosta notes, being "aware of the shifting meaning of one's parents for negotiating ethnic belonging, many multiracial respondents reported at times going out of their way to make known their kin ties to their parents in public and at other times, downplaying those connections."[113] Evelyn demonstrates a common dilemma that multiracial individuals face—the myopic categorization of mixedness either as a novel state of existence or as not ethnically enough to be fully Asian. Evelyn opts not to disclose her ethnic background to Yasako from either a fear of objectification or a fear of rejection—two positions she has no doubt experienced before.[114]

Evelyn's development as a character mirrors a political shift in the zeitgeist from the mid-1990s to the early 2000s. This can be seen in Houston's revision of dialogue from the 1997 published version to the 2011 Dramatist version and provides insight into Evelyn's motivation and source of anxiety.[115] The metamorphosis also reflects the growing recognition of the racial multiplicity present in the U.S. population, as demonstrated by the change of policy on the 2000 U.S. census. Evelyn's lines, "Well, it seemed unnecessary to point it out. Unless you had asked," become bolder in 2011. Evelyn responds instead, "Well, I guess I wanted you to like me for me and not just because I'm half Japanese."[116] Her revised response indicates not a fear of rejection but a fear of objectification, whereby her mixedness would be marked as novel or exotic. The line is more pointed, direct, unapologetic, and it asserts a desire to be acknowledged outside ethnic and racial ties or "boxes," regardless of whatever privileges those memberships might afford. The exchange also illustrates the shape shifting quality of multiraciality, which defies society's notions of race. Through the instability of its porous boundaries, multiraciality exposes the slippage that occurs when forcing these bodies into monoracial designations, revealing the fallacy in classifying bodies according to racial phenotype.

In her understanding of two different cultural perspectives, Evelyn illustrates her empowered position as a doubly liminal, mixed-race subject. During one of the visits to Yasako in jail, it is Evelyn who encourages Yasako to embrace the possibility of life, dissuading her from suicide and convincing her that Kuniko would have wanted her to live. Evelyn stands squarely in the center of the narrative, having successfully navigated both cultures in her own upbringing. As Masami Usui asserts, through the exploration of a Japanese woman's trauma and difficulty in readjusting to the cultural disparities she encounters, Evelyn is also a representation of Houston acting as intermediary between two different countries and their cultures.[117] Tamara Ruppart, the director of the 2011 and 2014 productions of the play, has similarly asserted that the multiethnic Evelyn is "the Velina role" in the play.[118] Evelyn, as Houston, becomes a kind of *waki*, a translator for the audience—most likely a mainstream American audience—who may not understand the cultural circumstances that would drive a mother to kill her own child. This mixed perspective is demonstrated through Evelyn's double liminality, on the microlevel. On a macrolevel, it is demonstrated in the body of the play's narrative and in the architecture of the dramatic form, which blends Japanese and Western theatrical traditions. The work itself represents Houston's mixed cultural perspective and creates a play with a mixed identity.

Through a supporting character, Evelyn Lauderdale, Houston develops the complexity of being mixed-race in a play that is ultimately about a Japanese woman's journey to survive in a foreign land. It is through her friendship with a mixed-race woman that she is able to see possibility in such a transition. Yet the hope-inspiring role of Evelyn Lauderdale remains fraught with assumptions about race, both as evinced in the character's words and historically, in the embodiment of the character through casting choices that have perceived the role as half-Asian and half-white.[119]

Houston wrote *Thirst* and *Kokoro (True Heart)* at a time when seminal mixed race scholars like psychologist Maria P. P. Root had just begun to write about mixed-race subjectivity. Houston's dramas illustrate the ways in which theater not only followed the social movements of the 1980s and 1990s but more importantly the way it helped shape these movements. The plays of Velina Hasu Houston thrust the issues of transnationalism and mixed-race subjectivity into the national discourse and contributed to the shifting cultural tide that paved the way for the mixed-race grassroots movement to change the racial categorization on the U.S. census in 2000. Her work opened the doors for playwrights in the coming millennium to prime the theatrical landscape for a new kind of racial discourse.

5

Multiraciality in the Post-Racial Era

● ●

In January 2016, Stage Left Theatre, together with Red Tape Theatre, produced the political satire *Mutt* (2014) by Christopher Chen in a North Side neighborhood of Chicago. The dark comedy revolves around an Asian mixed-race presidential candidate who garners enough support to be elected to the White House. He accomplishes this despite having murdered his opponent on national television. In an uncanny instance of life imitating art, within ten days of the play's opening, 2016 presidential candidate Donald J. Trump told supporters at a political rally in Sioux Center, Iowa, that he could "stand in the middle of 5th Avenue and shoot somebody" and still get elected.[1] More than a macabre coincidence, the play illuminated Chen's chilling observation that political and racial perception can eclipse even the most egregious of crimes. It also exposed how race, a central issue in both Chen's fictional and the real 2016 presidential election, becomes powerful fodder for American political rhetoric. Considered together, the play and the real-life incident elucidate how whiteness, the master monoracial category, is held to different standards of unhampered privilege. In *Mutt*'s mixed-race candidate, Chen shows us how the supposed acceptance of all races under the guise of colorblindness perpetuates a racially divisive system and furthers the interests of the white hegemony.

Frances Ya-Chu Cowhig's play, *Lidless* (2011), also demonstrates how the hands of the state manipulate race. The play follows Bashir, a political detainee at the Guantánamo Bay detention camp, and his torturer, Alice, who uses "invasion of space by a female," or rape, as a means of extracting information from her prisoner. The assault results in a pregnancy that Alice sees to term. Their mixed-race child, although different from the presidential candidate in *Mutt*, highlights another facet of political discourse—the invisibilization of the mixed-race body in contemporary American culture.

Together, these two plays foreground the ways that the fluidity of multiraciality becomes clouded by polarizing monoracial designations. The mixed-race characters of *Lidless* and *Mutt* become absorbed by whiteness in different ways, whether by disappearing into the monoracial category or by upholding the hegemonic ideals of white patriarchy. The plays elucidate the ways in which mixed-race identity also becomes co-opted to further the problematic rhetoric of colorblindness. Both projects expose the underpinnings of the persisting cultural amnesia that fail to recognize and valorize the prevalence of mixed-race heritage and identity.

In this chapter, I examine how contemporary performances of hapa, or mixed-Asian, characters complicate the identity narratives of the twenty-first century and highlight the ability of mixed-race individuals to shape shift, or sidestep predetermined racial categories, due to their ethnic ambiguity. This shape shifting ability is what enables hapa figures to slip into monoracial categories—a shift they must perform to gain subjectivity in American social, cultural, and political frameworks.

At first glance, the mixed characters in *Mutt* and *Lidless* seem to reify archaic, Jim Crow and Coolie era tropes, such as the "half-breed" as a troubled pathological figure rather than a malleable shape shifter.[2] Yet these dramatic narratives surreptitiously work to reveal larger mechanisms of racial discourse by illuminating how multiculturalism and colorblindness work within political and legal structures that grant subjectivity only on their own terms. I contend that mixed-race identity is dependent on the performance of historical and genealogical knowledge. Without this crucial understanding, multiracial bodies slip into reified categories of race, leaving their mixed histories inevitably behind. The plays work in tandem to demonstrate how political policies succeed in erasing mixedness and how the ability of the mixed-race body to shape shift across racial lines then becomes contingent on social and historical context and the reception of the individual.

Significantly, reading the plays also reveals a drastic departure from the mixed-race dramas of the late twentieth century. The mixed characters of *Mutt* and *Lidless* do not actively work to reconcile their angst about conflicting cultural values, nor do they wrestle with a desire to belong. Rather, the dramatizations reflect the growing awareness of mixed-race identity in the twenty-first century, a complex, yet perhaps hopeful political period marked by a change in the racial self-identification policies of the 2000 U.S. census. For the first time in the census enumeration, mixed-race individuals were permitted to identify with more than one racial category. This subtle change in the zeitgeist has slowly seeped into theatrical discourse, as evident in these postmillennial plays.

The Midwest production of the play opened in Chicago on January 13, 2016. With the title shortened simply to *Mutt*, the performance was presented as a coproduction between Stage Left Theatre and Red Tape Theatre. My examination of the play will include a close semiotic reading complemented by my observations recorded from a short-term ethnographic study of the production. I was fortunate enough to attend one combined technical and dress rehearsal, three previews, and the first two performances of the Chicago run. My research methodology combined participant observation and co-performer witnessing. I participated in production meetings, helped clear set pieces from the stage, interviewed various members of the cast, and conducted audience surveys. The entire production team was warm and welcoming, especially the director, Vanessa Stalling, with whom I developed a special affinity. These observations are also complemented by two interviews with playwright Christopher Chen, conducted before and after the ethnographic research, and a follow-up interview with Stalling. Additionally, I will conclude with a close reading of *Lidless*, supported by archival research of the play's productions and an interview with Frances Ya-Chu Cowhig.

Double Liminality and Racial Transgression

When junior Illinois senator Barack Obama became the first African American to be elected president, his campaign and election signaled to a vast majority of Americans that a post-racial society had finally dawned. Upon hearing President Obama's 2010 State of the Union speech, television pundit Chris Matthews declared, "He is post-racial, by all appearances. I forgot he was black tonight for an hour."[3] Matthews's comment, of course, tellingly contradicts its own sentiment, since it implies that after an hour, even Matthews remembered that the president was Black. It was a clear indication that quite the opposite had occurred. The post-racial era had failed to arrive.

In light of this false premise about a post-racial society, this chapter investigates how multiracial subjectivity can be understood by performance theorists to interrogate and challenge the desired belief in racial transcendence that some people desire. Taking into account Brandi Wilkins Catanese's notion of racial transgression, I explore the ways that mixed-race figures transform and clarify our understanding of the racial scaffolding in contemporary America. I advance the notion that what I call double liminality, or the fluidity of mixed identity, illustrates how the mixed body slips between the boundaries of race in *Mutt* and *Lidless*.

Brandi Wilkins Catanese astutely observes that the term *transcendence* is often called upon in racial discourse as a means of celebrating cultural triumph over the ugliness of race. Racial transcendence, or "colorblindness," purports not only to look beyond the physical markers of race but, naively, to not see race at all. Cultural theorists SanSan Kwan and Kenneth Speirs similarly call this racial transcendence the "egalitarian multicultural paradigm," which evades racial complexities through a belief in a "brownwashed," raceless society.[4] All three scholars note that the desire of many white people for racial transcendence becomes a political maneuver and a revered cultural objective with the underlying message that people of color should simply "get over it."[5] These scholars further argue that the more humane pursuit is not to ignore race but to acknowledge the division and destruction that racialization has caused. Through acknowledgment, we can instead interrogate and dismantle the violence of race. Catanese calls this approach racial transgression. She advocates for performances that defy racial frameworks to expose the "limitations of transcendence as a viable strategy for social change" and to acknowledge the histories that racial hierarchies have inscribed on individual bodies.[6] She contends that the antidote to transcendence is an awareness of the divisions put in place by race, rather than a denial of their existence.

The moral limits of transcendence are apparent in Catanese's analysis of the film performances of Black actor/director Denzel Washington. Catanese affirms that an audience will read the "surplus meanings his presence as a black actor will or will not introduce into the film."[7] That is, the idea that the audience never sees Washington's race is a fallacy. His racialized materiality may not be relevant to the character he portrays, but nonetheless his skin color and the assumptions ascribed to his racial physiognomy are always present. Washington does not stop being Black, but rather the audience presumes not to notice his Blackness.

Catanese also observes the way that hip-hop artist Ice Cube's 2006 reality television show, *Black. White.*, purported to give members of different racial groups a glimpse into one another's everyday life. White participants were "made up" to appear Black through the use of cosmetics, costumes, and "raced" performances, while Black individuals were made to look white by the same means. In this way, Black and white bodies superficially switched one racialized state for another. But interculturalist Leo Cabranes-Grant has keenly noted that Ice Cube's transracial experiment "actualized" an experience "that was neither white nor black: *Black. White.* performed a mixing of colors that still remains underrepresented in our visual repertoire."[8] Cabranes-Grant acknowledges this unlikely nod toward miscegenation and points out a lack of representation of mixed-race bodies that Catanese perhaps misses.

Building on Catanese's argument and continuing Cabranes-Grant's observation regarding a lack of multiracial performances in general, I wonder how mixed-race bodies, which embody two or more sets of difference, negotiate multiple racial states in performance. In our cultural conditioning, are they allowed to inhabit more than one? How does the material presence of the mixed-race body expose the limitations of the racial hierarchy and our misguided belief in the possibility of a colorblind utopia in this current moment?

I contend that the very portrayal and embodiment of mixed-race characters are performances of racial transgression. Their racially ambiguous physiognomy defies prescribed racial codes and foregrounds the process by which we see and assign racial difference. When we encounter a mixed-race body, far from "not seeing race," often we vigorously pursue the "mystery" of its racial identity. The racially nebulous body troubles our ability to organize individuals into accepted racial groups and, in doing so, dismantles the fixity of monoracial categories. For example, individuals of mixed-Asian descent cannot easily fit into a single Asian category. The mixed-race body makes apparent how disparate the multiracial experience is. Mixed Asians are *doubly liminal*. They exist on the margins, at the thresholds, of the categories of monoraciality, such as categories of Blackness, whiteness, or Asianness. While they are often not quite Asian enough to be fully accepted as Asian, neither are they fully accepted as white, for example.

Yet the mixed-race body is perhaps a conundrum, as it is not two "halves" of a cultural experience fused together but rather two "wholes" experienced simultaneously. While racial expectation assumes that a perceived phenotype ensures an assignment to a supposedly correct racial category, mixed-race bodies shape shift and slip into many different racial designations, including some that are not part of those individuals' ethnic histories. This process is contingent on many things, such as an observer's reception, the geographical location, the subject's personal genealogical knowledge, and the performance of self. Plays like *Mutt* and *Lidless* can take Catanese's theory one step further by acknowledging the myriad histories that make up the mixed-race body. As Kwan and Speirs keenly note, the various racial histories inscribed on individual bodies carry with them different lineages of power and oppression.[9] Rather than insisting that multiracial bodies identify as one specific race, they advocate that individuals embrace the multitude of ethnic experiences that make up the mixed identity and acknowledge the vastly different tensions that a multiethnic body possesses.

And yet these various historical lineages also separate mixed individuals from each other. This variegated mixed-race experience is also an aspect of double liminality, as a multiethnic person cannot entirely fit into a monoracial group, but neither can she neatly fit into a mixed-race category. For example, the Chinese-white character, Nick, in *Mutt* has a vastly different experience in his multiethnic upbringing than that of his political rival, Len Smith, who claims to know every ethnic ancestor in his mixed-race lineage. Both characters, however, are identified in *Mutt* as hapa, although neither of them shares a similar Asian or mixed cultural experience.

This demonstrates a particular dilemma of mixed race. Although the experience of mixedness may be a commonality among multiracials, a subject's particular ethnic background and exposure to those cultures varies drastically between individuals. This further distances them from each other. Nonetheless, contemporary racial politics force mixed-race bodies into monoracial categories in an attempt to systematically organize individuals into easily legible racial codes. While this is shifting in the new millennium with the ability to self-identify on the census, the rule of hypodescent still governs hegemonic perceptions of race.

While many multiracials no longer have to choose between two or more different parental lineages, the persisting paradigm in society still organizes them into dominant racial groups. This denial of the mixed-race body produces its own kind of violence, as mixed individuals are often not fully accepted into the racialized group to which they are assigned.

As theater scholar Joshua Takano Chambers-Letson notes, American legal structures grant subjectivity only to those who are racialized. Chambers-Letson's analysis of Bashir's subjectivity in *Lidless* is useful here. Bashir, a political prisoner at the Guantánamo Bay detention center, becomes a subject in the eyes of the state only because of his race.[10] His interrogator, Alice Jones, finally recognizes him years later *only* after he performs his previously assigned role as a prisoner of Middle Eastern Asian descent. In this way, as Chambers-Letson contends, the law is "structured by acts of performance."[11] Chambers-Letson's observations about the legal creation of racialized personhood shed light on the mixed-race individual's desire to yield to the rule of hypodescent and to allow the self to be absorbed into monoraciality. Racialization as a means of becoming a subject also clarifies the subdominant's hesitation, even refusal, to recognize mixed-race subjectivity, which reveals an anxiety over losing members who may claim mixedness. Even though multiracial individuals must endure some erasures that accompany belonging to a specific racialized group, such as identifying solely as African American, those who do not subscribe to an established racial category run the risk of not existing at all. In *Lidless*, Bashir's mixed-race daughter, Rhiannon, avoids this invisibility by shape shifting into whiteness. Her mixed-race ability to morph across multiple racial lines, in conjunction with her lack of personal genealogical knowledge, is what, in fact, causes the erasure of her mixed self.

Sublime Superhapa: Optics, Representation, and the American Presidency

The work of international award-winning, mixed-race playwright Christopher Chen features dramatic narratives in which racial transgression interrogates transcendence. His plays explore the instability of cultural perception and the dynamics of transracial relationships. His postmodern sensibilities play with disruptions in time, alluding to surrealistic spheres where his characters grapple with real-world problems in the theatrical realm. In 2014, he was commissioned by Impact Theater and Ferocious Lotus Theatre Companies in San Francisco to write a play about mixed-Asian identity. His response was a political satire originally entitled *Mutt: Let's All Talk about Race!* that first premiered in San Francisco in May of the same year.

Chen's stylized comedy is perhaps the first millennial play on the U.S. mainland to use the Hawaiian word *hapa* to identify individuals of mixed-Asian descent. He thus introduces the word to mainstream American theatrical audiences. The play examines shifting racial perceptions in a fictitious 2016 presidential election. It focuses on the depiction and commodification of multiraciality as envisioned by Chen, who exposes the absurd tenacity with which society clings to tenuous racial scaffolding. In *Mutt*, Chen not only interrogates racial politics in contemporary America but also examines how mixed-race sensibility navigates the often perplexing and treacherous terrain of what Evelyn Alsultany calls "monoracial cultural logic."[12] In the play, party leaders are on the lookout for a "superhapa," a multiethnic candidate who can morph into any race, in the hopes of appealing to all racial groups and securing every "race" vote possible. Through this premise, Chen imagines the dire and darkly humorous consequences that only a relentless search for the "perfect mix" can bring.

Mutt performs in two acts and is written in the vein of episodic, nonlinear sketch comedy. Rather than following an inevitable linear plot, the chronological narrative progresses in what playwright David Edgar refers to as "disconnected time," where a collection of stories unfold that do not at first seem to be related.[13] In the stylized staging, the actors employ indirect audience address, and projected titles of scenes provide mile markers for the audience along the way. The show's nonillusionistic requirements transform the set into many locales: a therapist's office, a D.C. bar, and a Thai Mexican restaurant, among others.

Central to the narrative are the journeys of three hapa characters. Hanna, a "race management consultant," introduces the idea of a mixed-race presidential candidate to white Republican Party leaders, Miriam and Zach. She sees a multiracial candidate as a solution to the problems stemming from the party's refusal to acknowledge race. Hanna asserts that an individual with an "appealing" amalgamation of whiteness and the model minority, would be safer than someone like Obama, whose "presidency proved that the country isn't ready for an African American president."[14] Hanna coaxes the truth from Miriam and Zach, crooning, "Let's be honest . . . you're still scared of black people. Aren't you?"[15] Swayed by Hanna, the Republican leaders admit that their party's unpopularity is due to its fear of minorities and their wish that the race issue didn't exist.[16] Hanna then proposes that they embrace a half-Asian, half-white figure as a safer candidate and reminds them that "optics" and public perception are of the utmost importance to win the election.

Enter two potential contenders: Nick Wong, a congressman of mixed-Asian descent with little connection to his Chinese heritage, and Len Smith, a decorated war hero, who has just returned home from a tour in Afghanistan. Len is introduced as a mix of every major race in the world.[17] He is what the Republicans refer to as a "superhapa," someone who can "optically appeal" to any voter. Quite frankly, he's the party's wildest dreams come true.

For Chen, *Mutt* becomes a study in the behavior of the political machine and its encounters with the physical bodies of others. In his astute vision, these interactions range from the hyperbolic to the ephemeral to the invisible as characters fail to physically see some bodies while wildly misperceiving others. For instance, in a keenly crafted sight gag, the cleaning lady at the Democratic national head-quarters, a Latina, is corporeally nonexistent. Not actually played by an actor onstage, the character is embodied by a voiceover alone, and neither the other characters nor the audience can see her. She is only discovered to be in the room when the Democratic Party leader supposedly trips over her. After a brief verbal exchange with the confounded group of politicians, in the Chicago production the door to the room seemingly opens by itself, and the "invisible minority" makes an exit. As this invisible Latina reminds us, in this system the only body that can ultimately be seen is one that fits the hegemonic ideal.

Amid eye-opening exchanges like these, the playwright creates a mixed-genre style that parallels the mixed-race subjectivity underscoring the play. He initiates a subplot written as a procedural drama with neo-noir characteristics in which a character known only as the "Inspector" is on the hunt for a serial killer. The quick jumps between a procedural drama, political talking heads, and comedic sketches mirror the act of surfing television channels where viewers receive their information in snippets. As the Inspector interviews witnesses at various crime scenes, the suspect's race keeps morphing. The witnesses are not quite sure they can actually identify the race of the killer whose descriptions range from Korean to Black to "Aztec." (The last one is, in fact, a complete conundrum to them since they cannot decide if Aztec is Native American or not.) Nevertheless, the Inspector is confident in the accuracy of all their testimonies and sends all of them to his sketch artist to craft a composite that will incorporate each racialized account.

Ironically, this uncertainty is exactly what the hegemony counts on in the narrative's main plot. Enamored by his stories of multiculturalism, the Republicans select superhapa Len to be their nominee. In his preliminary interview, he confidently assures Hanna, Miriam, and Zach, "I am all people, so I can literally be whoever you want me to be."[18] As Cynthia L. Nakashima has asserted, "These days just about every political and ideological camp utilizes mixed-race people in support of their arguments. . . . The representation of mixed-race people as the 'children of the future' sporting 'global identities' has continued, manifesting itself . . . as the racial expression of an Everyman."[19] In a climate dependent on the rigidity of racial codes, Len's shape shifting abilities become an asset in securing the nomination. He promises a transcendent society that superficially acknowledges racial difference even as it holds the racial hierarchy in place (see figure 5.1).

By contrast, Nick is interested in exploring the disparities created by race. Disillusioned by the colorblind Republicans, he has switched parties and begins to self-identify as a mutt. He vehemently asserts that the United States is a mutt, too, and that collectively, Americans need to "get out of the pound."[20] Upon hearing Len's stump speeches about a new utopian society, Hanna echoes Nick's unnerved frustration, declaring, "He's not *saying* anything! He's letting people

FIGURE 5.1 "The cast of *Mutt, 2016*." (Photo by Tom McGrath/TCMcG Photography.)

see whatever they want to see in him."[21] Nick's passion and her own disgust prompt Hanna to join him in his bid for the Democratic nomination, which he eventually wins.

Through these prisms of mixedness, Chen examines the instability of racial perception. By unhinging the "pure" categories of monoraciality, he reveals how the multiplicity of ethnicities and experiences are subsumed within these fixed designations. All three of these hapa characters—Hanna, Nick, and Len—are identified as Asian, even though none of them share similar ethnic backgrounds. Furthermore, Chen demonstrates the separation experienced by multiracial figures, who not only fail to fit into a monoracial category but also cannot neatly fit into a mixed-race group. While Len knows his entire ancestral lineage, Nick barely relates to his own Chinese father and knows nothing about his father's upbringing. Hanna never reveals her ethnic background in the play. She only self-identifies as "hapa." Individually, they each occupy a liminal space of mixedness. They are separate from each other in spaces that call monoracial designations into question. The mutability of perception and the ambiguity of their phenotypes allow them to shape shift, a skill Len relies on for the success of his campaign. While mixed-race labels seemingly reinforce fixed racial codes by suggesting a mix of stable races, the doubly liminal bodies of multiraciality simultaneously dismantle them. This double liminality is the center from which Chen, a Chinese and white American playwright, pens *Mutt*. His bifurcated positionality fuels his writing, becoming the driving force behind the play's narrative.[22]

Rather than reifying the trope of the tragic Eurasian, *Mutt* legitimizes mixed-race bodies by empowering and foregrounding them in the play. Hanna, Len, and Nick are all in positions of political power. Indeed, Len and Nick are vying for perhaps the most powerful office in the free world, and Hanna is the mastermind behind their ascent. The rise of the mixed-race character to presidential candidate is significant, considering that multiracial people have historically been depicted in white mainstream theater as slaves, servants, prostitutes, and criminals.[23] While newer works written by mixed-race playwrights have slowly begun to feature multiethnic characters in a variety of professions, typically the mixed-race character has no known profession at all, such as the unemployed mixed woman Lee in Frank Chin's seminal play *The Chickencoop Chinaman* (1972). This is significant since, in works like Chin's play, mixed-race subjects cannot even aspire to a disenfranchised place in the community—they simply have no place at all. The inability of the mixed-race body to be racialized, therefore, bars the subject from achieving a kind of personhood, even one as an outcast in a tenuous social position. If in 1895, Patsy O'Wang aspires to be the alderman of his district in a white playwright's vision, it is not until 2014 that Len and Nick finally fulfill and surpass his dreams 119 years later. At the very least, it is a strong suggestion that multiracials may finally have found their place.

Beyond the sublation of the tragic Eurasian figure, the racial transgression of shape shifting bodies enables Chen to interrogate another multiracial trope: the messianic "Face of the Future" imaginary.[24] This hope that a futuristic multiethnic society will end racism has been written about extensively since the appearance of "The New Face of America" on the cover of *Time* magazine in 1993.[25] The image featured the face of a woman who was purportedly a mix of several races and sought to demonstrate what society would look like in the future. While critical scholars have problematized its use as a symbol for the advent of a post-racial era, its rhetoric still circulates in popular culture in television and films like the popular Wachowski sisters' *Matrix* trilogy (1999–2003).[26] Through Len's nebulous shape shifting character, Chen challenges the trope's pernicious embrace of a transcendent, colorblind society in order to demonstrate how the system has failed to acknowledge the presence of multiethnic bodies.

In the play, Chen charges Hanna with introducing and reinforcing the idea of the Face of the Future. Her reference to the trope demonstrates the insidious ways that bodies of color become complicit in their own straitjacketing. Midway through the play, a despondent Hanna anticipates a mixed-race future, but Nick dismisses this as an excuse to be complacent in the present.

HANNA By 2050 every race will have screwed every other race so the political machine will just move on finding other ways of dividing us.
NICK So you're saying we just have to wait it out for the population to interbreed its way out of racial issues? . . . Isn't that passing the buck?[27]

This exchange is ironic because according to Len, every race has already "screwed every other race." When television pundit Dave Matthews asks Len what contributed to his multiethnic heritage, Len replies, "A lot of screwing, Dave."[28] In fact, Hanna has unknowingly described the present—a multiracial society that the political machine has found a way to divide. Chen dispels the notion that a mixed-race utopia is on the horizon by revealing the existence of the Face of the Future now. Superhapa Len knows his entire ethnic makeup. Like the computer-generated *Time* image, he, too, is Asian, white, Middle Eastern, and African. Far from being a genetically inferior "creature," television pundits describe Len as "sensuous," "magnetic," and as someone who can appeal "to everyone of every background and persuasion."[29] Len delivers the future now, which is, as he puts it, "exciting and non-threatening at the same time."[30] But the presence of the mixed-race body does not in actuality represent racial transcendence, as the Face of the Future would have us believe. On the contrary, a mixed-race person represents an interracial union that disrupted the racial divide and chose transgression rather than dismissive transcendence.[31] Resultantly, the status quo and the rule of hypodescent continue to force mixed-race persons into specific monoracial categories.

Nonetheless, Len's superhapa persona reinforces the idea that we are all mixed, even though we may not know it. While television pundits are impressed by his ability to rattle off his diverse parentage, it becomes clear that what separates us from multiracials like Len is mere knowledge—personal histories that would reveal our mixed selves if only those histories had not become lost to us. As Hanna observes, these erasures are how we have become divided, since there is a concomitant pressure to identify monoracially—an impossibility for many Americans. The truth is that the intermixing she believes is forthcoming has already taken place.

Furthermore, Len's "beigewashed" superhapa becomes a symbol for the desired universality that underlies the notion of a transcendent, raceless society. By problematically sidestepping the very real challenges of racism faced by many Americans, this beigewashing attempts to "homogenize us all."[32] As Chen has affirmed about Len, though he may be a supermix of every major race, part "of the joke is that he's a blank slate"; that is, in his embodiment of many races, his racial mixedness becomes homogenized and consequently, erased.[33] The supposed representation of many different cultures and communities, united under the umbrella of the universal, is merely a matter of perception, of "optics," rather than a true reflection of the reality of different life experiences. Nick reminds us that the American hegemony only cares "about a racial culture's greatest hits collection of American-like attributes."[34] In the refusal to acknowledge the histories of oppression housed in the racialized body, we see the danger that universality brings.

Chen sees societal erasure and cultural amnesia as hastened by the evolving dependency on technology and social media—a dependency that rapidly expedites the loss of our own personal histories. Nick attempts to rediscover his cultural roots because he is genuinely interested in his family's history. Yet modern technological culture changes so quickly that Nick's Chinese father, Carruthers, cannot remember moments that happened the day before much less oral histories that were handed down decades ago. In this digital world of perpetually renewed information, our genealogical and cultural memories evaporate, and Chen sees this evanescence as an unfortunate "product of American culture."[35] Though Nick tries in vain to help his father recall superficial details of his life in China, Carruthers warns him not to romanticize the past and not to trust memory. In a broader sense, Carruthers's dismissal of Nick's cultural soul-searching could serve as a way to disrupt the romantic persistence of Orientalism and the West's attempts to reduce Asian culture to stereotypes. But as a prisoner of digital culture, Carruthers has also lost his connection to his ethnic past in his desire to be relevant and keep up with the times.

Chen highlights the devastation of cultural amnesia through Carruthers's confusion and through the manipulation of temporal space onstage. Within surreal scene transitions, a disembodied voice interrupts the action by announcing, "It's night time! It's daytime!" The performers stop the action, frozen in place, and then reanimate, seemingly not affected by this loss of time. What has become "real time" in this world is time without contemplation. Only the Inspector, who moves about in a noir space that progresses more slowly than the main narrative, seems to have the time to reflect. Indeed, days and nights move by so quickly that Nick's father cannot remember what is happening from moment to moment.

Curiously, the third and final witness interviewed by the Inspector revels in this quirky version of virtual time. As she tracks a delivery online, she delights in how quickly her package "pings" across the globe.[36] She praises the enlightened members of our technologically enhanced society and vehemently asserts that here there is no race and no time. In her world, or our world, she is beyond the confines of time and, as a result, believes she is beyond the confines of race, much to the Inspector's confusion. Nevertheless, when she is asked to speculate on the race of the suspect, she unquestionably identifies him as an African American, which exposes her ability to see race after all. Chen thus sharply interrogates our blind adoption of a technological culture that would aid us in forgetting cultural memories and the lessons of the past. It perpetuates a belief in colorblind transcendence that is actually an internalized lie.

In this savvy appraisal of the erasures committed in the digital age, the Inspector identifies Len, the embodiment of the universal, as the serial killer. His sketch artist compiles varied eyewitness descriptions and produces a composite sketch that is reminiscent of the Face of the Future imaginary. The rendering is a portrait of Len (see figure 5.2). Yet the Inspector, who has been overtaken by his own white guilt, allows Miriam to dissuade him from charging her candidate with the murders. In the frenzied conclusion that follows, Len stabs Nick in the neck during a campaign speech on live national television. Despite this

FIGURE 5.2 "The Inspector and Miriam assess the composite sketch." (Photo by Tom McGrath/TCMcG Photography.)

heinous act, Len—heralded as the candidate who can "save us all"—ultimately wins the election amid an overt, hubristic display of violence, willfully overlooked by the body politic.[37] The play culminates in a frenetic clamor of techno music, which is intertwined with the chorus of "We Are the World" and video projections that proclaim America's victory over race—such as "America Defeats Race Issue" and "National Nightmare Over!" In the play's final moments, the hedonistic din builds to a crescendo before the stage goes black.

Len's character embodies the false acceptance of cultural and ethnic multiplicity in American society. As the invisible Latina earlier in the narrative reminds us, in this system the only body that ultimately can be seen is one that fits the hegemonic white ideal. Len's shape shifting physiognomy morphs into a manifestation of the universal, which methodically proceeds to erase histories of color. His actions reveal a fallacy in the myth of American racial democracy. Metaphorically, the philosophy of transcendent colorblindness kills difference. It is a serial killing that singles out people of color. The consequences of this action are dire. The failure to recognize race means that racism does not end. In our refusal to discuss race, as Nick endeavors to do, we overlook these erasures of color as a result of social conditioning and entrainment. As Nick asserts, "America is a mutt," but the dominant desire for a beigewashed universality systematically attempts to eliminate these cultural and racial differences in America.

In an alarming indication that the colorblind mentality is alive and well in the United States, many of the Chicago reviewers found Chen's script to be an ineffective and unnecessary critique of race. One critic in particular believed that race was nonexistent. Reviewer Tom Williams from the *Chicago Critic* called the production "loud, stupid, and witless."[38] He objected to race as the play's central theme by asserting, "Chen didn't realize that Obama made that a non-issue."[39] Williams's comment ignited a maelstrom among Chicago theater artists of color, who called for a ban of the critic from their shows.

The show also illuminated the colorblind rhetoric present in the 2016 presidential election, a series of events that Williams did not believe was adequately represented in the performance. He recommended that the production cull YouTube for video clips of real 2016 candidates and contended that if "the producers really want to satirize presidential politics in 2016, all they need do is act out what the misfit collection of Republican contenders, led by Trump, are actually doing on the campaign trail!"[40]

Interestingly, it is exactly these moments of art imitating life that Stageandcinema.com critic Lawrence Bommer found disturbing and horrific. Bommer disbelieved Len's extensive ethnic background and was disgusted by the audience's positive reaction to Len's tendency to "shoot people in the face."[41] Bommer criticized the opening night audience for finding this "perversely" funny, adding, "This creature, who apparently has ancestors in every country, inevitably morphs into a stateside serial killer—but that's no hindrance to his race (pun intended)."[42] He found the play implausible and condescending. Most significantly, he understood that Chen's argument about a "mongrelized" United States was destroyed in a "final grotesquery,"[43] although he failed to recognize that this grotesque erasure was, in fact, Chen's point.

This "cynical ending" demonstrates the brutality inherent in a colorblind society and replicates the climate of the 2016 political landscape.[44] The election of a presidential candidate who openly incites violence keenly parallels Donald J. Trump's own rise to political fame. During the run of the production, Trump boasted to a crowd of supporters in Iowa that, "I could stand in the middle of 5th Avenue and shoot somebody and I wouldn't lose voters."[45] His comment drew laughter from the Iowa rally much like the opening night audience's amused reaction at Len's desire to shoot people in the face. Jeremy Diamond of CNN has observed that Trump "repeatedly pointed to the loyalty of his supporters, many of whom tell reporters and pollsters that almost *nothing* could make them change their mind about voting for Trump in the presidential race."[46] In *Mutt*, Len's questionable character is also no deterrent for the Republicans, who continuously stand behind him, drawn to his ability to garner unabashed loyalty from the voters. Len mirrors Trump's broad appeal as a member of a white, privileged class, who panders to racial and cultural groups solely to win elections. In this way, Chen's drama feels like a chilling prophetic vision, especially considering that the play was written two years prior to Trump's presidential rise. Furthermore, Len's hypocritical, Janus-faced policies mirror Trump's Machiavellian campaign rhetoric. In Len's unquestioned and unbridled confidence, Chen literalizes Trump's "killer" mentality and makes manifest an embodiment of the political landscape.[47] The play unwittingly satirizes Trump's mind-boggling political ascent, from his contradictory points of view to his penchant for violence, which is precisely what Williams accused the production of failing to do.

Bommer's review also highlighted the tenacity of the tragic Eurasian trope in which race mixing produces an impure, pathological subject. Bommer identified Len as a "creature," an unreal abomination reminiscent of the Jekyll and Hyde character Patsy O'Wang and Cynthia L. Nakashima's "mythological multiracial monster."[48] Bommer repudiated the claim that Len could possess an extensive mixed-race background, even though he believed that this creature could "morph" into a criminal. Bommer's assessment of Len reveals the persistence of the nineteenth-century racial trope in which defects of character can be passed through a mixed racial biology. Unbeknownst to Bommer, the play illuminated the multiracial's ability to shape shift, not to serve as evidence of the tragic Eurasian's criminality but rather to interrogate the malevolence of systemic colorblindness.

The mixed-race individual's ambiguous racial physiognomy exposes our reliance on racial markers and reveals the fallacy of a colorblind society. *Chicago Theater Beat* reviewer Lauren Whalen praised the *Mutt* production for its timeliness and overall understood the play's ultimate goals. Interestingly, though, even Whalen failed to recognize the depth of the play's critique of persistent racial tropes. As Whalen recounts, "Some jokes are right on the money and hilariously tragic. . . . Others don't make quite as much sense, like the subplot in which a white police officer attempts to find a prolific serial killer whose description keeps changing."[49] Whalen refers to the subplot in which the Inspector cannot determine the suspect's racial profile because the criminal continuously shape shifts. These shifts occur not only because of Len's complex ethnic background but also because of the shifting perception of the witnesses, who read his racial makeup differently. Whalen's confusion surrounding these dramatic details perhaps stems from a misunderstanding of the centrality of mixed-race personhood in the drama. The work was, after all, originally commissioned to explore hapa identity, and Chen's multiracial perspective is what drives the narrative. In a 2019 interview, Chen affirmed, "I've always had a complicated relationship with my ethnic and cultural heritage, because I am half and half. On the one hand, I very much identify with my white side, culturally. But at the same time, I also identify as Chinese American. Because of that, a lot of my work deals with shifting perspectives of one culture to another."[50] Without this key component, the play is seemingly just another parody about race. Its focus on multiraciality illuminates fissures in the racial hierarchy—slippages that can create confusion in observers like the witnesses in *Mutt*. Mixedness slips in between fixed categories and, in doing so, dismantles colorblindness as a viable tool for social transcendence.

The Chicago production of *Mutt*, directed by Goodman Theater directing fellow Vanessa Stalling, focused on Chen's examination of racial politics and public misperceptions. Stalling, sensitive to the racial violence and tension present in Chicago, worked closely with Chen to add an African American character to a script about race, which, at that point, had none. In the Chicago version, Nick and Hanna encounter Karen, an African American woman, who is a political science professor at Georgetown University. Nick asks Karen to describe the Black experience to him in an effort to be more racially sensitive. Skeptical about his intentions, Karen gently reminds him that one experience cannot be distilled into a single sound bite for political gain nor can it represent all racialized experiences. Stalling highlighted Karen's message throughout the production by having the same actress play all the witnesses. Under the chameleon-like prowess of actress Nicole Michelle Haskins, the audience viewed the same Black body in different cultural circumstances. This directorial choice effectively illuminated Karen's point that while we might assume that all Black bodies are the same—in this production they were the same body—not all experiences are alike. The embodied racial commentary was sensitive and smart. The creation of Karen developed under Stalling's perceptive collaboration with Chen was a necessary and effective addition to a production having its Midwest premiere in Chicago, a city dominated by Black and white racial politics. Furthermore, Stalling mindfully cast her actors in roles against the script to illuminate how race changes or problematizes our social expectations. For example, her casting of Haskins as the third witness, who in the text is a white hippy living in a religious commune, disrupts and modifies the audience's perception of what a religious zealot might look like.

I applaud Stalling's bold, visual direction and her sensitive, compassionate choices about racial politics, and I wonder if perhaps a closer consideration of mixedness would have crystallized her vision even more. This occurred to me as I sat in the dark, watching the final dress rehearsal unfold at Theater Wit in Chicago. I noticed that while the focus of the burgeoning show concentrated on the discrepancies of race, the idea that the three most powerful people in the play were mixed was not entirely addressed. While textual interpretation is the prerogative of the director and the production team, it seemed to me that perhaps a sparse exploration of mixedness in rehearsals would have had an impact on the final product.

In a show about race, especially in a play where the plot revolves around the experiences of mixed-race hapa subjects, a discussion of mixedness in the rehearsal process is perhaps crucial in fully communicating the essence of the play's central themes. Interestingly, the three hapa actors who played Len, Hanna, and Nick admitted to me in a group interview that their ethnic backgrounds were never discussed in the initial table reading or at subsequent rehearsals. All of them also had similar, though varied, life experiences with misperception. They each expressed moments of double liminality, which means they felt distanced from one another through different cultural as well as generational experiences.

Other than in the casting appointments, the material presence of mixed-race bodies onstage and their centrality to the production were seemingly overlooked.

In fact, when I first saw the performance of Autumn Walsh, the actress who played Hanna, I questioned whether or not she was actually mixed.[51] When her character reveals that she is mixed-race in the play, Walsh did not seem to draw on her deep understanding of hapa subjectivity to communicate Hanna's embodied sense of self. I was later pleasantly surprised to learn that Walsh was half-Japanese and half-white. I surmised that her somatic awareness as a mixed-race individual was not translating on stage initially, because her experiences as a multiethnic subject had not been incorporated into the rehearsal process. According to Walsh, when her ethnic background did come up in side conversations, these took place in down times between cast members outside rehearsal. This seems a missed opportunity, especially since I found Walsh to be the most vocal of the three hapa actors. In her interview, she seemed both politically and socially aware of the impact of her mixedness and understood that she related to society in a way that is different from those who are monoracial. She shared stories about subverting pointed questions regarding her ambiguous ethnic physiognomy as her peers tried to figure out "who she was" and how to categorize her.

Furthermore, Walsh realized that the white community around her saw her as monoracially Asian even though she also identified as white. This is problematic because it illustrates the persistence of the rule of hypodescent,[52] which also often applies to those of African/African American ancestry as well as to other groups of color.[53] For instance, she recounted how a friend asked "about my ethnicity in the worst possible way and he's a very sweet kid, but he was like, "[Autumn,] are your, were your ancestors born here?" And I was like . . . if my ancestors were born here, I would be a Native American, so no. I know what you're asking me."[54] Likewise, the rule of hypodescent perpetuates the monoracial cultural paradigm and erases the notion of mixedness from our social consciousness.

While I commend the Chicago production of *Mutt* for confronting stereotypes and assumptions in racial perception, I offer that a further exploration of the mixed-race experience would have provided the production with a deeper interrogation of the status quo's fascination with monoraciality. The multiracial's ability to shape shift into a monoracial group is contingent on the reception of a viewer and the perceived phenotype of the mixed-race body. The shift completes when the mixed-race figure verbally confirms her ethnic background. Because of her physical ambiguity, this can initiate a shift because the ethnicity revealed may be different from the viewer's presumptions about her parentage.

Mixed individuals especially trouble the racial status quo when they refuse to shift into monoracial categories. As Nakashima notes, mixed-race people frequently "resist the oppressiveness of having to [publicly] "choose" . . . by maintaining" their privacy.[55] One of the *Mutt* actors, Carl George, often refrains from answering the "what are you" question.[56] His unwillingness to participate in the co-creation of his racialization illustrates the two-sided nature of the shape shifting process, one that is contingent on the observer's reception of an individual's perceived race. George is reticent to engage in these exchanges and to disclose his ethnic makeup. "You know, I'm not going to say it's en vogue or whatever, but . . . I don't readily offer it up. I mean, I identify as an American. . . . I just hold onto it a little more. If I'm comfortable with you, you know, I'll go through the list of it. . . . If I don't really know you, you're not going to get anything from me. I'll just say a lot of different things or I'm a mutt, you know? . . . [Or why] do you want to know? . . . Why are you asking?"[57] George reveals his skepticism at the viewer's intentions in these last two questions. Far from being colorblind, experience has shown him that because observers cannot readily identify his racial background, they will vigorously pursue information about his parentage. George's reticence then prevents the shape shifting process from taking place. In this way, he leaves observers uncomfortably colorblind. Without their knowledge of his ethnic background, he remains racially ambiguous since the viewer's mind fails to complete the shape shifting transformation.

George's experiences foreground ruptures in the efficacy of colorblind transcendence. Observers belie their dependency on racial markers when presented with an ethnically ambiguous body. Walsh, who is fourth-generation Japanese American, has also experienced this phenomenon. In an interview, she expressed her annoyance at being asked the dreaded but familiar "what are you" question from men who tried to pick her up. "Eventually we'll get there, you know. They'll get real specific on what it is that they want, and I'm like, I'm half-Japanese. There you go. That's the answer you're looking for. That was a great conversation."[58] Exchanges like these reveal the failure of transcendent colorblindness in society. Far from not seeing race, these interracial encounters demonstrate how racial categorization is embedded in our social consciousness. Our society is not color neutral. When a mixed-race body fails to immediately fit into a monoracial category, it creates what Maria Root calls an "emotional/psychic earthquake" that disrupts a belief in racial immutability.[59] Rather than transcending color, we rely on it.

In theater, as in life, monoraciality and racial transcendence continue to trouble theatrical spaces. Performances of racial transgression must actively dismantle the prevalence of the racial transcendence that has permeated theater institutions and their art. Just as mixed-race bodies fade into singular racial categories in society, on stage they may also disappear. An example of this can be seen in the controversial casting of The Engineer in the musical Miss Saigon (1989). To date, no mixed-race actor has ever played the role, even though the character is of mixed-Asian descent.[60] Furthermore, all three multiethnic Asian actors in the Chicago production of Mutt said they had never had the opportunity to play a hapa character, even though they have collectively worked at over twenty-five different theaters in both Chicago and New York. Mutt was the first time any of them had ever encountered a mixed-Asian character, and they doubted whether other hapa roles existed. The actors' experiences simultaneously illustrate the continued invisibility of the mixed-race body in theater. Chen's drama succeeds in foregrounding mixedness at his play's center, while director Stalling, to her credit, sensitively and tirelessly worked to bring mixed-Asian actors to auditions for the multiracial roles.

The mixed-race actors' life experiences also successfully mirrored the doubly liminal experiences of the characters. This crucial similarity illuminates the complexity of double liminality because, while ethnic backgrounds can differ between mixed-race individuals, the extent of these differences is further complicated by how much access each person has to their familial cultures. Actor Paul King, who played Nick and identifies as half-Filipino and half-white ("mostly Dutch"), leaped at the chance to audition for the role.[61] This was not only because the character was hapa but also because, like King, he felt isolated from his father's Asian heritage. King said he explained his connection to the character in his audition, and as a result, he never felt the need to discuss it again.

> They announce the season, and they announce the play, and I'm like look, that's exactly me. It's not just because I happen to be half-Asian, but because I happen to be a half-Asian guy who doesn't really know anything about his father's ethnic background. It's sad. It's really, really sad. I don't know anything about the Philippines at all. . . . Anyway, my point is that I kind of laid all that out. I said, hey, you know that part of it, at least for me, I think I kind of got. . . . So, I don't recall having specific conversations about me in particular [after the audition].[62]

The role of Nick was an opportunity for King to play a mixed-race character with whom he specifically identified. Nick and King did not share the same ethnic background (Chinese and Filipino), but they both had similar experiences with Asian fathers and paternal cultural backgrounds with which they could not relate. Furthermore, while the actors' mixed-race histories were not discussed in the rehearsal process, the director gave the actors the space to discuss them in auditions. This is important because it acknowledges and validates their mixed-race subjectivities. An opportunity for King to bring his individual experiences into discussion during rehearsal could have additionally enriched the theater-making process even more.

While multiracial experiences were explored in auditions, some scenes about mixedness were ultimately cut from the final performance. In an interview with Vanessa Stalling, the director, I asked her about these omissions and whether or not she considered multiraciality to be a driving force in the play. She said that in trying to find the musicality of the piece she felt that, in certain scenes, the "rhythms of the play overall weren't working" in terms of narrative flow.[63] She made the decision, in consultation with Chen, to cut scenes that she felt made the play veer off in another direction. Her artistic choices aimed to assess how to make the play, which had only been produced once before, work rhythmically. Stalling, who acknowledged that a non-white director would perhaps have seen different underlying thematic threads, remained committed to the narrative's interrogation of race and misperception in a broader sense. In her words, she chose to highlight "how misguided our thinking of race is in general."[64] While Chen himself asserted that the play is about "all race, not just hapa identity," he also conceded that the play was written "from my subconscious" or the collection of mental processes that were surely informed by his mixed-race identity.[65] From this perspective, Stalling may have had a blind spot about the mixed-race subjectivity driving the play due to her own positionality as a white director.

In a serendipitous, Orwellian moment in the show's climax, it was the physical shape shifting qualities of Carl George that illustrated how mixed-race individuals become subsumed by monoraciality. Even though George is half-white and half-Asian, the prop that the sketch artist produced was a portrait of an "Anglicized" version of the actor's face. In the Chicago production, the character of Len, who is ridiculously multiple, literally morphs into a reflection of the dominant. While the "whitening" of George's facial features in the onstage prop was perhaps unintended and arguably captured the actor's ability to shift into whiteness, the rendering ironically served to demonstrate the core of Chen's larger project. Len Smith is the embodiment of a political climate that peddles a belief in racial transcendence. While colorblindness purports to embrace all peoples and all colors, in refusing to acknowledge race, it only reflects the interests of white hegemony. We realize that Len represents all of us, living and accepting a monoracial system of categorization created by a white society.

The Colorblind That Cannot Be: *Lidless*

If Len Smith knows every ancestral ethnicity that makes up his mixed-race background, in contrast, Frances Ya-Chu Cowhig's Rhiannon Jones knows nothing of her multiethnic lineage. Like *Mutt*, Cowhig's play *Lidless* illuminates the limited visibility of mixedness in contemporary American theater. The work of the critically acclaimed, transnational mixed-race playwright has been described as "salty, surreal and bombastic."[66] *Lidless* is Cowhig's debut drama and has received professional productions in London, Edinburgh, New York, Philadelphia, and Tucson. Most recently, the Horse Head Theater Company in Houston presented the play in the summer of 2016.

Cowhig has written about mixed-race erasure in a play that is also not singly about mixed race. Rather, *Lidless* explores the traumatic effects of war and political evasion after the September 11 attacks. In the play, the decisions of the political elite play out in personal, domestic spheres. Although neither Chen nor Cowhig would solely characterize either of these scripts as "hapa" plays, I contend that, like *Mutt*, a bifurcated sensibility undergirds Cowhig's narrative. This is significant as it demonstrates the shift in mixed-race drama that differs from the ethnic "identity" plays produced before the turn of the millennium. These plays demonstrate a more sophisticated awareness about mixed race than ever seen before.

In *Lidless*, Cowhig explores how the systematic, political erasure that occurs in the aftermath of war results in cultural amnesia. By pitting a misguided military woman against an incarcerated racialized prisoner, she keenly elucidates how legal decisions filter down and affect our everyday lives. In Cowhig's narrative, one of the by-products of this amnesia is also the expunction of mixed race. Whereas Chen's superhapa Len highlights his extensive multiracial background, Cowhig's character, Rhiannon, demonstrates how quickly genealogical knowledge can be lost. This intervention is significant because it critiques how mixed-race subjects may become complicit in their own oppression. Rhiannon represents those of us who, through no fault of our own, have forgotten our mixed histories.

While U.S. military conflict is only hinted at in *Mutt* vis-à-vis Len's tour in Afghanistan, the war on terror is the soil on which Cowhig's drama grows. The play's narrative is nonlinear, beginning at the Guantánamo Bay detention center in 2004 and flash forwarding fifteen years later to middle-class life in Minnesota. The play features nonillusionistic staging with locations delineated only by squares of stage light. The props are also minimal.

The play's searing critique about the ethics of one's actions revolves around a cultural amnesia that subtly condones violence in imperialistic projects. Rhiannon Jones is a fourteen-year-old girl who knows nothing of her true biological parentage and cultural past. She is the product of a rape committed by her mother, Alice, a white, U.S. Army interrogator. Rhiannon's biological father is Alice's Muslim prisoner, Bashir, a former Guantánamo detainee of Pakistani descent. Alice has been authorized by the U.S. government to use rape, an "enhanced interrogation technique" referred to as "invasion of space by a female," in order to extract information from Bashir.[67] While Alice's best friend, Riva, an army medic of Assyrian Iraqi descent, tries to dissuade her from using the sexual tactic, Alice relishes the idea of spoiling her prisoner's chances of entering Heaven. So determined is Alice to extract information that she will use any means necessary as long as she does not have to remember the events. To ensure this, she takes government-issued pills designed to erase her memory and above all, to absolve her of her "sins." This premise provides the background for the unlikely examination of the invisibility of mixed race in America.

Erasure of the truth in the face of war is not new to the history of the United States. In her critique of the U.S. policies during the Vietnam War, Yen Lê Espiritu has noted "the unsettling entanglement between military acts of violence and recovery, with recovery overlaying and at times disappearing (the memory of) violence."[68] In an effort to maintain a reputation as the global "do-gooder," the United States justifies acts of violence as a "humanitarian" means of keeping the world safe. Cowhig highlights the irony of this policy as Alice uses sexual tactics, or mechanisms of war, to bring the salve of democracy to the Middle East. As she says to Riva before she commits the assault, "I am what democracy looks like."[69] She then forgets the crime and lives her life in "recovery." As the representation of white American hegemony, Alice suffers a self-imposed fugue, which serves to exonerate her of past behavior in the service of war. She believes that her compliance with military policy protects her from taking responsibility for past events. In a broader sense, Alice's actions also mirror larger political erasures committed by the American government.

But, as Cowhig asserts, cultural blindness and amnesia are never permanent. Fifteen years after the incidents at Guantánamo, Bashir reenters Alice's life. She is now a florist with no memory of the brutal events she committed fifteen years earlier. Having contracted hepatitis during his time at the detention center, Bashir begs Alice for her liver. He reasons that the gift of a liver transplant will absolve Alice of her sins.

The encounter between Alice and Bashir makes clear who colorblindness serves. Alice, a character of white privilege who carries out atrocities of the imperialist project, is the only one who forgets these sins. Bashir, on the other hand, still grapples with the effects of the past. Rhiannon, their mixed-race child, without knowledge of her ethnic background, nor of the imperialist violence in her history, shape shifts into whiteness.[70] This transformation occurs like it has for many individuals whose mixed-race heritage has been lost to time. They, too, shift into the monoracial category most readily available, or deemed acceptable, for them. This racial state is a space that is created and then inhabited, and the erasure of those individuals' mixed subjectivity allows the current racial framework to continue.

Rhiannon's circumstances demonstrate how the process of shape shifting is a co-constitutive project between the subject and the observer. This process creates a perceived racial identity that is often based on context and influences how the subject self-identifies. Like the character Evelyn in Velina Hasu Houston's *Kokoro (True Heart)*, Rhiannon "passes" into monoraciality. Cowhig includes the actual spectators in the audience as part of this process as well. Similar to the characters in Rhiannon's respective "family," the audience members ostensibly have no idea that Rhiannon is mixed-race until the end of the play. The spectators also accept Rhiannon's supposed parentage (Alice and her husband, Lucas) and the monoraciality of her character, which demonstrates the ways that context and reception collaborate to mark the mixed-race body.

Cowhig points to the contextual mechanisms that facilitate this process of racialization at different moments in the play. This is crucial in understanding how racial identities get assigned and become internalized by mixed-race subjects. When Bashir purports to recognize Alice's "true self," she scoffs, "Spare me the true-self bullshit. No one is anything *except their situation*."[71] Later, Bashir tells Rhiannon, "When you can't see, everything is only what you make it."[72] As shown in *Mutt*, a raced body comes into being through perception and context. Cowhig elucidates how circumstances play a key role in enabling these shifts to take place. Context influences the perception of the observer.

Joshua Chambers-Letson has keenly noted how the U.S. legal system grants personhood through a process of racialization.[73] Without this necessary context, an individual runs the risk of becoming a nonentity. Alice tells Bashir, "You have a role. An identity. That's what you've really lost. You got out of prison but you never found a new self."[74] She highlights how Bashir benefits from becoming a raced person in the American political system. Though he gained his freedom from a racialized state, he cannot be "seen" in the eyes of the white hegemony. That is, Alice does not recognize him unless he resumes his performance as a racialized prisoner of Middle Eastern Asian descent.

Intriguingly, Lucas, Rhiannon's "adoptive" father, is possibly multiracial. He is described in the cast of characters only as "racially ambiguous." In the logic of realism, this makes sense as Rhiannon, a mixed-race child, could not unquestionably be Lucas's daughter unless he was a person of color or mixed as well. Yet, throughout the entire narrative, Lucas's ethnic background is never discussed nor questioned. It seems that Lucas has shape shifted, too. Both he and his daughter, Rhiannon, have quietly "passed" into monoraciality. This is not to say that the characters are not mixed, but through casting choices and under the paradigm of race, these figures shift into a normative racial designation.

Aided by casting, Lucas and Rhiannon could, in effect, shift into whiteness. This demonstrates how the racial paradigm has co-opted the institution of theater in its political project and how in the casting of characters, white bodies are more apt than mixed ones to be cast in racially ambiguous roles. Indeed, in two different casts of *Lidless*, Lucas's racial ambiguity has seemingly slipped past the production teams. In the 2011 InterAct production in Philadelphia and the 2012 Borderlands production in Tucson, both actors playing Lucas were phenotypically white. In all productions of *Lidless* to date, except for one at the 2010 Contemporary American Theatre Festival, Rhiannon has also been cast as a white character. This is striking when considering that Bashir is always cast as a person of color. Like Len Smith in *Mutt*, the racially ambiguous characters Lucas and Rhiannon silently transform into embodiments of whiteness.

While the American hegemonic system strives to forget the crimes born from the traumas of racism and war, Cowhig demands that both her characters and her audience bear witness to these atrocities. The play's title, *Lidless*, does not seem to reference any specific moment in the play, but I argue that for Cowhig, this state of being "lidless" means that one is never able to not see the consequences of their actions. Cowhig, in effect, removes the lids from her characters' and her spectators' eyes. In this way, all the theater participants are faced with the same realities of war and its aftermath—the residual, sedimented, and generational trauma.

These reverberations of the past set Rhiannon on a journey to discover her lost identity. Like Nick, she also interviews her father in an attempt to collect his personal oral history, though she does not realize that Bashir is, in actuality, her biological father. When Rhiannon asks to interview Bashir, he counters, "Which history do you want?" Confused, she answers, "How many you got?"[75] Bashir explains that history is never straightforward but complex, multilayered, and contingent. In many ways, Rhiannon is like Len Smith in *Mutt*, the product of a vast history of ethnicities and cultural narratives. The difference, however, is that, like most of us, she does not know about the entirety of her genealogical history as a result of the invisibilization caused by monoracial cultural logic. The expectation that we identify monoracially causes us to lose our ethnic histories.

Yet Rhiannon perseveres because she is determined to get to the truth. She feels a profound connection to Bashir that she cannot explain. As she tells him during her interview, "I feel like I've known you my whole life."[76] However, while she desperately tries to question her family about the past, they refuse her requests. Frustrated by her imposed ignorance, Rhiannon accuses her mother of deliberately keeping her in the dark and asks Riva, her godmother, to fill in the missing pieces of her history. But Riva refuses, insisting that, "It's hard to focus on the present when you're thinking about the past."[77] Crucially, the characters' desires to leave the pain of the past behind also cause other truths to vanish.

Plays like *Lidless* provide a necessary venue for exploring forgotten truths, including the existence and prevalence of mixed-race personhood. Early in the play, Rhiannon explains her strategy for identifying with the interviewee of her oral history project, saying, "If I want to understand someone, I need to dress like them, walk like them, talk like them. I need to become them."[78] At the end of the play, Rhiannon tries to become Bashir in an effort to understand him, understand his past, and ultimately, to understand herself. Since all she knows about him is his life as a detainee, she dons his orange jumpsuit, puts on blackout goggles, and handcuffs herself. She then tries out a stress position that Bashir was placed in at Guantánamo Bay. Because Bashir's American subjecthood is inextricable from the performance of his perceived race, Rhiannon, through her performance of Bashir, changes her racialized state as well. In doing so, she actualizes her mixed-race self and performs a reclamation of her Middle Eastern Asian parentage as understood in the American political system.

These mixed-race bodies threaten the neatly, racially organized social structure. Rhiannon's attempt to embrace mixedness becomes a stark contrast from the uncompromising persistence of monoraciality in the American status quo. And yet Rhiannon's tenacity also becomes her downfall. While restrained, she suffers an asthma attack. Unable to access the handcuff key, she fails to grasp her inhaler and succumbs. Her suffocation metaphorically illustrates the consequences of attempting to claim another racial identity. In Cowhig's narrative, the woman in search of the truth dies, which signifies, for Cowhig, punishment for those who resist surveillance and containment. Like the serial killer in Chen's *Mutt*, the dominant hegemony thwarts Rhiannon's attempt to transgress a racial system that enjoins her to forget and "get over it."[79] After Rhiannon's death, Bashir receives her liver, and, in this process, a part of her lives on in a racialized body. Her mixed self has now disappeared. Rhiannon then "vanishes" into a new monoracial category, a process facilitated by the rule of hypodescent.

In *Mutt*, political progressive Quinn Hernandez reminds Nick and Hanna that the "system of racial categorization . . . is actually a tool of social dominance based on false science."[80] She innervates their newfound racial platform by asserting that "We're actually all big mixed-race stews."[81] In Christopher Chen's *Mutt* and Frances Cowhig's *Lidless*, we see how the fluidity of mixed-race identity becomes buried under polarizing monoracial cultural logic. The mixed-race characters of *Lidless* and *Mutt* are subsumed by whiteness, whether by disappearing into monoracial categories or by upholding the hegemonic ideals of white assimilation and universality. The dramas also illustrate and critique the ways that mixed-race subjectivity becomes appropriated to further the transcendent rhetoric of colorblindness. Cultural amnesia follows, erasing the histories of ethnic multiplicity and intermixing in American society. Through Chen and Cowhig's theatrical narratives, we see how performances of racial transgression seek to reclaim dramatic narratives from the racialized project of transcendence. Their ruptures of established racial norms and categories illuminate how theater can carve out new spaces for the representation of mixed-race subjectivity in the new millennium.

6

Beyond Monoracial Hierarchies

• •

Recovering Lost Selves

> We greet you as liberators. . . . This "we" is
> that us in the margins, . . . I am speaking
> from a place in the margins where I am
> different—where I see things differently.
> —bell hooks

> I am mixed blood, it is true, but I differ
> from the party line in that I consider it
> neither an honor nor a shame.
> —Zora Neale Hurston

Might we reshape our current monochromatic racial vision into a more complex and radical understanding of a multiracial hybridity? In the first epigraph above, bell hooks asserts that those who live life in the margins can free society from the bonds of the extant racial codes that normalize separatism. In my application, the ability for mixed-race persons to simultaneously occupy and integrate multiple racial constructions shows us that race is not a biologically determined state, nor is it a sound and accurate marker through which to *cast* people. On the contrary, dominant racial constructs falsely produce diacritical bodies for the purpose of easy organization and the preservation of white hegemonic control.

As sociologists Michael Omi and Howard Winant remind us, race is neither fixed nor stable, but the "racial state inhabits us, so to speak; it is within our minds, our psyches, our hearts."[1] In other words, the construction that determines difference vis-à-vis race is neither real nor static, but the system of classification that enforces the use of racial semiotics doggedly persists. Its existence lies within social inscription and the compliance of the body politic.

This book has examined the discursive and artistic practices that contribute to the formation of a doubly liminal mixed-race identity within this racialized system. Multiracial subjects encounter a white hegemonic discourse that identifies them solely as people of color rather than as an amalgamation of various ethnic backgrounds. Conversely, the subdominant discourse (in this case, in the Asian community) may deny the mixed-race subject full group membership because of a mixed heritage, thus barring them from the very designations assigned to them by the dominant. Harvey Young refers to these cultural assumptions about the body as social habiti. These are external social expectations that become internalized and incorporated in the subject's identity. Habiti instruct the racialized body how to behave.[2] Young, however, applies this process exclusively to monoracial identities.

Extending Young's observations, I have applied this process of identity construction to the mixed-race experience and have suggested that multiple habiti leave the multiethnic person at the limen of several different groups. This learned separation includes being set apart from other mixed-race persons who may not share the same cultural or ethnic backgrounds. But I suggest that another complex process is also at work. The act of shape shifting serves mixed-race people with a tactic for managing the confines of the dominant culture (and its current racial scaffolding) and the subdominant discourse where mainstream racial codes may be internally inscribed. As discussed in chapter 5, these shape shifting acts are racially transgressive performative moments that expose society's problematic reliance on racial phenotypes as a means to classify individuals. The performances of mixed-race subjects in daily life and the representation of these experiences in theater evince the fallacy of race as a viable social marker and subvert the power of the racial hierarchy.

Thus far, I have traced the doubly liminal subject and the act of shape shifting represented in theater from the Progressive Era to the present. This inquiry has attempted to illuminate the world in which each play was written and to contextualize the interventions that these dramas may have made in the historical period in which they were situated. Specifically, I began with the depiction of mixed-race Asian Americans in 1890 and arrived crucially at the plays by hapa playwrights in the first twenty years of the new millennium. In the midcentury, I followed Omi and Winant and considered the political shift from racial domination to racial hegemonic control after World War II and beyond the national Black Freedom Movement of the 1950s and 1960s.[3] In this historical moment, Omi and Winant have astutely observed that right-wing counter movements reframed "the emancipatory politics of the Black movement" and ultimately transformed them into a desirable erasure of race vis-à-vis colorblindness.[4] Mixed-race individuals have then been co-opted as the "poster children" for a post-racial era that will be bathed in a racial transcendence. This designation of multiracial people as the "Faces of the Future" problematically fails to recognize the histories of oppression and violence that have been imposed on racialized communities.

Antonia Nakano Glenn has astutely identified the tragic Eurasian and Face of the Future imaginary as the mixed-race Asian tropes that have bookended the twentieth century.[5] These tropes together construct an invisible/visible binary to which mixed-race persons inevitably find themselves assigned, effectively erasing their subjectivity in contemporary representations. Popular culture at the turn of the twentieth century depicted the mixed-race figure as pathological, biologically impure, weak, and often monstrous. In these portrayals, the tragic Eurasian is physically and emotionally incapable of productively functioning in society and unworthy of recognition; any actual mixed person is rendered invisible.

By contrast, the Face of the Future imaginary curiously elevated the mixed-race figure to that of a visible racial savior. The trope was popularized with the appearance of the 1993 *Time* magazine cover "The New Face of America" that featured a woman's face who was supposedly a mix of several racial backgrounds.[6] In the Face of the Future imaginary, mixed-race persons, who are prized as physically novel or exotic, are asked to shoulder the burden of alleviating racial tension and to serve as a salve to heal the wounds of racial violence. In political rhetoric and public discourse, the mixed-race Face of the Future transforms into a visible beacon that will illuminate the way to an enlightened, post-racial future, where a beige or gray mixed-race population will render society colorblind. Yet these portrayals of multiethnic people as aesthetically appealing are often, as Maria P. P. Root observes, "used as tools to reduce discomfort" couched "in the guise of something special or positive being offered."[7] Although these depictions may appear to be positive, they nonetheless illuminate the social distance typically assigned to mixed-race people who have been othered in society. Thus the Face of the Future imaginary cannot help but acknowledge the marginalization and abjection endured by the mixed-race subject.

Likewise, the Face of the Future imaginary is always suspended in time. This delay is a crucial element in the futuristic trope. The attractive glimpse of a "beige" (read: "colorless" and by extension, white) future offered in the present, vis-à-vis the mixed-race subject, attempts to reduce the multiethnic subject's racial strife and frame it as temporary. Under the paradigm supported by this trope, the much-desired post-racial society never arrives. The Face of the Future imaginary inevitably exists as an extension of invisibility deployed by white hegemony to erase the racial tension of the present. As seen in chapter 5, playwrights like Christopher Chen and Frances Ya-Chu Cowhig subvert the Face of the Future in their plays by exposing the hegemonic, monoracial universality embedded within the construct. Will the next generation of hapa playwrights continue to resist the Face of the Future? Can the new millennium cultivate and encourage other paradigmatic possibilities, like shape shifting, that will resist the invisible/visible binary?

The case studies in the previous chapters have also demonstrated the limitations of hypodescent. The normalized process of racial and social assignment forces individuals to abandon entire family histories through disassociation from one parentage. Through this process, the dominant culture can control groups of color by collapsing mixedness into a monoracial framework. Hapa subjects must deny family histories that linger and swirl around them like ghosts, until, eventually, through lack of recognition and acknowledgment, they fade away. Multiethnic individuals become monoracialized then and solely identify with one monoracial group. As playwrights Chen and Cowhig persistently remind us, this process begets a cultural amnesia that is transferred to subsequent generations. That this erasure has taken place is undeniable. Where then are the mixed-race populations of previous generations? Where, for instance, are the children of the "seventy or so" interracial Chinese Irish unions from New York City's Chinatown in 1882?[8] Have they been, like Anna Leonowens and her children, absorbed by the racial framework and lost to a monoracial system? Has the racial hierarchy also made many of us and our histories invisible, even to ourselves? Are all of our bodies potentially racially transgressive through an unknown, invisible mixed-race heritage? Perhaps when the current racial paradigm acknowledges the existence of doubly liminal space, our ways of seeing will cease to be monovisual.

Theater has been historically complicit in this process of erasure. Yet, at times, theater has also offered up its space and its practices as a hopeful sanctuary. While it has succumbed to the system in which it lives, it also remains at its core, a nebulous, open space, full of possibility. As performance theorist Anurima Banerji reminds us, it is in performance that these alternative possibilities come into being.[9] Theater has the opportunity and the ability to hasten a new way of seeing and to continue to explore narratives about the multiraciality as rendered through the consciousness of hapa playwrights. Theater can expose audiences to the mixed-race experience and encourage visibility and representation of the mixed-race subject.

The theater makers in these case studies have ignited the stage in a way that has changed subsequent mixed-race performances. In the 1986 Asian American Theater Company's production of *Thirst*, Velina Hasu Houston constructed a racially transgressive play that empowered the theater and future playwrights to carve out a new space for multiracial representation. In one particular moment in the production, actress Nadja Kennedy (as Plinka) coolly declares her doubly liminal position to Michael O'Brien's Joseph. Plinka states, "I like being Japanese and I like being white."[10] She easily negates Joseph's claim that her whiteness is a burden to her..Rather, Plinka defiantly proclaims her right and her ability to embrace both cultural and ethnic backgrounds simultaneously. While the monoracial hierarchy may be real, through Plinka, Houston asserts that hapa identities are not tragic subjects or prophetic figures of the future, but are fully integrated (corpo)realities now.[11] This small fissure of transgression in theater in the face of a white masculine hegemonic subjectivity has paved the way for other mixed-race Asian artists to tell their own stories through similar "cosmopolite" sensibilities.[12] Houston became an early voice in the mixed-race movement that vitally emerged to its full force in the following decade. This transgressive yet hopeful moment opened up and claimed new space in Asian American theater.

Future productions point to inquiries of research about the audience reception of mixed race and can provide another robust locus of analysis. Chapter 5 features an interview with Carl George, a mixed-race actor who affirmed that in his personal life he often refuses to disclose his ethnic background to the uninitiated observer.[13] His refusal to participate in the social performance of his racialized body by "going off script," that is, not saying the lines expected of him ("I am x, y, and z") opens up a site for a critical hermeneutic.[14] His nebulous, phenotypic characteristics then move and shape shift, easily bending under a monoracial perception and reading. Exchanges such as these reveal a dependence on the racial hierarchy to maintain order, and George's refusal to participate in the process of racialization exposes the porous boundaries that exist between racial categories. Can playwrights actively illuminate this slippage for their audiences?

My proposed extensions of habiti and racially transgressive performance to encompass the mixed-Asian experience moves the terms away from restrictive monoracial applications. In turn, I have examined the process of shape shifting in theatrical performance as a powerful way that mixed-race persons have freed themselves from monoracial designations, thus allowing them to perform their double liminality. Can playwrights, therefore, take a more active role in dramatizing the shape shifting process on stage through new narratives? Can theater makers actively and ethically seek out and cast mixed-race actors in these roles? I suggest that future research expand to determine the use of race-conscious casting practices that account for mixedness. This research could also examine the efficacy of dramatizing the shape shifting process on stage and deduce if the visibility of the ambiguous, nonidentifiable, mixed-race performer onstage will continue to *recast* the audience's perceptions of mixedness and race.

In the new millennium, mixed-Asian theater has seen the emergence of multiracial voices like Frances Ya-Chu Cowhig, Christopher Chen, and newcomer Japanese American hapa playwright Leah Nanako Winkler. In their work, these artists have begun to talk back to the social status quo by challenging the racial and legal structures persistently put in place. They push beyond an articulation of what it means to be mixed-race and instead investigate the reasons that these ideologies fall short in the first place. Their theater clarifies the human condition under these regimes of control.

In light of all this, how will mixed-race playwrights continue to address and interrogate the shifting racial landscape of the twenty-first century? How will they persist in developing and expanding representation in theater as the incendiary political and social climates continue to evolve? What new challenges await these dramatists? How many more burgeoning mixed-race playwrights will emerge and transform the current canon of mixed-race plays?

The current American theater landscape has perhaps begun to finally open its generative space to the mixed-race Asian experience, its representations, and its artists. In chapter 1, I began with a memory of the 2011 National Asian American Theatre Conference and Festival and a theater community of color still grappling with an ambivalent acceptance toward the mixed-race Asian artists in their midst. Yet the contemporary moment brings us to new terrain in which the Consortium of Asian American Theaters and Artists (CAATA) currently supports the Mixed-Asian American Artists Alliance, an artists' interest group within the CAATA organization, which builds community among hapa artists.[15] Additionally, the 2020 Steinberg Playwrighting Award winners, Christopher Chen and Leah Nanako Winkler, are both mixed-race playwrights of Asian descent.[16] Each of these dramatists writes with bifurcated insight as they critically examine racial dynamics in America. Their plays reach into political and domestic spheres and question archaic Jim Crow and Coolie-era racial constructs in a new millennium. Currently, Winkler has risen to the national spotlight. Besides winning the 2018 Yale Drama Series Prize for her play *God Said This* (2018),[17] Winkler's play *Kentucky* (2016), about a mixed-race Asian family in the American South, received a world premiere at East West Players in Los Angeles. Her play specifically about race and whiteness, *Two Mile Hollow* (2017), saw a 2018 "rolling" world premiere at Artists at Play in Los Angeles, Mu Performing Arts and Mixed Blood Theatre in Minneapolis, Ferocious Lotus Theatre Company in San Francisco, and First Floor Theater in Chicago.[18] Winkler's emergence in the mixed-race Asian American theater canon continues to point to a new generation of multiethnic Asian playwrights who continue to push the boundaries of race in America.

The new artistic leadership at East West Players also seems to be engaged in this new national conversation about mixed-Asian representation. Tim Dang's successor as Producing Artistic Director of East West Players,[19] Snehal Desai, proudly asserted his desire to develop and produce the hapa canon at the theater's reading of Chen's play *Mutt* in November 2016.[20] His shift in the theater's focus and vision, at the site of the 2011 National Asian American Theatre Conference and Festival only five years earlier, seems like a promising step toward the embrace of mixed-race Asian subjects in theater and the critically important preservation of mixed-Asian American histories in theatrical texts. The mixed-race body onstage calls into question the soothing balm of colorblind racial transcendence and quickly lays bare any assumption that a post-racial era is upon us. What new hopeful moments then will these plays, their playwrights, and their performers spark in the potential for a radically redemptive cartography in this millennium? Future ethnographic studies of the productions of these new plays, including in-depth audience surveys and analysis, will lead to a more comprehensive understanding of the ways in which playgoers view the mixed-race Asian subject and will measure how theater continues to nurture racially transgressive performances, social change, and the preservation of our diverse, polychromatic American history.

Acknowledgments

I am especially grateful for the opportunity to formally thank my doctoral committee—Christina S. McMahon, Ninotchka Bennahum, and Paul Spickard—for their endless support, crucial mentorship, enthusiastic cheerleading, and abundant wisdom.

I thank the faculty, the staff, and my colleagues and mentors in the Departments of Theater and Dance, Asian American Studies, and History at the University of California, Santa Barbara; in the Department of Theatre and Dance at California State University, Los Angeles; in the Department of Theatre Arts at Loyola Marymount University; and in the School of Dramatic Arts at the University of Southern California. I am the recipient of their unwavering belief in my endeavors, their many hours of caring feedback, and their welcome, good cheer.

I am endlessly grateful to the archivists who came to my aid and went above and beyond to assist me in this research, most notably Mark E. Swartz of The Shubert Archive and Allison Wagner with the Archives and Special Collections at the University of Calgary. None of my work on Winnifred Eaton would have been possible without them. I am also indebted to the dedicated archivists at the Billy Rose Theatre Division at the New York Public Library; the Department of Special Research Collections at University of California, Santa Barbara; and the many, many archivists over the years at the Special Collections & University Archives at University of California, Riverside, for assisting me with the work on Sadakichi Hartmann.

I personally thank Diana Birchall and Elizabeth Mooney, the descendants of Winnifred Eaton, whose gracious insights into Eaton's personal life were invaluable to this work.

The following people and organizations deserve recognition and my gratitude for their generous contributions to this research and to my personal growth as a scholar: Ellen Anderson; Lynda and Jerry Baker; Nic Barilar; Fay Beauchamp; Michael W. Butchers; Kirstin Candy; Mary Chapman; Christopher Chen; Alex Chester; Frances Ya-Chu Cowhig; Tim Dang; Snehal Desai; Kristin DiBernardo; Robert Garcia; Christopher Goodson; Brian Granger; Sarah Grant; Hiwa Elms; Charls Hall; Kimberly Kay Hoang; Christina Holdrem-Markulich; Velina Hasu Houston; Robert Hsiang; Miglena Ivanova; Laura Kina; Jessica Kubzansky; Hannah Kunert; Shishir Kurup; Teresa Williams-León; Elizabeth Liang; Laura MacCleery; Tom McGrath; Justine Nakase; Laura Pancake; Jeff Rankin; Jenn Robbins; Tamara Ruppart; Lisa Schebetta-Jackson; Kara Leigh Severson; Lawrence D. Smith; Vance Smith; Vanessa Stalling; Kymm Swank; Lily Anne Y. Welty Tamai; Marie-Reine Velez; Kristina Wong; Pamela Wu-Kochiyama; Ynika Yuag; Annie Zamora; the entire cast and production team of the 2016 Chicago production of *Mutt*; my colleagues at California State Parks; Japan Studies Association; Red Tape Theatre; Stage Left Theatre; and the Transracial and Mixed-Race working groups of the American Society of Theatre Research Annual Conferences, 2016 and 2017.

Contrary to popular belief, writing is not a solitary exercise, and it never happens in isolation. I am deeply indebted to the contributions of my writing colleagues and fellow scholars, Francisco Beltrán and Laura Hooton, whose keen insights and steadfast dedication to their own projects served as an inspiration to me throughout the entire revision process. Likewise, I thank my editor, Nicole Solano, and the production team at Rutgers University Press for supporting me and championing this work from the beginning. Without them, this book would not have come to be. Also, thank you to Esther K. Chae, Ann Pegelow Kaplan, and David McIntosh, my fellow comrades and researchers on the journey.

Finally, I am most grateful to my family: my parents Maria N. Lilagan and James A. Heinrich, my partner Roger Butchers, and my daughters Paige and Lillian Butchers for their never-ending love and support and without whom the journey of this book would never have been possible.

Portions of chapter 2 appear in a somewhat different form in Shape Shifters: Journeys across Terrains of Race and Identity, ed. Lily Anne Y. Welty Tamai, Ingrid Dineen-Wimberly, and Paul Spickard (Lincoln: University of Nebraska Press, 2020), 281–312.

Notes

Chapter 1   Stages of Denial

1 Reed Johnson, "Asian American Theater Conference Widens Its Embrace," *Los Angeles Times*, March 22, 2011, http://articles.latimes.com/2011/mar/22 /entertainment/la-et-asian-american-theater-20110322.

2 When referring to the academic field of study, mixed race is not hyphenated. Otherwise, I have elected to hyphenate mixed-race when referring to multiracial identity. Naomi Zack, "American Mixed Race: The United States 2000 Census and Related Issues," in *Mixing It Up: Multiracial Subjects*, ed. SanSan Kwan and Kenneth Speirs (Austin: University of Texas Press, 2004), 13.

3 Colorblindness purports not only to look beyond and "transcend" the physical markers of race but to naively not see race at all.

4 I have elected to capitalize the word "Black" when it refers to African Americans and their experiences. In this capacity, the term serves as a proper adjective and should be capitalized. By extension, I follow scholar Holly Roose and do not capitalize white. Roose clarifies: "Since whites do not share a similar historical struggle in terms of racial respect in American culture, I do not capitalize white." Holly Roose, *Black Star Rising: Garveyism in the West* (Lubbock: Texas Tech University Press, 2022), 132n5.

5 Robert G. Lee, *Orientals: Asian Americans in Popular Culture* (Philadelphia: Temple University Press, 1999), 11, 149; William Peterson, "Success Story: Japanese American Style," *New York Times Magazine*, January 9, 1966, http://inside.sfuhs .org/dept/history/US_History_reader/Chapter14/modelminority.pdf.

6 LeiLani Nishime, "Mixed Race Matters: What Emma Stone and Bruno Mars Can Tell Us about the Future of Asian American Media," *Cinema Journal* 56, no. 3 (2017): 152.

7 Evelyn Alsultany, "Toward a Multiethnic Cartography: Multiethnic Identity, Monoracial Cultural Logic, and Popular Culture," *Mixing It Up: Multiracial Subjects*, ed. SanSan Kwan and Kenneth Speirs (Austin: University of Texas Press, 2004), 141–162.

8 Michel de Certeau, *The Practice of Everyday Life*, trans. Steven F. Rendall (Berkeley: University of California Press, 1984), 29.

9   Brandi Wilkins Catanese, *The Problem of the Color[blind]: Racial Transgression and the Politics of Black Performance* (Ann Arbor: The University of Michigan Press, 2011), 21.

10 Mary Beltrán and Camilla Fojas, eds., *Mixed Race Hollywood* (New York: New York University Press, 2008); Kimberly McClain DaCosta, *Making Multiracials: State, Family, and Market in Redrawing of the Color Line* (Stanford: Stanford University Press, 2007); Helena Grice "Face-ing/De-Face-ing Racism: Physiognomy as Ethnic Marker in Early Eurasian/Amerasian Women's Texts," in *Re/collecting Early Asian America: Essays in Cultural History*, ed. Josephine Lee, Imogene L. Lim, and Yuko Matsukawa (Philadelphia: Temple University Press, 2002), 255–269; Jennifer Ann Ho, *Racial Ambiguity in Asian American Culture* (New Brunswick, NJ: Rutgers University Press, 2015); LeiLani Nishime, *Undercover Asian: Multiracial Asian Americans in Visual Culture* (Chicago: University of Illinois Press, 2014); Jayne O. Ifekwunigwe, ed., *Mixed Race Studies: A Reader* (New York: Routledge, 2004); Maria P. P. Root, ed., *Racially Mixed People in America,* (Thousand Oaks, CA: Sage, 1992); and Paul Spickard with Jeffrey Moniz and Ingrid Dineen-Wimberly, *Race in Mind: Critical Essays* (Notre Dame: University of Notre Dame Press, 2015).

11 Josephine Lee, *Performing Asian America: Race and Ethnicity on the Contemporary Stage* (Philadelphia: Temple University Press, 1997).

12 Karen Shimakawa, *National Abjection: The Asian American Body Onstage* (Durham: Duke University Press, 2002), 18.

13 Jonathan Marks, *Human Biodiversity: Genes, Race, and History* (New York: Walter de Gruyter, 1995), 11; Madison Grant, *The Passing of the Great Race or the Racial Basis of European History* (New York: Charles Scribner's Sons, 1916).

14 W. E. B. Du Bois, *The Souls of Black Folk* (Oxford: Oxford University Press, 2008), 3.

15 For further discussion, see G. Reginald Daniel, "Black and White Identity in the New Millennium: Unsevering the Ties That Bind," in *The Multiracial Experience: Racial Borders as the New Frontier*, ed. Maria P. P. Root (Thousand Oaks, CA: Sage, 1996), 121–139.

16 I use "hypolineal" here as an adjectival form of hypodescent.

17 Anna Leonowens was of mixed Anglo-Indian descent. For further discussion and relevant sources, see chapter 3 in this book.

18 Literary historian Sterling Brown described the problematic paradox of the stereotype in 1933 in which "the mulatto inherits the vices of both races and none of the virtues." Sterling Brown, "Negro Character as Seen by White Authors," *Journal of Negro Education* 2, no. 2 (1933): 192–195; Carole DeSouza, "Against Erasure: The Multiracial Voice in Cherrie Moraga's *Loving in the War Years*," in *Mixing It Up: Multiracial Subjects*, ed. SanSan Kwan and Kenneth Speirs (Austin: University of Texas Press, 2004), 182.

19 Brown, 193.

20 Langston Hughes, *Mulatto: A Tragedy of the Deep South*, in *Five Plays by Langston Hughes*, ed. Webster Smalley (Indianapolis: Indiana University Press, 1963), 16.

21 Dion Boucicault, *The Octoroon: or, Life in Louisiana*, in *Representative American Plays*, ed. Arthur Hobson Quinn (New York: The Century Company, 1917), 429–458.

22 Joseph Roach, *Cities of the Dead: CircumAtlantic Performance* (New York: Columbia University Press, 1996), 220.

23 Roach, 232.

24 Caroline A. Streeter, "Ambiguous Bodies: Locating Black/White Women in Cultural Representations," in *The Multiracial Experience: Racial Borders as the New Frontier*, ed. Maria P. P. Root (Thousand Oaks, CA: Sage, 1996), 310.

25 Cynthia L. Nakashima, "An Invisible Monster: The Creation and Denial of Mixed-Race People in America," in *Racially Mixed People in America,* ed. Maria P. P. Root (Newbury Park: Sage, 1992), 174.

26 Antonia Nakano Glenn, "Racing and E-Racing the Stage: The Politics of Mixed Race Performance" (PhD diss., University of California, San Diego, 2004), 46; Elaine H. Kim, *Asian American Literature: An Introduction to the Writings and Their Social Context* (Philadelphia: Temple University Press, 1982), 9.

27 Paul Spickard with Jeffrey Moniz and Ingrid Dineen-Wimberly, "What Must I Be? Asian Americans and the Question of Multiethnic Identity," in *Race in Mind: Critical Essays* (Notre Dame: University of Notre Dame Press, 2015), 185. I reference Reuter's dissertation as quoted in Spickard.

28 I refrain from using the term *Eurasian* to identify mixed-race individuals more broadly. The word is employed in the trope of the tragic Eurasian as an analogue to the tragic mulatto/a. Originally, the term referred to "Anglo-Indians" with both English and Indian parentage and emerged from the rigid caste structures of colonial India.

29 Onoto Watanna, "A Father," *Conkey's Home Journal*, January 1900, 9–10. The mixed-race protagonist is named Yuri, which is Japanese for "lily." Lillie Winifred was Eaton's given name at baptism.

30 Onoto Watanna, "The Wickedness of Matsu," *Smart Set* (May 1900): 140.

31 Glenn, "Racing and E-Racing the Stage," 3–4; T. S. Denison, *Patsy O'Wang*, in *The Chinese Other 1850–1925: An Anthology of Plays*, ed. Dave Williams (Oxford: University Press of America, 1997), 125–148.

32 DaCosta, *Making Multiracials*, 1–20.

33 Edward W. Said, *Culture and Imperialism* (New York: Alfred A. Knopf, 1993), xxii.

34 Dominika Ferens, "Winnifred Eaton's 'Japanese' Novels as a Field Experiment" in *Middlebrow Moderns: Popular American Women Writers of the 1920s*, ed. Lisa Botshon and Meredith Goldsmith (Boston: Northeastern University Press, 2003), 66.

35 Oberon (1911–1979) was one-eighth Sri Lankan descent, though she may also have had some Maori heritage.

36 Lawrence Wright, "One Drop of Blood," *New Yorker* 70, July 1994, 134.

37 Wright, 134.

38 DaCosta, *Making Multiracials*, 25.

39 DaCosta, 25; Nakashima, "An Invisible Monster," 174.

40 From this point forward, all references to Teresa Kay Williams will be made using her current name, Teresa Williams-León. However, her work will be cited with the name used at the time of publication. Teresa Kay Williams, "Race as Process: Reassessing the 'What Are You?' Encounters of Biracial Individuals," in *The Multiracial Experience: Racial Borders as the New Frontier*, ed. Maria P. P. Root (Thousand Oaks, CA: Sage, 1996), 196–197; Wright, "One Drop of Blood," 134.

41 DaCosta, *Making Multiracials*, 25.

42 Marks, *Human Biodiversity*, 134.

43 DaCosta, *Making Multiracials*, 25.

44 Wright, "One Drop of Blood," 137.

45 Paul Spickard, "Shape Shifting: Reflections on Racial Plasticity," in *Shape Shifters: Journeys across Terrains of Race and Identity*, ed. Lily Anne Y. Welty Tamai, Ingrid

Dineen-Wimberly, and Paul Spickard (Lincoln: University of Nebraska Press, 2020), 1–53.

46 Ric Knowles, *Reading the Material Theatre* (Cambridge: Cambridge University Press, 2004). Knowles identifies the performance text as the translation of a performance into a "recollected experience" that is then "read" and interpreted.

47 Catanese, *The Problem of the Color[blind]*, 21–22.

48 Rebecca Schneider, *"Never, Again," The Sage Handbook of Performance Studies*, ed. D. Soyini Madison and Judith Hamera (Thousand Oaks: Sage, 2006), 28.

49 Williams, "Race as Process," 210.

50 Williams, 208.

51 Maria P. P. Root, "The Multiracial Experience: Racial Borders as a Significant Frontier in Race Relations," in *The Multiracial Experience: Racial Borders as the New Frontier,* ed. Maria P. P. Root (Thousand Oaks, CA: Sage, 1996), xvii.

52 DaCosta, *Making Multiracials*, 1–20; Cynthia L. Nakashima, "Servants of Culture: The Symbolic Role of Mixed-Race Asians in American Discourse," in *The Sum of Our Parts: Mixed Heritage Asian Americans*. ed. Teresa Williams-León and Cynthia L. Nakashima (Philadelphia: Temple University Press, 2001), 45.

53 Adriane E. Gamble, "Hapas: Emerging Identity, Emerging Terms and Labels and the Social Construction of Race," *Stanford Journal of Asian American Studies*, no. 2 (2009): 12–13.

54 Haunani-Kay Trask, *From a Native Daughter: Colonialism and Sovereignty in Hawaii* (Monroe, ME: Common Courage Press, 1993), 26.

55 When used as nouns to identity a person's ethnic or racial background, the words Hapa, Haole, and Hapa Haole are capitalized. In the Hawaiian language, when using these words as adjectives, they are spelled in lowercase, and so I follow suit in this book.

56 Glenn, "Racing and E-Racing the Stage," 12.

57 Robert Keao NeSmith, "The Etymology of Hapa," Japanese American National Museum, July 19, 2018, YouTube, 1:21:12, https://www.youtube.com/watch?v=ZZPa_yyoJc8&t=1461s&ab_channel=janmdotorg; Robert Keaoopuaokalani NeSmith, *"Hapapū,* Completely Hapa," in *Hapa.Me: 15 Years of the Hapa Project*, Kip Fulbeck (Los Angeles: Japanese American National Museum, 2018), 86–87.

58 I have refrained from using the terms *Amerasian* and Wasian in this book. The word Amerasian specifically refers to individuals who qualified for the Amerasian Immigration Act of 1982 and the Amerasian Homecoming Act of 1988. Coined by Pearl S. Buck in the novel *East Wind, West Wind* (1930), the term *Amerasian* identifies mixed-race children—born of American GI fathers and Southeast Asian or Korean mothers only—who were permitted to immigrate to the United States and receive refugee benefits. While these individuals are hapa, the term *Amerasian* is narrow in its political scope. I have also refrained from using Wasian, Blasian, or other similar iterations. Originally derogatory, the term Wasian emerged around the early 2000s and referred to white-identifying individuals who expressed an affinity for Asians or Asian culture. By 2017, the term had been appropriated by mixed-Asian persons to describe their mixedness and has subsequently been popularized on social media platforms. Rebecca Chiyoko King-O'Riain, "#Wasian Check: Remixing 'Asian + White' Multiraciality on *TikTok*," *Genealogy* 6 (2), no. 55 (June 2022). https://doi.org/10.3390/genealogy6020055.

59 Stephen Cornell and Douglas Hartmann, *Ethnicity and Race: Making Identities in a Changing World* (Thousand Oaks, CA: Pine Forge Press, 1998), 19.

60 Cornell and Hartmann, 24.

61 Michael Omi and Howard Winant, *Racial Formation in the United States*, 3rd ed. (New York: Routledge, 2014), 7, 110.

62 Claire Jean Kim, "The Racial Triangulation of Asian Americans," *Politics and Society* 27, no. 1 (March 1999): 105–138.

63 Ngai also recognizes members of the Latinx or Latiné community as often perceived to be "alien citizens." Mae M. Ngai, *Impossible Subjects: Illegal Aliens and the Making of Modern America* (Princeton: Princeton University Press, 2004), 2–9.

64 Spickard, Moniz, and Dineen-Wimberly, "What Must I Be," 182.

65 Paul Spickard, "Who Is An Asian? Who Is a Pacific Islander? Monoracialism, Multiracial People, and Asian American Communities," in *The Sum of Our Parts: Mixed Heritage Asian Americans*, ed. Teresa Williams-León and Cynthia L. Nakashima (Philadelphia: Temple University Press, 2001), 18.

66 Harvey Young, *Embodying Black Experience: Stillness, Critical Memory, and the Black Body* (Ann Arbor: The University of Michigan Press, 2010), 20.

67 Young, 20.

68 Young, 12–13.

69 Though Asians and Pacific Islanders are sometimes differentiated, these different groups of people are often placed together in the same racial category and identified as "Asian."

70 Lee, *Orientals*, 9; Krystyn R. Moon, *Yellowface: Creating the Chinese in American Popular Performance, 1850s–1920s* (New Brunswick, NJ: Rutgers University Press, 2005), 2–9; Celine Parreñas Shimizu, *The Hypersexuality of Race: Performing Asian/American Women on Screen and Scene* (Durham: Duke University Press, 2007), 59–61.

71 I used a pseudonym to identify this participant. Paul King (actor) in discussion with the author, January 2016.

72 Young, *Embodying Black Experience*, 20.

73 Anurima Banerji, "Paratopias of Performance: The Choreographic Practices of Chandralekha," in *Planes of Composition: Dance, Theory, and the Global*, ed. André Lepecki and Jenn Joy (Calcutta, India: Seagull Books, 2009), 346–347.

74 Foucault defines heterotopias as "counter-sites," which exist as alternative spaces meant to represent or invert reality within a culture. For example, a garden is a heterotopia; it is a real, concrete space, yet, because of its varied collection of plants, represents many different places in a single space. See Michel Foucault, "Of Other Spaces," trans. Jay Miskowwiec, *Diacritics* 16, no. 1 (1986): 22–27.

75 Banerji, "Paratopias of Performance," 346–371.

76 Banerji, 350.

77 Banerji, 354.

78 Banerji, 354.

79 Christopher Chen, *Mutt* (unpublished manuscript, December 8, 2015), private collection of Christopher Chen, 48.

80 bell hooks, "Marginality as a Site of Resistance," in *Out There: Marginalization and Contemporary Cultures*, ed. Russell Ferguson, Martha Gever, Trinh T. Min-ha, and Cornell West (Cambridge: Massachusetts Institute of Technology Press, 1990), 341–343.

81 hooks, 341.

82 Chen, *Mutt*, 47.

83 Stefanie Dunning, "Brown Like Me: Explorations of a Shifting Self," in *Mixing It Up: Multiracial Subjects*, ed. SanSan Kwan and Kenneth Speirs (Austin: University of Texas Press, 2004), 125.

84 For further discussion, see Pierre Bourdieu, *Outline of a Theory of Practice*, trans. Richard Nice (Cambridge: Cambridge University Press, 1977).

85 Spickard, "Not Passing—Shape Shifting," 1–53.

86 SanSan Kwan describes how the production of race and social space are intricately intertwined as racial cartography. SanSan Kwan, "Performing a Geography of Asian America: The Chop Suey Circuit," *TDR* 55, no. 1 (2011): 121–122.

87 Dunning, "Brown Like Me," 127. (Dunning discussing Maria P. P. Root.)

88 Omi and Winant, *Racial Formation in the United States*, 126.

89 De Certeau, *The Practice of Everyday Life*, 29, 37.

90 De Certeau, 32.

91 Angela C. Pao, *No Safe Spaces: Re-casting Race, Ethnicity, and Nationality in American Theater* (Ann Arbor: The University of Michigan Press, 2010), 1.

92 Pao, 38.

93 Lee, *Performing Asian America*, 97.

94 I refer here to the establishment of Saint Malo by Filipino "Manilamen" in eighteenth century Spanish Louisiana. See Jonathan H. X. Lee and Kathleen M. Nadeau, *Encyclopedia of Asian American Folklore and Folklife*, vol. 1 (Santa Barbara: ABC-CLIO, LLC, 2011), 387–388.

95 Eunhye Kim, "Interracial Marriages among Asian Americans in the U.S. West, 1880–1954" (PhD diss., University of Florida, 2011), 114.

96 Lee observes that fewer than 150 Chinese residents were reported in New York's Chinatown on the 1880 census. Lee, *Orientals*, 75.

97 Lee, 76.

98 Jack Kuo Wei Tchen, "Quimbo Appo's Fear of Fenians: Chinese Irish-Anglo Relations in New York City," in *The New York Irish*, ed. Ronald H. Bayor and Timothy J. Meagher (Baltimore: The John Hopkins University Press, 1996), 129.

99 Sui Sin Far, "Half-Chinese Children: Those of American Mothers and Chinese Fathers, Some of Their Troubles and Discomforts," in *Mrs. Spring Fragrance and Other Writings*, ed. Amy Ling and Annette White-Parks (Chicago: University of Illinois Press, 1995), 187–191.

100 Kim, *Asian American Literature*, 9.

101 DeSouza, "Against Erasure," 182–183.

102 Lee, *Orientals*, 10.

103 Moon, *Yellowface*, 148–149, 207.

104 Moon, 148.

105 Moon, 149–150.

106 *The Magical Life of Long Tack Sam*, directed by Ann Marie Fleming (AMF Productions, 2003), 1:30, https://www.nfb.ca/film/the_magical_life_of_long_tack_sam/.

107 *The Magical Life*, 1:02:08.

108 *Forbidden City, USA*, directed by Arthur Dong (DeepFocus Productions, 1989), 8:14, https://video.alexanderstreet.com/watch/forbidden-city-usa.

109 Mixed-Asian actress France Nuyen also shape shifted into monoracial Asianness as the character Suzie Wong. *The World According to Suzie Wong* by Paul Osborn, Perf. France Nuygen and William Shatner, Broadhurst Theatre, October 14, 1958.

110 For further discussion, see T. V. Reed, *The Art of Protest: Culture and Activism from the Civil Rights Movement to the Present*, 2nd ed. (Minneapolis: University of Minnesota Press, 2019).

111 For further discussion see Karen Umemoto, "On Strike!" San Francisco State College Strike, 1968–69: The Role of Asian American Students," *Amerasia Journal* 15, no. 1 (1989): 3–41.

112 Pao, *No Safe Spaces*, 17.

113 After the midcentury, each generation of emerging Asian American playwrights is referred to as a "wave." Playwrights Frank Chin, Wakako Yamauchi, and Edward Sakamoto, for example, are considered as "first wave" playwrights. For further discussion, see Velina Hasu Houston, "Respecting History: Asian American Forum Response," Discovernikkei.org, June 24, 2012, http://www.discovernikkei.org/en/journal/2012/6/24/forum-velina-hasu-houston/.

114 Frank Chin, *The Chickencoop Chinaman/The Year of the Dragon: Two Plays* (Seattle: University of Washington Press, 1981), 59.

115 Founded in 1965, East West Players in Los Angeles holds the distinction of being the oldest Asian American theater company in the United States. Tisa Chang, the longest active Asian American artistic director, founded Pan Asian Repertory Theatre in New York in 1977.

116 Knowles champions a "materialist semiotics," which combines theories of semiotics and the study of reception with cultural materialist practice. Knowles, quoting Scott Wilson, identifies the four main strands of cultural materialist practice as historical context, theoretical method, political commitment, and textual analysis. See Ric Knowles, *Reading the Material Theatre*, 13.

Chapter 2 Tragic Eurasians

1 This author first transcribed the play from Hartmann's handwritten manuscript in 2016.

2 "Americanisms," *America: A Journal for Americans* 4, no. 8 (1890): 206; "Theatrical Chronology 1890," *New York Clipper Annual* (1891), 6, http://www.columbia.edu/cu/lweb/digital/collections/cul/texts/ldpd_5655288_003/pages/ldpd_5655288_003_00000014.html?toggle=image&menu=maximize&top=&left=.

3 "Madame Butterfly" (1898) is a short story by John Luther Long, who was inspired by Pierre Loti's novel *Madame Chrysanthème* (1887). Long's short story was adapted into a one-act play written by David Belasco in 1900. In turn, Puccini saw the play in London in the same year and was inspired to write the 1904 opera. See John Luther Long, *Madame Butterfly* (New York: The Century Company, 1917); David Belasco, *Madame Butterfly: A Tragedy of Japan*, in *Representative American Plays* (New York: The Century Company, 1917), 649–664; and Giacomo Puccini and John Luther Long, *Madama Butterfly: Opera in Three Acts: Founded on the Book by John L. Long and the Drama by David Belasco* (New York: G. Ricordi and Company, 1905).

4 See Alain Boublil and Claude-Michel Schönberg, *Miss Saigon: A Musical* (Milwaukee: Hal Leonard Corporation, 1990); David Henry Hwang, *M. Butterfly* (New York: Penguin Group, 1986).

5 It is significant to note that the narrative function of the mixed-race Asian child persists in other cultural products deep into the twentieth century. Kent A. Ono discusses how a mixed-race Japanese child functions to explore "monoracial experiences and relations" in the film *Come See the Paradise* (1990). Though the character "Mini" speaks, she has no subjectivity. See Kent A. Ono, "The Biracial Subject as Passive Receptacle for Japanese American Memory in *Come See the Paradise*" in *Mixed Race Hollywood*, ed. Mary Beltran and Camilla Fojas (New York: New York University Press, 2008), 136–154.

6 Joyce Flynn, "Melting Plots: Patterns of Racial and Ethnic Amalgamation in American Drama before Eugene O'Neill," *American Quarterly*, 38 (1986): 417–438.

7 See Winnifred Eaton as Onoto Watanna, "A Japanese Girl," *Cincinnati Commercial Tribune*, November 8, 1896; T. S. Denison, *Patsy O'Wang*, in *The Chinese Other 1850–1925: An Anthology of Plays*, ed. Dave Williams (Oxford: University Press of America, Inc., 1997), 125–148.

8 Emerging performance scholarship interprets Hartmann as an Asian immigrant who was perhaps the first to write a play in English in the United States. As is clear in this chapter, this author finds this to be a mischaracterization of Hartmann's background and his approach to theater. However, it has been gratifying to see a long-awaited uptick in the attraction toward Hartmann and his life's work as this book is going to press.

9 Paul Spickard, "Shape Shifting: Reflections on Racial Plasticity," in *Shape Shifters: Journeys across Terrains of Race and Identity*, ed. Lily Anne Y. Welty Tamai, Ingrid Dineen-Wimberly, and Paul Spickard (Lincoln: University of Nebraska Press, 2020), 1–53.

10 de Certeau, *The Practice of Everyday Life*, 37.

11 Elizabeth Bell, *Theories of Performance* (Thousand Oaks: Sage, 2008), 229.

12 Rebecca Schneider, "Never, Again," 28.

13 Schneider, 29.

14 Timothy J. Gilfoyle, "In the Tenderloin," in *A Pickpocket's Tale: The Underworld of Nineteenth-Century New York* (New York: W.W. Norton, 2006), 420.

15 Lee, *Performing Asian America*, 97.

16 Celine Shimizu discusses a similar phenomenon in the portrayal of Asian American actresses in productions of *Miss Saigon*. Shimizu contends that although the actors craft performances of female power, the audience continues to witness hypersexualized Asian women in positions of subservience, due to what she refers to as the "bind of representation." No doubt George Appo's portrayal of his criminal past served to reinforce the white audience's anxiety about the ills of miscegenation. See Celine Parreñas Shimizu, *The Hypersexuality of Race: Performing Asian/American Women on Screen and Scene* (Durham: Duke University Press, 2007), 30–57. For a description of the Appo production, see Gilfoyle, "In the Tenderloin," 260–270.

17 Shannon Steen, *Racial Geometries of the Black Atlantic, Asian Pacific and American Theatre* (New York: Palgrave MacMillan, 2010), 68.

18 Lee, *Orientals*, 75.

19 For further discussion, see David R. Roediger, *The Wages of Whiteness: Race and the Making of the American Working Class*, rev. ed. (New York: Verso, 1999).

20 Denison, *Patsy O'Wang*, 125–148.

21 Jolie A. Sheffer, *The Romance of Race: Incest, Miscegenation, and Multiculturalism in the United States, 1880–1930* (New Brunswick, NJ: Rutgers University Press, 2013), 9.

22 Sheffer, 4.

23 For examples, see Onoto Watanna [Winnifred Eaton], *"A Half Caste" and Other Writings*, ed. Linda Trinh Moser and Elizabeth Rooney (Urbana: University of Illinois Press, 2003).

24 Eaton's older sister, Edith Eaton (1865–1914), also wrote fictional accounts about the mixed-race experience, often under the "Chinese" pen name Sui Sin Far. The Eaton sisters grew up in Europe, in the United States (like Hartmann), and in Canada.

25 Sheffer, *The Romance of Race*, 1.

26 Lee, *Orientals*, 76.

27 Jane Calhoun Weaver, "Introduction," in *Critical Modernist: Collected Art Writings*, ed. Jane Calhoun Weaver (Berkeley: University of California Press, 1991), 43.

28 In his essay "Three Years in Philadelphia," Hartmann describes falling in love with the theater upon seeing the famous American actor Thomas Wallace Keene onstage. "And when Thomas Keene came, and I saw him in MacBeth and Richard III, it happened that I became despairingly in love with the stage." Sadakichi Hartmann, "Three Years in Philadelphia: June 1882–February 1885," Box 6, Sadakichi Hartmann Papers, Special Collections & University Archives, University of California, Riverside.

29 Sadakichi Hartmann, *Critical Modernist: Collected Art Writings*, ed. Jane Calhoun Weaver (Berkeley: University of California Press, 1991), 30.

30 Linda Thinh Moser, "Sadakichi Hartmann (1867–1944)," in *Asian American Poets: A Bio-Bibliography Critical Sourcebook*, ed. Guiyou Huang (Westport: Greenwood Press, 2002), 129.

31 Hartmann mentions two plays he wrote in Boston: *A Child Actress* and *Abraham Lincoln*. Sadakichi Hartmann, "Aspirations of a Playwright," 1920–1930, Box 5, Sadakichi Hartmann Papers, Special Collections & University Archives, University of California, Riverside.

32 Esther Kim Lee, *A History of Asian American Theatre* (Cambridge: Cambridge University Press, 2006), 13. Lee quotes Hartmann's biographer, Jane Calhoun Weaver.

33 In "Aspirations of a Playwright," Hartmann notes that of all his plays, *Boston Lions* is his favorite. In the comedy, he writes about his experiences on the lecture circuit in Boston and names the caricature of himself Nichi Swartzman. See Hartmann, "Aspirations of a Playwright."

34 Hartmann.

35 Daniel Gerould, "The Art of Symbolist Drama: A Re-assessment," in *Doubles, Demons, and Dreamers: An International Collection of Symbolist Drama*, ed. Daniel Gerould (New York: Performing Arts Journal Publications, 1985), 7.

36 Hartmann never knew the exact year or month of his birth, an omission that troubled him his entire life. His father, unsure of the date, chose November 8 as his birthday, which was the birthday of Hartmann's paternal grandmother. "Program to Sadakichi's 63rd Birthday," 8 November 1933, Box 29, Sadakichi Hartmann Papers, Special Collections & University Archives, University of California, Riverside.

37 Frits Vos, "Forgotten Foibles: Love and the Dutch at Dejima (1641–1854)," *East Asian History*, no. 39 (2014):139–152.

38 Richard J. Evans, *Death in Hamburg: Society and Politics in the Cholera Years 1830–1910* (Oxford: Clarendon Press, 1987), 28–34.

39 Hartmann claimed he was anywhere from two to four months old when his mother died. See Sadakichi Hartmann, "A Youngster Dons Mikado Garb: A Confession," Box 8, Sadakichi Hartmann Papers, Special Collections & University Archives, University of California, Riverside, 3.

40 Hartmann, 3–6.

41 Hartmann alleged he had no association with the Japanese community. See Sadakichi Hartmann, "Banning California August 27 1942," Box 29, Sadakichi Hartmann Papers, Special Collections & University Archives, University of California, Riverside.

42 Hartmann, "A Youngster Dons Mikado Garb," 1–2.

43 Hartmann, *Critical Modernist*, 39.

44 Sadakichi Hartmann, "Races and the Melting Pot," in *White Chrysanthemums: Literary Fragments and Pronouncements*, ed. George Knox and Harry Lawton (New York: Herder and Herder, 1971), 119.

45 Michelle Legro, "A Trip to Japan in Sixteen Minutes," *The Believer*, May 2013, http://www.believermag.com/issues/201305/?read=article_legro.

46 Sadakichi Hartmann, "At the Training School," Box 5, Sadakichi Hartmann Papers, Special Collections & University Archives, University of California, Riverside.

47 Before Hartmann was sent to Philadelphia, his older brother, Taru, was sent to work as an apprentice on a farm in Holstein, Germany. Taru eventually immigrated to the United States and settled in Denver, Colorado. His life in Denver is largely unknown. See Sadakichi Hartmann, "Kiel," 1915, Box 6, Sadakichi Hartmann Papers, Special Collections & Archives, University of California, Riverside, CA.

48 Hartmann, "A Youngster Dons Mikado Garb," 2.

49 George Knox and Harry Lawton, "Introduction," in *The Whitman-Hartmann Controversy: Including Conversations with Walt Whitman and Other Essays*, ed. George Knox and Harry Lawton (Frankfurt: Herbert Lang Bern, 1976), 13.

50 In Strindberg's *The Father*, the character Laura can push her own agenda by convincing authorities that her husband is mad, although the play can also be read as a woman trying to outwit a system that is intrinsically patriarchal. Hartmann translated the play in 1889. See Sadakichi Hartmann, "Aspirations of a Playwright."

51 Hartmann, "A Youngster Dons Mikado Garb," 2.

52 This essay includes multiple revisions in the same version. The essay was written in 1891 and revised in 1915 and 1933. See Hartmann, "Three Years in Philadelphia."

53 Sadakichi Hartmann, "On the Lack of Culture," in *Sadakichi Hartmann: Critical Modernist: Collected Art Writings*, ed. Jane Calhoun Weaver (Berkeley: University of California Press, 1991), 168.

54 In September 1888, Hartmann proposed to mount a season of plays at Union Hall in Boston featuring *Pillars of Society*, *A Doll House*, and *Ghosts*. Hodges notes that the repertory was to be completed with Hartmann's translations of *The Father* and Heyse's *The Death of Don Juan*. See Peter B. Hodges, "The Plays of Sadakichi Hartmann" (PhD diss., City University of New York, 1991), 27–28.

55 This brief period of fascination with the Japanese culture began to wane in the twentieth century. The Japanese military success during the Russo-Japanese War (1904–1905) cultivated anxiety about Japanese expansion and turned popular opinion against the Japanese. Sheffer, *The Romance of Race*, 57.

56 Knox and Lawton, "Introduction," in *The Whitman-Hartmann Controversy*, 15.

57 Note how Hartmann conflated his Japanese ethnicity with nationality, even though he was a German national. Hartmann became a naturalized U.S. citizen in 1894. Knox and Lawton, 15.

58 Sadakichi Hartmann, "My First Visit," in *The Whitman-Hartmann Controversy: Including Conversations with Walt Whitman and Other Essays*, ed. George Knox and Harry Lawton (Frankfurt: Herbert Lang Bern, 1976), 68.

59 Hartmann, "A Youngster Dons Mikado Garb," 1.

60 Knox and Lawton, "Introduction," in *The Whitman-Hartmann Controversy*, 15.

61 George Knox and Harry Lawton, "Introduction Notes," in *The Whitman-Hartmann Controversy: Including Conversations with Walt Whitman and Other Essays*, ed. George Knox and Harry Lawton (Frankfurt: Herbert Lang Bern, 1976), 48.

62 Simon Williams, *Wagner and the Romantic Hero* (Cambridge: Cambridge University Press, 2004), 165.

63 Simon Williams, *Shakespeare on the German Stage: Volume 1, 1586–1914* (Cambridge: Cambridge University Press, 1990), 185–186.

64 After moving to the United States, Hartmann returned to Europe multiple times in 1885, 1886, 1887, 1888, and 1892. Hartmann wrote to Walt Whitman upon his return from Europe in 1888. See Walt Whitman Papers in the Charles E. Feinberg Collection: General Correspondence, 1841–1892; Hartmann, C. Sadakichi, July 24, 1888. Manuscript/Mixed Material. https://www.loc.gov/item/mss1863000211/.

65 Hartmann published a wealth of articles on acting and European dramatists and even ran advertisements for dance and acting lessons in *The Theatre: An Illustrated Weekly Magazine, Drama, Music, Art*, vol. 6., ed. Deshler Welch (New York: Theatre Publishing Company, 1889–1891).

66 According to Fuchs, an unmarked copy of *Christ* can be found in Strindberg's library. See Elinor Fuchs, "Strindberg 'Our Contemporary': Constructing and Deconstructing *To Damascus* (I)," in *Strindberg's Dramaturgy*, ed. Göran Stockenström (Minneapolis: University of Minnesota Press, 1988), 77.

67 Stéphane Mallarmé, "Letter to Sadakichi," 1893, Box 30, Sadakichi Hartmann Papers, Special Collections & University Archives, University of California, Riverside.

68 George Knox and Harry Lawton, "Introduction," in *White Chrysanthemums: Literary Fragments and Pronouncements*, ed. George Knox and Harry Lawton (New York: Herder and Herder, 1971), xix.

69 Sadakichi Hartmann, *Buddha* (New York: privately printed, 1897), 23. On the back of page 104 in the *Osadda's Revenge* manuscript, Hartmann has similarly listed colors that seem to accompany the drama's three different acts. See C. Sadakichi Hartmann, *Osadda's Revenge*, 1890, Box 7, Sadakichi Hartmann Papers, Special Collections & University Archives, University of California, Riverside, 104.

70 Tia Anne Vasiliou, "'The Power of Suggestiveness': Sadakichi Hartmann, Thomas Wilmer Dewing, and American Modernism" (master's thesis, University of California, Riverside, 2011), 76.

71 Christina Bradstreet, "*A Trip to Japan in Sixteen Minutes*: Sadakichi Hartmann's Perfume Concert and the Aesthetics of Scent," in *Art, History and the Senses: 1830 to the Present*, ed. Patricia Di Bello and Gabriel Koureas (Burlington: Ashgate Publishing Company, 2010), 53.

72 Bradstreet, 53.

73 "Perfume Concert Fails," *New York Times*, December 1, 1902, 5.

74 "Program of Rice's Sunday 'Pops'" 1902, Box 28, Sadakichi Hartmann Papers, Special Collections & University Archives, University of California, Riverside.

75 "Perfume Concert Fails," 5.

76 "Comparisons Most Odorous," *New York Times*, October 6, 1902, 8.

77 Comparisons Most Odorous, 8.

78 "Perfume Concert Fails," 5.

79 Cynthia L. Nakashima, "An Invisible Monster: The Creation and Denial of Mixed-Race People in America," in *Racially Mixed People in America*, ed. Maria P. P. Root (Newbury Park: Sage, 1992), 165–167.

80 Bradstreet, "*A Trip to Japan in Sixteen Minutes*," 62.

81 Bradstreet, 62.

82 Simon Williams (theater historian) described small Parisian theaters during a discussion with the author, March 2017.

83 Hartmann's financial ability to produce his theater projects is nebulous. To support himself and his family, he sold manuscripts, lectured on various topics, and asked acquaintances and friends for money, often receiving checks from contemporaries like Alfred Stieglitz and Ezra Pound. Hartmann's second wife, Lillian Bonham,

wrote about their financial hardships in her diary in 1917, recalling, "It is hard for him to make up his mind to taking a steady job." A few months after the House of Mystery production, Hartmann was arrested in Redwood City, California, for failure to adequately support his wife and children. He pled guilty and spent three days in jail after which he returned to the lecture circuit. See "Poet Arrested for Theft of L.A. Taxicab," *Oakland Tribune*, May 23, 1933, C7; Lillian Bonham diary entry, 24 July 1917, Box 43, Sadakichi Hartmann Papers, Special Collections & University Archives, University of California, Riverside.

84 Sadakichi Hartmann, "Program: The House of Mystery" 1917, Box 30, Sadakichi Hartmann Papers, Special Collections & University Archives, University of California, Riverside.

85 Sadakichi Hartmann, "Sadakichi's Autobiography," in *White Chrysanthemums: Literary Fragments and Pronouncements*, ed. George Knox and Harry Lawton (New York: Herder and Herder, 1971), 27.

86 Hartmann, 27.

87 "Hartmann to Read Own Play Tuesday," *San Francisco Chronicle*, March 11, 1917, 24.

88 Hartmann, "Races and the Melting Pot," 115.

89 Hartmann, *Critical Modernist*, 39.

90 Hartmann proclaimed himself the "King of Bohemia" when he lived in New York's Greenwich Village. See George Knox and Harry W. Lawton, "Introduction," in *The Valiant Knights of Daguerre*, ed. George Knox and Harry W. Lawton (Berkeley: University of California Press, 1978), 1.

91 Knox and Lawton, 18.

92 Knox and Lawton, 15.

93 Sadakichi Hartmann, "In Search of My Likeness," Box 6, Sadakichi Hartmann Papers, Special Collections & University Archives, University of California, Riverside.

94 Hartmann.

95 Knox and Lawton, "Introduction," in *White Chrysanthemums*, xxiv.

96 Hartmann, "Aspirations of a Playwright."

97 Hartmann had produced *Ghosts*, a favorite play of his, multiple times in both Boston and San Francisco. He was also well versed in Shakespeare's plays and had translated Wilhelm Hauff's *Othello* from German. Hartmann, "Aspirations of a Playwright."

98 Sheffer, *The Romance of Race*, 56.

99 Main character Kiku in "A Half-Caste" specifically wants to see her father suffer for the pain he caused her deserted mother. Onoto Watanna, "A Half-Caste," *Frank Leslie's Popular Monthly*, vol. 48, September 1899, 489–496; Onoto Watanna, "A Father," *Conkey's Home Journal*, January 1900, 9–10.

100 Hartmann, *Osadda's Revenge*.

101 Hartmann.

102 Hodges, "The Plays of Sadakichi Hartmann," 54–55.

103 Hartmann, *Osadda's Revenge*, 5.

104 Browning died in December 1889, six months before the play was produced.

105 Hartmann, *Osadda's Revenge*, 13.

106 Hartmann, 14.

107 William Shakespeare, *Othello*, in *The Complete Works of William Shakespeare*, ed. William Aldis Wright (Garden City, NY: Doubleday, 1936), 942.

108 Hartmann, *Osadda's Revenge*, 13.

109 Henrik Ibsen, *Ghosts; An Enemy of the People; The Wild Duck*, ed. William Benfield Pressey (New York: Holt, Rinehart and Winston, 1966). The incestuous sibling

relationship is also found in many European dramatic plots, any of which could also have influenced Hartmann's play. See, most notably, John Ford, 'Tis a Pity She's a Whore (London: Nick Hern Books, 2002); John Webster, The Duchess of Malfi (Mineola, NY: Dover, 1999); and Richard Wagner, Die Walküre, ed. and trans. Rudolph Sabor (London: Phaidon Press, 1997).

110 George Knox and Harry Lawton, "Introduction," in The Whitman-Hartmann Controversy: Including Conversations with Walt Whitman and Other Essays, ed. George Knox and Harry Lawton (Frankfurt: Herbert Lang Bern, 1976), 18.

111 Hartmann, Osadda's Revenge, 94.

112 Hartmann, 101–102.

113 In Belasco's play, the mixed-race child is named Trouble. See Belasco, Madame Butterfly, 649–664.

114 Hartmann, Osadda's Revenge.

115 Hartmann, "Races and the Melting Pot," 117.

116 Early in the play, Miss Blueblood enjoins her party "to speak about the foreigner to everyone we meet." Later Clarissa confesses, "I love this foreigner with all my heart and soul." Hartmann, Osadda's Revenge, 6, 9.

117 Hartmann, 70.

118 "Theatrical Chronology 1890," New York Clipper Annual, 1891, 5, http://www .columbia.edu/cu/lweb/digital/collections/cul/texts/ldpd_5655288_003/pages/ldpd _5655288_003_00000014.html?toggle=image&menu=maximize&top=&left=.

119 Built in 1887, Apollo Hall was rebuilt as the Lyceum Theatre and reopened in 1905. Harry Houdini performed at the same theater in 1926, less than two months before he died in Detroit. See Hodges, "The Plays of Sadakichi Hartmann," 55–56; Craig Morrison, Theaters (New York: Library of Congress, 2006), 130.

120 Hodges, "The Plays of Sadakichi Hartmann," 55–56. Hodges quotes Hartmann's biographers Harry Lawton and George Knox.

121 "Americanisms," 206. This is ironic, as Hartmann regularly wrote articles in German for the New Yorker Staats-Zeitung, a popular German-language newspaper, from 1898 to 1902 to make money. See Weaver, "Introduction," in Critical Modernist, 118.

122 "Americanisms," 206.

123 Hartmann, "A Youngster Dons Mikado Garb," 1. This author's emphasis.

124 Sadakichi Hartmann, "Statement March 11, 1942," Box 29, Sadakichi Hartmann Papers, Special Collections & University Archives, University of California, Riverside.

125 "How to Tell Japs from Chinese," Life, December 22, 1941, 81.

126 Those faced with internment were well aware of the racialization in these primers and took a variety of measures to avoid incarceration. Japanese American Fred Korematsu went so far as to undergo plastic surgery to avoid being phenotypically read as Japanese. He informally changed his name to Clyde Sarah and claimed to be a "Spaniard," but was arrested, nonetheless, in June 1942. See "3 Japanese Defy Curbs: Army Says One Tried to Become a 'Spaniard' by Plastic Surgery," New York Times, June 13, 1942, 8.

127 Hartmann, "A Youngster Dons Mikado Garb," 1.

128 According to Jennifer Ann Ho, as of September 1943, 568 persons of Japanese descent, including mixed-race individuals, were living freely in the Western United States. For further discussion on the Mixed Marriage Policy of 1942, see Jennifer Ann Ho, Racial Ambiguity in Asian American Culture (New Brunswick, NJ: Rutgers University Press, 2015), 22–43; Paul Spickard, "Injustice Compound:

Amerasians and Non-Japanese Americans in World War II Concentration Camps," *Journal of American Ethnic History* 5, no. 2 (Spring 1986): 5–22.

129 Sadakichi Hartmann, *A History of American Art* (London: Hutchinson and Company, 1903).

130 Hartmann, *Osadda's Revenge*, 101–102.

131 Hartmann, 104.

132 Sadakichi Hartmann, "Erbschleicherei," Box 6, Sadakichi Hartmann Papers, Special Collections & University Archives, University of California, Riverside, 3.

133 Historian Robert G. Lee distills and articulates Asian stereotypes as "Six Faces of the Oriental," which includes the subservient coolie as well as the threat of the pollutant, the deviant, and yellow peril. He includes the model minority and the gook, stereotypes that evolve in the twentieth century, as the final two "faces." See Lee, *Orientals*, 8–12.

134 Lee, 10; Sheffer, *The Romance of Race*, 57.

135 Denison, *Patsy O'Wang*, 126.

136 In the analysis that follows, I use the name "Patsy" when referring to the mixed-race main character. In the play, "Chin Sum" refers to the Chinese cook before he transforms into the Irish Patsy O'Wang. It is understood from the beginning that the character is mixed, but his cultural selves are never embodied at the same time.

137 Denison, *Patsy O'Wang*, 126.

138 Denison, 126.

139 For further discussion on Denison's publishing career, see Kevin Bryne, "'Simple Devices are Always Best': An Examination of the Amateur Play Publishing Industry in the United States," *Papers of the Bibliographical Society of America* 108, no. 2 (2014): 217–237.

140 Hsin-yun Ou, "Ethnic Presentations and Cultural Constructs: The Chinese/Irish Servant in Patsy O'Wang," *Canadian Review of American Studies* 43, no. 3 (2013): 481.

141 "Clubs and Women's Societies," *Washington Post* (February 23,1908): E3.

142 "Clubs and Women's Societies," E3.

143 Ou, "Ethnic Presentations and Cultural Constructs," 482.

144 Lee, *Orientals*, 43. The yellowface role is reminiscent of the minstrel character John Chinaman. See Lee, 34–35.

145 Krystyn R. Moon, *Yellowface: Creating the Chinese in American Popular Performance, 1850s–1920s* (New Brunswick, NJ: Rutgers University Press, 2005), 49–50.

146 Moon, 51.

147 Lee, *Orientals*, 75.

148 As quoted in Lee, 75–76.

149 "California Legislature—Assembly, Twenty-third Session," in *California State Assembly Journals* (1880): 146 and 449.

150 SanSan Kwan and Kenneth Speirs, "Introduction," in *Mixing It Up: Multiracial Subjects*, ed. SanSan Kwan and Kenneth Speirs (Austin: University of Texas Press, 2004), 3.

151 Steen, *Racial Geometries*, 68.

152 See Boublil and Schönberg, *Miss Saigon: A Musical*.

153 T. S. Denison, *Lively Plays for Live People* (Chicago: T.S. Denison and Company, 1895), 79.

154 Denison, 79.

155 Note Denison's addition of "girl" in the parenthetical stage directions. Denison, *Patsy O'Wang*, 129.

156 Lee, *Orientals*, 36–37; Moon, *Yellowface*, 144.

157 Thomas Stewart Denison, *Mexican Linguistics: Including Nauatl or Mexican in Aryan Phonology, The Primitive Aryans of America* (Chicago: T.S. Denison and Company, 1913), 3.

158 Paul Spickard, *Almost All Aliens: Immigration, Race, and Colonialism in American History and Identity* (New York: Routledge, 2007), 158.

159 Denison, *Patsy O'Wang*, 127–128, 140.

160 Denison, 128.

161 Dave Williams contends that the character Patsy and his ability to shift between two opposing personas was most likely inspired by the title character in Robert Louis Stevenson's *The Strange Case of Dr. Jekyll and Mr. Hyde* (1886). Wildly popular at the end of the century, Stevenson's novella was published just nine years before Denison's play was written. Dave Williams, "Introduction to *Patsy O'Wang*," in *The Chinese Other 1850–1925: An Anthology of Plays*, ed. Dave Williams (Oxford: University Press of America, Inc., 1997), 125.

162 Denison, *Patsy O'Wang*, 129.

163 A similar account can be seen in Clara A. N. Whitney, *Clara's Diary: An American Girl in Meji Japan*, ed. William Steele and Tamiko Ichimata (Tokyo: Kodansha International Limited, 1979), 25. Clara Whitney was fourteen years old when she arrived in Meji-era Japan with her American missionary parents in 1875. The first section of her diary, in which she recounts her life in Asia, is entitled, "In the Land for Which We Have So Often Prayed," mirroring Simper's sentiments in Denison's play. Whitney later married a Japanese man and had six Japanese English children.

164 Edward W. Said, *Culture and Imperialism* (New York: Alfred A. Knopf, 1993), xix.

165 Denison, *Patsy O'Wang*, 129.

166 Denison, 129.

167 Denison, 139.

168 Spickard, *Almost All Aliens*, 160.

169 Nayan Shah, *Contagious Divides: Epidemics and Race in San Francisco's Chinatown* (Berkeley: University of California Press, 2001), 79.

170 Shah, 77.

171 Denison, *Patsy O'Wang*, 127–128.

172 Mrs. Fluke says, "I hope the wretch doesn't smoke opium." See Denison, 130.

173 Denison, 131.

174 Denison, 131.

175 Shah, *Contagious Divides*, 27.

176 Lee, *Orientals*, 39.

177 Denison, *Patsy O'Wang*, 130.

178 Shah, *Contagious Divides*, 89.

179 Shah, 27.

180 Denison, *Patsy O'Wang*, 138.

181 Denison, 138.

182 Denison, 148.

183 Spickard, *Almost All Aliens*, 108.

184 Ou, "Ethnic Presentations and Cultural Constructs," 494.

185 Ou, 494–495.

186 Spickard, *Almost All Aliens*, 181.

187 Gregory T. Carter, "'A Shplit Ticket, Half Irish, Half Chinay': Representations of Mixed-Race and Hybridity in Turn-of-the-Century Theater," *Ethnic Studies Review* 31, no. 1 (2008): 32–54; Ou, "Ethnic Presentations and Cultural Constructs," 480–501.

188 Denison, *Patsy O'Wang*, 147.

189 Ou, "Ethnic Presentations and Cultural Constructs," 495.

Chapter 3 Shape Shifting Performances in the Twentieth Century

1 David Belasco, *Madame Butterfly: A Tragedy of Japan*, in *Representative American Plays* (New York: The Century Company, 1917), 649–664.

2 Actress Fannie Ward played Yuki in a yellowface characterization. See *A Japanese Nightingale*, directed by George Fitzmaurice (Pathé, 1918), 50 min.

3 For examples of other popular, contemporary travelogues, see James Anthony Fronde, *Oceana: or, England and Her Colonies* (London: Longmans, Green, and Company, 1886); Charles Kingsley, *A Christmas in West Indies* (Leipzig: Bernhard, Tauchnitz, 1871).

4 Eve Oishi, "Introduction," in *Miss Numè of Japan: A Japanese-American Romance*, Onoto Watanna (Baltimore: Johns Hopkins University Press, 1999), xvii.

5 Eaton wrote her early work under the pseudo-Japanese pen name Onoto Watanna, who served as a kind of literary alter ego.

6 Harvey Young refers to external social expectations that become internalized and incorporated in the subject's identity as social habiti. Eaton and her siblings experienced different social expectations from white and Asian monoracial groups in their childhood, causing them to make discrete choices about how to self-identify. For further discussion of social habitus, see Young, *Embodying Black Experience*, 20.

7 Karen Shimakawa articulates abjection as bodies that are othered in American society yet are fundamentally part of the whole and constantly negotiating visibility versus invisibility. For further discussion, see Shimakawa, *National Abjection*, 18.

8 Sara Jane Bailes, *Performance Theatre and the Poetics of Failure: Force Entertainment, Goat Island, Elevator Repair Service* (New York: Routledge, 2011), 2.

9 I follow Celine Parreñas Shimizu who classifies the lotus blossom and the dragon lady archetypes as femme fatales. The former's obsession with her lover will lead to death by suicide. The latter will fatally deploy her sexual power to entrap men. A relationship with either of these two figures almost always ends in death. See Shimizu, *The Hypersexuality of Race*, 59–65.

10 The play was performed at Daly's Theatre in New York City from November 19, 1903, to December 30, 1903.

11 Bailes, *Performance Theatre and the Poetics of Failure*, 2.

12 Crystal Parikh, *An Ethics of Betrayal: The Politics of Otherness in Emergent U.S. Literatures and Culture* (New York: Fordham University Press, 2009), 2.

13 Parikh, 4, 12.

14 Jean Lee Cole, *The Literary Voices of Winnifred Eaton: Redefining Ethnicity and Authenticity* (New Brunswick, NJ: Rutgers University Press, 2002), 3.

15 Amy Ling, "Winnifred Eaton: Ethnic Chameleon and Popular Success," *MELUS: The Journal of the Society for the Study of Multi-Ethnic Literature of the United States* 11, no. 3 (1984): 8, 13; Yuko Matsukawa, "Onoto Watanna's Japanese Collaborators and Commentators," *Japanese Journal of American Studies*, no. 16 (2005): 37; and Sheffer, *The Romance of Race*, 59.

16 Eve Oishi, "Introduction," in *Miss Numè of Japan*, xi.

17 Oishi, xxi.

18 Diana Birchall, *Onoto Watanna: The Story of Winnifred Eaton* (Chicago: University of Illinois Press, 2001), 18.

19 Eaton also wrote the Japanese-themed novels *The Wooing of Wistaria* (1902), *The Heart of Hyacinth* (1903), and *The Love of Azalea* (1904) among others.

20 The Russo-Japanese war ended in Russian defeat in 1905 and thwarted Russia's expansion into Asia.

21 Sui Sin Far, "Leaves from the Mental Portfolio of an Eurasian," in *Mrs. Spring Fragrance and Other Writings*, ed. Amy Ling and Annette White-Parks (Chicago: University of Chicago Press, 1995), 218–230.

22 Grace and Edward Eaton had fourteen children, but two, Ernest George and Lawrence, died in childhood.

23 Sui Sin Far, "Leaves from the Mental Portfolio of an Eurasian," 220.

24 Sui Sin Far, 220.

25 Sui Sin Far, 220.

26 Sui Sin Far, 219.

27 As appropriate for the period, Edith identified as a Eurasian. See Sui Sin Far, "Leaves from the Mental Portfolio of an Eurasian," 218–230.

28 Diana Birchall, "Calgary Notes" (unpublished manuscript, n.d.), private collection of Diana Birchall, 41. This author's emphasis.

29 Sui Sin Far, "Leaves from the Mental Portfolio of an Eurasian," 228.

30 Sui Sin Far, 227.

31 According to Birchall, Grace wrote "the first published history of women lawyers in the United States" in *Woman Lawyers' Journal* in 1947. See Birchall, *Onoto Watanna*, 24.

32 Birchall, 25.

33 Birchall, 19.

34 Sui Sin Far, "Leaves from the Mental Portfolio of an Eurasian," 223.

35 Sui Sin Far, 223.

36 Oishi, "Introduction," in *Miss Numè*, xvii.

37 Birchall speculates that she arrived in Chicago in May. She had left Jamaica in July 1896 shortly before her twenty-first birthday. See Birchall, *Onoto Watanna*, 42.

38 "Onoto Watanna, the Writer," *Saint Paul Globe*, December 25, 1902, 7.

39 Birchall, *Onoto Watanna*, 58.

40 "Onoto Watanna, the Writer," *Saint Paul Globe*, 7; "Onoto Watanna, the Writer," *San Francisco Call*, August 10, 1902, 24; and "A Japanese Novelist," *Evening Times*, October 11, 1902, 4.

41 Birchall, *Onoto Watanna*, 44.

42 Birchall, 44.

43 Oishi, "Introduction," in *Miss Numè*, xvii.

44 "Onoto Watanna, the Writer," *Saint Paul Globe*, 7.

45 "A Japanese Girl Who Writes Clever Short Stories," *Defiance Democrat*, April 13, 1899, 5.

46 Onoto Watanna, *A Japanese Nightingale* (New York: Harper and Brothers, 1901), 24.

47 Watanna, 24.

48 Dominika Ferens, "Winnifred Eaton's 'Japanese' Novels as a Field Experiment," 70.

49 Edward Said, *Orientalism* (New York: Vintage Books, 1994), 3.

50 Said, 5.

51 Maria P. P. Root, "A Bill of Rights for Racially Mixed People," in *The Multiracial Experience: Racial Borders as the New Frontier* (Thousand Oaks: Sage, 1996), 9.

52 Nakashima, "An Invisible Monster," 174.

53 Watanna, *A Japanese Nightingale*, 15.

54 Spickard, Moniz, and Dineen-Wimberly, "What Must I Be," 182.

55 Watanna, *A Japanese Nightingale*, 15.

56 Watanna, 192.

57 Watanna, 16.

58 Watanna, 17. This author's emphasis.

59 "David Belasco Dies; Dean of Theatre Had Long Been Ill," *New York Times*, May 15, 1931, 1; Craig Timberlake, *The Life and Work of David Belasco: The Bishop of Broadway* (New York: Library Publishers, 1954), 220–224.

60 Timberlake, 224.

61 Alice Kauser's office stamp appears on the cover of the script for "A Japanese Nightingale." See William Young, *A Japanese Nightingale*, 1903, Box 135, Scripts, K and E Series, The Shubert Archive, New York, New York.

62 "Homespun Dramatic Yarns," n.d. [1900s], Box 14, Winnifred Eaton Reeve Fonds, Archives and Special Collections, University of Calgary, Alberta, Canada.

63 Eaton married writer Bertrand Babcock on July 16, 1901, and used her married surname at the time of the production. The author on the cover of the playscript for *A Japanese Nightingale* is identified in handwriting as "Winifred Babcock." However, the first page of the script reads, "A Japanese Nightingale, Adapted from Onoto Watanna's Novel by William Young." Archival materials, including the program and the poster for the production, corroborate that Young wrote the adaptation; the contract between Eaton and Klaw and Erlanger granted the producing team the right to choose the dramatist for the play and to credit Eaton as the author of the novel only. This author has been unable to confirm the reason for Eaton's married name on the script cover. See "Winifred Babcock and Marc Klaw and A.L. Erlanger Agreement: The Japanese Nightingale," 30 June 1902, Box 36, Series 2, American Play Company records, Billy Rose Theatre Division, The New York Public Library, 72–76.

64 Young adapted the mega-hit *Ben-Hur* from Lew Wallace's novel *Ben-Hur: A Tale of Christ* (1880). "Japanese Nightingale," *Montreal Gazette*, November 28, 1903.

65 Young, *A Japanese Nightingale*, 1.4. Young's emphasis.

66 Said, *Orientalism*, 3–6.

67 Emily Goodell, "Before Crenshaw: A Historiographical Look at Intersectional Identity in Three Twentieth-Century American Plays by Eaton, Grimke, and Treadwell" (master's thesis, Binghamton University State University of New York, 2017), 31; Watanna, *A Japanese Nightingale*, 57.

68 Young, *A Japanese Nightingale*, 1.3.

69 Goodell, "Before Crenshaw," 14.

70 Young, *A Japanese Nightingale*, 1.7.

71 Young, 1.41. This author's emphasis.

72 Watanna, *A Japanese Nightingale*, 30.

73 Watanna, 41–42.

74 Young, *A Japanese Nightingale*, 2.5–6.

75 Watanna, *A Japanese Nightingale*, 84. Eaton's emphasis.

76 Watanna, 85. Eaton's emphasis.

77 Watanna, 90.

78 Young, *A Japanese Nightingale*, 1.41.

79 Melissa Eriko Poulsen, "Writing Madame Butterfly's Child: Japonisme and Mixed Race in Winnifred Eaton's 'A Half Caste,'" *Amerasia Journal* 43, no. 2 (2017): 168.

80 Poulsen, 168.

81 Young, *A Japanese Nightingale*, 2.7.

82 Young, 2.44.

83 Young, 3.13.
84 Watanna, *A Japanese Nightingale*, 150.
85 Watanna, 150.
86 Sui Sin Far, "Leaves from the Mental Portfolio of an Eurasian," 222.
87 Young, *A Japanese Nightingale*, 2.42.
88 Watanna, *A Japanese Nightingale*, 145–146.
89 Young, *A Japanese Nightingale*, 3.22.
90 Young, 4.1.
91 Archaic designation for the emperor of Japan.
92 Watanna, *A Japanese Nightingale*, 109.
93 Watanna, 114.
94 Watanna, 114–115.
95 Watanna, 114–115.
96 Watanna, 115.
97 Watanna, 141.
98 Watanna, 141.
99 Winnifred Eaton, "Notes for Lawyer Regarding Infringement by Belasco of 'The Wooing of Wistaria,'" [1900s], Box 14, Winnifred Eaton Reeve Fonds, Archives and Special Collections, University of Calgary, Alberta, Canada, 3.
100 Esther Kim Lee, *Made-Up Asians: Yellowface during the Exclusion Era* (Ann Arbor: The University of Michigan Press, 2022), 134.
101 Eaton, "Notes for Lawyer Regarding Infringement by Belasco," 3.
102 Eaton, 3.
103 Timberlake. *The Life and Work of David Belasco*, 226.
104 "Mrs. Babcock Wins the Belasco Suit," 7 February 1903, Box 14, Winnifred Eaton Reeve Fonds, Archives and Special Collections, University of Calgary, Alberta, Canada.
105 "Mrs. Babcock Wins the Belasco Suit."
106 "Mrs. Babcock Wins the Belasco Suit."
107 "In The Theatres This Week," *New York Times*, November 15, 1903.
108 "Japanese Nightingale Suffers from Locomotor Ataxia and Influenza," 21 November 1903, Box 14, Winnifred Eaton Reeve Fonds, Archives and Special Collections, University of Calgary, Alberta, Canada.
109 Watanna, *A Japanese Nightingale*, 81, 220. I reference Alan Dale's review as quoted in Birchall.
110 "A Japanese Nightingale," *New York Daily Tribune*, November 20, 1903.
111 Watanna, *A Japanese Nightingale*, 142.
112 "A Japanese Nightingale: Dramatized Novel at Daly's Has Rich Trimmings," *New York Times*, November 20, 1903.
113 Young, *A Japanese Nightingale*, 2.4.
114 This character does not exist in the novel but bears a striking similarity to Cho-Cho-San's maid Suzuki in *Madame Butterfly*.
115 "A Japanese Nightingale: Dramatized Novel at Daly's Has Rich Trimmings," *New York Times*.
116 "A Japanese Nightingale," *New York Daily Tribune*. This author's emphasis.
117 For further discussion of yellowface caricatures in vaudeville, see Moon, *Yellowface*.
118 "Double Bill at the Grand Opera House," *New York Times*, November 27, 1900, 5.
119 "Belasco's Japanese Play," *New York Times*, November 21, 1902, 9.
120 "A Japanese Nightingale: Dramatized Novel at Daly's Has Rich Trimmings," *New York Times*.

121 Loie Fuller, a performer of proto-modern dance, was a predecessor of Isadora Duncan and Martha Graham. She was famous for dancing in swathes of undulating fabric, under colored electrical lights. The advancements in illumination stunned audiences and drew huge crowds to her performances.

122 "A Japanese Nightingale: Dramatized Novel at Daly's Has Rich Trimmings," *New York Times*.

123 "Madame Butterfly: Blanche Bates Talks About Her Role in the Japanese Play," *New York Times*, March 18, 1900, 18.

124 Mari Yoshihara, *Embracing the East: White Women and American Orientalism* (Oxford: Oxford University Press, 2003), 79.

125 Birchall, *Onoto Watanna*, 75.

126 Garrick, "A Japanese Nightingale," n.d. [1900s], Box 14, Winnifred Eaton Reeve Fonds, Archives and Special Collections, University of Calgary, Alberta, Canada.

127 One of Eaton's closest friends was the powerful Lois Weber, the first female director to own her own studio.

128 In an alternative version, Gloria is raised by her father's family, but her mixed blood prevents her from truly fitting in. See Winnifred Eaton Reeve, "A Savage in Silks," Collection No. 204, Folder 546, William Wyler Papers, Margaret Herrick Library, Academy of Motion Picture Arts and Sciences and Winnifred Reeve, "A Savage in Silks," n.d. [1920s], Box 9, Winnifred Eaton Reeve Fonds, Archives and Special Collections, University of Calgary, Alberta, Canada.

129 Eaton divorced Bertrand Babcock in 1917. She married American businessman turned cattle rancher Francis Fournier Reeve later that same year.

130 Birchall, *Onoto Watanna*, 159.

131 Universal Pictures was one of the first studios to comply with the rules established by the Production Code Administration. An original subplot in *Show Boat* featured an interracial relationship between a Black woman and a white man, which the studio eliminated. Eaton is uncredited on both projects. See Cole, *The Literary Voices of Winnifred Eaton*, 136–137, 196; *The Phantom of the Opera*, directed by Rupert Julian (Universal Pictures, 1925), 1:32; and *Show Boat*, directed by Harry A. Pollard (Universal Pictures, 1929), 2:26.

132 *Shanghai Lady* was based on the play, *Drifting*, by John Colton and Daisy H. Andrews. *East Is West* was based on the similarly titled play by Samuel Shipman and John B. Hymer. Jean Lee Cole notes that the earlier silent version of *East Is West* (1922) had been written by Eaton's friend, Frances Marion. See Cole, *The Literary Voices of Winnifred Eaton*, 170; *East Is West*, directed by Monta Bell (Universal Pictures, 1930), 1:15; and *Shanghai Lady*, directed by John S. Robertson (Universal Pictures, 1929), 1:06.

133 *East of Borneo* was adapted from a story by the same name by the feminist playwright and screenwriter Fred de Gresac. *East of Borneo*, directed by George Melford (Universal Pictures, 1931), 1:17.

134 Cole, *The Literary Voices of Winnifred Eaton*, 136.

135 Ralina L. Joseph, *Transcending Blackness: From the New Millennium Mulatta to the Exceptional Multiracial* (Durham: Duke University Press, 2013), 19.

136 *Barbary Coast*, directed by Howard Hawks (Metro-Goldwyn-Mayer, 1935), 1:31.

137 *Reeve Theatre*, 1981, University of Calgary Photo Archives, University of Calgary, Alberta, Canada, https://cdm22007.contentdm.oclc.org/digital/collection/uc50/id /44799/rec/4.

138 Based on Leonowens's memoir first published in 1870. See Anna Harriette Leonowens, *The English Governess at the Siamese Court: Being Recollections of Six Years in the Royal Palace at Bangkok* (Oxford: Oxford University Press, 1988).

139 Morgan quotes Mary Martha Sherwood in *Stories Explanatory of Church Cat-echism*. This author has not been able to locate the original reference. Additionally, in Landon's account, Leonowens was born in Carnavon in Wales. See Susan Morgan, *Bombay Anna: The Real Story and Remarkable Adventures of the King and I Governess* (Berkeley: University of California Press, 2008), 28; Margaret Landon, *Anna and the King of Siam* (New York: The John Day Company, 1943), 4.

140 Morgan, *Bombay Anna*, 5.

141 Morgan, 207.

142 In various film versions, Leonowens has also been portrayed by white actresses: Irene Dunne in 1946, Deborah Kerr in 1956, and Jodi Foster in 1999. It is worth noting that Yul Brenner, who was of Mongol, Russian, and Swiss-German ancestry, played the monoracial Asian king in the 1956 film opposite Kerr. By the same token, hapa actress France Nuyen shape shifted into Japaneseness in the film *A Girl Named Tamiko* (1962), which ironically followed a mixed character of Chinese and Russian descent, who was played by European actor Laurence Harvey. Chinese-English actress Nancy Kwan also shape shifted into monoracial Asianness in films like *The World According to Suzie Wong* (1960) and *Flower Drum Song* (1961). *The King and I*, directed by Walter Lang (20th Century-Fox, 1956), 2:13; *A Girl Named Tamiko*, directed by John Sturges (Paramount Pictures, 1962), 1:50; *The World According to Suzie Wong*, directed by Richard Quine (Paramount Pictures, 1960), 2:06; *Flower Drum Song*, directed by Henry Koster (Universal Pictures, 1961), 2:13.

143 Chin, *The Chickencoop Chinaman/The Year of the Dragon*, 3.

144 Frank Chin has sharply criticized Asian American writers who betrayed Asian America by authoring "fake" Asian American stories. Ironically, Chin aggrandized Edith Eaton, Diana Chang, and Han Suyin for being writers of "real" Asian American literature, although all three were multiracials. See Frank Chin, "Come All Ye Asian American Writers of the Real and the Fake," in *The Big Aiiieeeee!: An Anthology of Chinese American and Japanese American Literature*, ed. Jeffery Paul Chan et al. (New York: Meridan, 1991), 12; Wei Ming Dariotis, "Teaching Edith Eaton/Sui Sin Far: Multiple Approaches," *Asian American Literature: Discourses and Pedagogies* 1, no. 10 (2010): 70–72.

145 Chin, *The Chickencoop Chinaman/The Year of the Dragon*, 2.

146 Chin, 59. This author's emphasis.

147 Morgan, *Bombay Anna*, 5.

148 Shimakawa, *National Abjection*, 96

149 Nakashima, "An Invisible Monster," 176, 178. For a further discussion on the casting history of *Miss Saigon*, see Glenn, "Racing and E-Racing the Stage," 4, 62–158; Lee, *A History of Asian American Theatre*, 177–199; Moon, *Yellowface*, 163–165; and Pao, *No Safe Spaces*, 55–61.

150 In a similar move in film more recently, Cameron Crowe cast Emma Stone to play a character who was half-Asian/Pacific Islander in the motion picture *Aloha* (2015). See Nishime, "Mixed Race Matters," 149–150.

151 Chin, *The Chickencoop Chinaman/The Year of the Dragon*, 3.

152 However, in Chin's drama, marriage has not provided Lee respectability nor stability, even though he depicts her as successfully passing before she is outed by Tam. Streeter, "Ambiguous Bodies," 310.

153 Streeter, 311.

154 Parikh, *An Ethics of Betrayal*, 35.

155 Parikh, 36.

156 Parikh, 38.

157 Eaton was also not in its reprinting as *The Big Aiiieeeee!: An Anthology of Chinese American and Japanese American Literature* (1991), although her sister Edith, identified as Sui Sun Far, was included. See Jeffery Paul Chan et al., eds., *Aiiieeeee! An Anthology of Asian-American Writers* (Washington, DC: Howard University Press, 1974) and Jeffery Paul Chan et al., eds., *Aiiieeeee The Big Aiiieeeee!: An Anthology of Chinese American and Japanese American Literature* (New York: Meridan, 1991).

Chapter 4 Cosmopolitan Identity in Mixed Dramatic Forms

1 Houston told me that Plinka's unusual name was inspired by music. Houston attended a "home concert," which featured Spanish guitar music, and she felt that the music captured the essence of who Plinka is. The sounds she heard were integrated into her main character. Velina Hasu Houston (playwright) in discussion with author, January 2018.

2 Boublil and Schönberg, *Miss Saigon: A Musical*; Shimizu, "The Bind of Representation," 30–57.

3 Belasco, *Madame Butterfly*, 649–664.

4 Root, "A Bill of Rights for Racially Mixed People," 5.

5 For examples of hapa characters played by white actors in the midcentury, see *The Chickencoop Chinaman* by Frank Chin, Perf. Randall "Duk" Kim, Sally Kirkland, and Sab Shimono, American Place Theatre, New York, May 27, 1972; *A Girl Named Tamiko*, directed by John Sturges (Paramount Pictures, 1958), 1:50; *The King and I* by Oscar Hammerstein II and Richard Rodgers, Perf. Yul Brynner and Gertrude Lawrence, St. James Theatre, New York, March 29, 1951; and *Love Is a Many-Splendored Thing*, directed by Henry King (Twentieth Century Fox, 1955), 1:42.

6 Velina Hasu Houston, "Playwright's Note," in *Tea* (New York: Theatre Communications Group, 1985), n.p. Houston states that many Japanese women prefer the term *international brides* to *war brides*, which is considered a derogatory term. Following Houston's lead, I use the term *international bride/s* hereafter in this chapter.

7 Velina Hasu Houston, "Notes from a Cosmopolite," in *The Color of Theater: Race, Culture, and Contemporary Performance*, ed. Roberta Uno and Lucy Mae San Pablo Burns (New York: Continuum, 2002), 88.

8 Houston, 83.

9 Houston, 88.

10 hooks, "Marginality as a Site of Resistance," 341–343.

11 Banerji, "Paratopias of Performance," 354.

12 Christina S. McMahon, *Recasting Transnationalism through Performance: Theatre Festivals in Cape Verde, Mozambique, and Brazil* (New York: Palgrave Macmillan, 2014), 8.

13 McMahon, 8.

14 Kim, *Asian American Literature*, 9; Spickard, Moniz, and Dineen-Wimberly, "What Must I Be," 185.

15 Winnifred Eaton was raised by her Chinese mother predominantly in Canada, while Houston was raised by her Japanese mother in the United States.

16 De Certeau, *The Practice of Everyday Life*, 37.

17 In Sadakichi Hartmann's play *Osadda's Revenge*, Hartmann's protagonist, Hidetada, identifies (and is identified) as Japanese, even though he has a white father. See Hartmann, *Osadda's Revenge*, 1–104.

18 Different than the dominant discourse, the subdominant discourse often does not fully recognize mixed Asians as members of the Asian American racial group due to a lack of blood purity. Spickard, Moniz, and Dineen-Wimberly, "What Must I Be," 182.

19 Spickard, Moniz, and Dineen-Wimberly, 109. For this author's take on this, see Rena M. Heinrich, "The White Wilderness," in *The Beiging of America: Being Mixed-Race in the 21st Century*, ed. Cathy J. Schlund-Vials, Sean Frederick Forbes, and Tara Betts (New York: 2Leaf Press, 2017), 99–101.

20 Julia Kristeva, *Desire in Language: A Semiotic Approach to Literature and Art*, ed. Leon S. Roudiez (New York: Columbia University Press, 1980), 92–93.

21 Houston writes in the manuscript that *The American Women* is inspired by *The Trojan Women* by Euripides. In *Calling Aphrodite* Houston invokes the Greek goddess Aphrodite into the space-time of performance in a play about the Japanese Hiroshima maidens. In *Kokoro (True Heart)* Houston references *Medea* in the text, noting that the circumstances of the protagonists Medea and Yasako are similar. Velina Hasu Houston, *Calling Aphrodite, Green Tea Girl in Orange Pekoe Country: Selected Plays of Velina Hasu Houston* (South Gate, CA; NoPassport Press, 2007), 197–258; Velina Hasu Houston, "The American Women" (unpublished manuscript, 2015), private collection of Velina Hasu Houston; and Velina Hasu Houston. *Kokoro (True Heart)* (New York: Dramatists Play Service, 2011).

22 Literally translated as "new first generation," *shin-issei* refers to the Japanese immigrants who migrated to the United States in the postwar era. They are differentiated from the issei generation who arrived before WWII. The *shin-issei* were typically entrepreneurs, students, or corporate employees, who had been transferred to Japanese companies in the United States. See Hirosuke Hyodo, "The Era of Dual Life: The Shin-Issei, the Japanese Contemporary Migrants to the U.S.," *Electronic Journal of Contemporary Japanese Studies (EJCJS)* 13, no. 1 (2013); Tritia Toyota, "The New Nikkei: Transpacific Shin-Issei and Shifting Borders of Community in Southern California," *Amerasia Journal* 38, no. 3 (2012): 1–27.

23 Cynthia L. Nakashima, "Voices from the Movement: Approaches to Multiraciality," in *The Multiracial Experience: Racial Borders as the New Frontier*, ed. Maria P. P. Root (Thousand Oaks: Sage, 1996), 80.

24 Maria N. Heinrich (now Maria N. Lilagan) chronicles the events that led to the multicultural and bilingual movement in education, including the passing of the Bilingual Education Act of 1968 and the landmark 1974 *Lau v. Nichols* case, which determined that the lack of supplementary language instruction violated the Civil Rights Act of 1964. Maria N. Heinrich, "Bilingual Education: A Misconception" (presentation, National Association for the Advancement of Asians and Pacific Islanders in Education Conference, New Orleans, LA, 1984).

25 DaCosta, *Making Multiracials*, 1–20.

26 Bernard Weiner, "Plays about Strangers in a Strange Land," *San Francisco Chronicle*, January 22 1986, 56.

27 Verna A. Foster, "After Chekhov: The Three Sisters of Beth Henley, Wendy Wasserstein, Timberlake Wertenbaker, and Blake Morrison," *Comparative Drama* 47, no. 4 (Winter 2013): 451–472; Richard Nelson, *The Apple Family: Scenes from Life in the Country* (New York: Theatre Communications Group, 2014.); and Richard Nelson, *Goodnight Children Everywhere and Other Plays* (New York: Theatre Communications Group, 2004).

28 Kristeva, *Desire in Language*, 92–93.

29 Houston, in discussion with the author.

30 Velina Hasu Houston, "Notes from a Cosmopolite," 87.

31 In the 1985 Asian American Theater Company production script of the play, the neighbors' last name is Zweigenbaum. The version of the play analyzed for this chapter is the revised 1990 manuscript unless otherwise noted. See Velina Hasu Houston, *Thirst*, 1985, Series VII, Folder 12, Asian American Theater Company Archives 1973–1993, University of California, Santa Barbara Special Collections, University of California, Santa Barbara, 1.

32 Bernard Weiner, "Plays about Strangers in a Strange Land," 56; Velina Hasu Houston, *Thirst* (unpublished manuscript, February 1, 1990), private collection of Velina Hasu Houston.

33 Houston, 21.

34 I reference the production as these lines were transcribed from the video of one of the performances and differ slightly from the playscript. Video of performance of *Thirst* by Velina Hasu Houston, January 1986, Database V0061/UM, Asian American Theater Company Archives 1973–1993, University of California, Santa Barbara Special Collections, University of California, Santa Barbara.

35 Houston, *Thirst* (1990), 39. This author's emphasis.

36 Caryl Churchill, *Cloud Nine* (New York: Samuel French, 1979).

37 Nakashima, "An Invisible Monster," 174.

38 Houston, *Thirst* (1990), 5.

39 The term *hypodescent* refers to the assignment of a mixed-race individual to the race of the parent deemed socially subordinate.

40 DeSouza, "Against Erasure," 182.

41 Houston, *Thirst* (1990), 25. This author's emphasis.

42 Houston, 3.

43 Houston, *Thirst* (1985), 47.

44 Houston, 47.

45 Houston, in discussion with the author and Lee, *A History of Asian American Theatre*, 149.

46 Houston, 149.

47 It is worth noting that this is a discussion of the accusation. However, the experience of the playwright is significant as it seems to mirror the discrimination that the mixed-race character experiences in the play. Houston, in discussion with the author.

48 Houston.

49 Houston.

50 Lee, *A History of Asian American Theatre*, 149.

51 Houston, *Thirst* (1990), 50.

52 Houston, *Thirst* (1985), 61–62.

53 Houston, *Thirst* (1990), 42.

54 Anton Chekhov, *Three Sisters*, in *The Plays of Anton Chekhov*, trans. Paul Schmidt (New York: Harper Perennial, 1997), 319.

55 Foster, "After Chekhov," 451.

56 Leon Katz calls this type of dramatic structure a "process plot," where an outside circumstance, such as the *process* of dissolving a familial estate, provides the frame for the narrative. See Leon Katz, *Cleaning Augean Stables: Examining Drama's Strategies* (Encino: Create Space Publishing, 2012), 92.

57 J. Douglas Clayton and Yana Meerzon, *Adapting Chekhov: The Text and Its Mutations* (New York: Routledge, 2013), 5.

58 Houston, in discussion with the author.

59 Houston, *Thirst* (1990), 12–13.

60 Houston, 12.

61 Houston, 7.

62 Chekhov, *Three Sisters*, 259–260.

63 David Edgar, *How Plays Work* (London: Nick Hern Books, 2009), 93.

64 Houston, "Playwright's Note," 37–39.

65 Houston, *Thirst* (1990), 7.

66 Houston, 45.

67 Chekhov, *Three Sisters*, 317.

68 Houston, *Thirst* (1990), 8.

69 Houston, 8.

70 Houston, 41.

71 Houston, 8.

72 Masami Usui, "Creating a Feminist Transnational Drama: *Oyako-Shinju* (Parent-Child Suicide) in Velina Hasu Houston's *Kokoro (True Heart)*," *Japanese Journal of American Studies*, 11 (2000): 181; Zvika Serper, "Between Two Worlds: 'The Dybbuk' and the Japanese Noh and Kabuki Ghost Plays," *Comparative Drama* 35 nos. 3/4 (2001–2002): 346–347. Obon festival is "one of the most important events in the Buddhist calendar." It would be unthinkable to miss this celebration, much like it would be unthinkable to miss a name-day in the Russian tradition. The name-day celebration is the equivalent of a birthday party in contemporary American culture. See Chekhov, *Three Sisters*, 319.

73 Plinka reminds Marina of the significance of the Obon festival: "Marina, it's O-bon! . . . The festival of the dead. Our holiday to visit with ancestral spirits and dance." Houston, *Thirst* (1990), 12–13.

74 See Brenda Wong Aoki, *The Queen's Garden*, in *Contemporary Plays by Women of Color: An Anthology*, ed. Kathy A. Perkins and Roberta Uno (New York: Routledge, 1996), 14–31; Amy Hill, *Tokyo Bound*, in *Asian American Drama: 9 Plays for the Multiethnic Landscape*, ed. Brian Nelson (New York: Applause Theatre Book Publishers, 1997), 43–70; Naomi Iizuka, *36 Views* (New York: The Overlook Press, 2003); Sandra Tsing Loh, *Aliens in America* (New York: Riverhead Books, 1997); and Dmae Roberts, *Breaking Glass*, in *But Still, Like Air, I'll Rise*, ed. Velina Hasu Houston (Philadelphia: Temple University Press, 1997), 271–330.

75 Noh plays are arranged into five different groups or "categories," depending on the identity of the main character known as the *shite*. See Serper, "Between Two Worlds," 349.

76 Usui, "Creating a Feminist Transnational Drama," 178; Houston, *Kokoro* (2011), 10.

77 Houston, "Notes from a Cosmopolite," 84.

78 I refrain from using the term *protagonist* as an analogue for the *shite*, although both are central figures in drama. While the Western protagonist struggles against an obstacle emplaced by an antagonist, the *shite* and the *waki* do not share a similar relationship in Noh.

79 Zvika Serper, "Japanese Noh and Kyogen Plays: Staging Dichotomy," *Comparative Drama* 39, nos. 3/4 (2005–2006): 308.

80 Serper, 308.

81 Serper, 308.

82 Serper, 312–314.

83 William Wetherall, "The Trial of Fumiko Kimura," *PHP Intersect Tokyo*, 2 (1986): 6–9.

84 For further discussion, see Maura Dolan, "Two Cultures Collide Over Act of Despair: Mother Facing Charges in Ceremonial Drowning," *Los Angeles Times*,

February 24, 1985; Janet Rae-Dupree and Jack Jones, "Children in Arms: Mother's Trek Into Sea Stuns Her Neighbors," *Los Angeles Times*, January 31, 1985; "Mother Placed on Probation in 2 Drownings," *Los Angeles Times*, November 21, 1985; and Myrna Oliver, "Cultural Defense—a Legal Tactic," *Los Angeles Times*, July 15, 1988.

85 Cynthia M. Wetzler, "Survival and off-off Broadway: Moments of Being," *The Pound Ridge Review* (Pound Ridge, NY: Acorn Press, March 16, 1995).

86 Houston, *Kokoro* (2011), 9.

87 Houston, 25.

88 Kanze Jūrō Motomasa, *Sumidagawa*, *The Noh*, 1–16, accessed June 8, 2018, http://www.the-noh.com/en/plays/data/program_012.html.

89 Houston, *Kokoro* (2011), 36.

90 Usui, "Creating a Feminist Transnational Drama," 179.

91 *Bun* means "divide" and *shin* means "of the body." Houston, *Kokoro* (2011), 36.

92 Houston, 36.

93 Motomasa, *Sumidagawa*, 11. This author's emphasis.

94 Houston, *Kokoro* (2011), 43.

95 Houston, 46.

96 Houston, 13–14.

97 Houston, 34.

98 Houston, 35.

99 Houston, 35.

100 Velina Hasu Houston, *As Sometimes in a Dead Man's Face*, in *Asian American Drama: 9 Plays from the Multiethnic Landscape*, ed. Brian Nelson (New York: Applause Theatre Book Publishers, 1997), 71–125; Velina Hasu Houston, *Asa Ga Kimashita (Morning Has Broken)*, in *The Politics of Life: Four Plays by Asian American Women*, ed. Velina Hasu Houston (Philadelphia: Temple University Press, 1993), 219–274; Velina Hasu Houston, *Calligraphy*, in *Green Tea Girl in Orange Pekoe Country: Selected Plays of Velina Hasu Houston* (South Gate: NoPassport Press, 2014), 315–377; and Velina Hasu Houston, *A Spot of Bother*, in *Green Tea Girl in Orange Pekoe Country: Selected Plays of Velina Hasu Houston* (South Gate: NoPassport Press, 2014): 378–420.

101 As a director, I admit my blind spot in this casting as I, too, envisioned a half-Asian and half-white performer in the role, which more closely aligns with my own ethnic background. This underscores the importance of the lived experiences of the director, producer, and casting director in casting decisions like these. *Kokoro (True Heart)* by Velina Hasu Houston, Perf. Jenny Woo, Timothey Fitzgerald, and Tamiko, Morgan-Wixson Theatre, September 5, 2003.

102 In the following educational productions, Evelyn was portrayed by monoracial student actors. *Kokoro (True Heart)* by Velina Hasu Houston, Perf. Jenny Chen, Patrick Scully, and Ana Rodriguez, Davidson College Second Stage, February 16, 2011; *Kokoro (True Heart)* by Velina Hasu Houston, Perf. Kyungseo Min, Brandon Wong, and Katie Peabody, University of Southern California Scene Dock Theatre, April 24, 2014; and *Kokoro (True Heart)* by Velina Hasu Houston, Perf. Rebecca Chan, Fadi Muallem, and Milan Levy, Nelda K. Balch Playhouse at Kalamazoo College, October 23, 2020.

103 Omi and Winant, *Racial Formation in the United States,* 12.

104 Nakashima, "An Invisible Monster," 174.

105 Sheng-mei Ma, "The Necessity and Impossibility of Being Mixed-Race in Asian American Literature," in *Reconstructing Hybridity: Post-Colonial Studies*, ed. Joel Kuortti and Jopi Nyman (New York: Rodopi, 2007), 164. This author's emphasis.

106 Sheng-mei Ma, 184.

107 Root, "A Bill of Rights for Racially Mixed People," 11–12.

108 Sheng-mei Ma, "The Necessity and Impossibility of Being Mixed-Race," 187.

109 Pao, *No Space Spaces*, 176.

110 Glenn, "Racing and E-Racing the Stage," 6. Glenn's emphasis.

111 Houston, *Kokoro* (1997), 116.

112 Heidi Durrow (class discussion, University of California, Santa Barbara, CA, March 5, 2015).

113 DaCosta, *Making Multiracials*, 130.

114 Paul Spickard discusses the rejection that many multiracials experience as a reaction from the subdominant discourse. See Spickard, Moniz, and Dineen-Wimberly, "What Must I Be," 182.

115 Houston, *Kokoro* (1997), 89–129.

116 Houston, *Kokoro* (2011), 35.

117 Usui contends that the exploration of the plight of transplanted Japanese women was personal for Houston. The notion of *oyako-shinju* haunted Houston for years as her mother admitted to Houston that she contemplated committing the practice after Houston's father's suicide. See Usui, "Creating a Feminist Transnational Drama," 193.

118 Tamara Ruppart (director) in discussion with the author, June 2021.

119 It is worth noting that director Ynika Yuag, whose senior thesis was a filmed production of *Kokoro (True Heart)* at Kalamazoo College during the COVID-19 pandemic in 2020, was constrained by the lack of people of color at her university. Nonetheless, when faced with casting Evelyn with a monoracial actor, she chose Milan Levy, who identifies as African American. Yuag asserted to me that "Americans are not just white. American could be theoretically any race. And I tried my best to . . . decenter whiteness at any point that I could. . . . I think people don't realize that Asians can also be Black." Director Tamara Ruppart, who was in a similar situation with casting at Davidson College in 2011, cast Latiné actress Ana Rodriguez as Evelyn. While these casting choices do not account for mixedness, they boldly signal a much broader vision of the term *American* in the current millennium. Ynika Yuag (director) in discussion with the author, July 2021, and Ruppart, in discussion with the author.

Chapter 5   Multiraciality in the Post-Racial Era

1 Jeremy Diamond, "Trump: I Could Shoot Somebody and I Wouldn't Lose Voters," CNN, January 24, 2016, http://www.cnn.com/2016/01/23/politics/donald-trump -shoot-somebody-support/.

2 In contemporary depictions, Ralina L. Joseph refers to this figure as the "new millennium mulatta." See Joseph, *Transcending Blackness*, part I.

3 Michael Calderone, "Matthews: 'I Forgot He Was Black Tonight for an Hour,'" *Politico*, January 27, 2010, http://www.politico.com/blogs/michaelcalderone/0110 /Matthews_I_forgot_he_was_black_tonight_ for_an_hour.html.

4 SanSan Kwan and Kenneth Speirs, "Introduction," in *Mixing It Up: Multiracial Subjects*, ed. SanSan Kwan and Kenneth Speirs (Austin: University of Texas Press, 2004), 3.

5 Catanese, *The Problem of the Color[blind]*, 21.

6 Catanese, 22.

7 Catanese, 88.

8 Leo Cabranes-Grant, "An Essay on Racial Understanding: Toward a Post-Obama State of Mind," *Theatre Survey* 55, no. 2 (May 2014): 254.

9 Kwan and Speirs, "Introduction," in *Mixing It Up*, 4.

10 Joshua Takano Chambers-Letson, *A Race So Different: Performance and Law in Asian America* (New York: New York University Press, 2013), 3.

11 Chambers-Letson, 3.

12 Alsultany, "Toward a Multiethnic Cartography," 143.

13 Edgar, *How Plays Work*, 113.

14 Chen, *Mutt*, 6.

15 Chen, 6–7.

16 Chen, 3.

17 Chen, 26.

18 Chen, 33.

19 Cindy L. Nakashima, "Servants of Culture," 42.

20 Chen, *Mutt*, 69.

21 Chen, 46, Chen's emphasis.

22 Christopher Chen (playwright) in discussion with the author, May 2015.

23 George Aiken, *Uncle Tom's Cabin* (Gloucester: Dodo Press, 2008); Boublil and Schönberg, *Miss Saigon: A Musical*; Dion Boucicault, *The Octoroon*, 429–458; William Wells Brown, *The Escape; Or, a Leap for Freedom*, in *Black Theatre USA: Plays by African Americans, The Early Period 1847–1938*, ed. James V. Hatch and Ted Shine (New York: The Free Press, 1974), 35–60; T. S. Denison, *Patsy O'Wang*, 125–148; Timothy J. Gilfoyle, "In the Tenderloin," 260–270; Jessica Hagedorn, *Dogeaters* (New York: Theatre Communications Group, 2003); Langston Hughes, *Mulatto*, 1–35.

24 Ralina L. Joseph explores a similarly troubled "problem-special" dichotomy and examines the post-racial promise of "the exceptional multiracial" in representations of multiracial Blackness. See Joseph, *Transcending Blackness*, part II.

25 *The New Face of America: How Immigrants Are Shaping the World's First Multicultural Society*, a special issue of *Time*, 142.21 (Fall 1993), cover. This future "Eve" is referenced widely in mixedrace scholarship. Jayne O. Ifekwunigwe, "Introduction: Rethinking 'Mixed Race' Studies," *Mixed Race Studies: A Reader*, ed. Jayne O. Ifekwunigwe (New York: Routledge, 2004), 1–3; Ono, "The Biracial Subject as Passive Receptacle," 149; Maria P. P. Root, "The Multiracial Experience," xiv; Danzy Senna, "The Mulatto Millennium," in *Half and Half: Writers on Growing Up Biracial and Bicultural*, ed. Claudine C. O'Hearn (New York: Pantheon Books, 1998), 12–14; Roberta Uno, "The Color of Theater," in *The Color of Theater: Race, Culture, and Contemporary Performance*, ed. Roberta Uno and Lucy Mae San Pablo Burns (New York: Continuum, 2002), 10; and Jan R. Weisman, "An 'Other' Way of Life: The Empowerment of Alterity in the Interracial Individual," in *The Multiracial Experience: Racial Borders as the New Frontier*, ed. Maria P. P. Root (Thousand Oaks: Sage, 1996), 159, to name a few.

26 For a further discussion of the "Face of the Future" trope in the Matrix trilogy, see Leilani Nishime, "The *Matrix* Trilogy and Multiraciality at the End of Time," in *Undercover Asian: Multiracial Asian Americans in Visual Culture* (Chicago: University of Illinois Press, 2014), 85–106.

27 Chen, *Mutt*, 49.

28 Chen, 26.

29 Chen, 45.

30 Chen, 45.

31 Root, "A Bill of Rights for Racially Mixed People," 9–10.

32 Kwan and Speirs, "Introduction," in *Mixing It Up*, 3.

33 Christopher Chen (playwright) in discussion with the author, October 2016.

34 Chen, *Mutt*, 19.

35 Christopher Chen (playwright) in discussion with the author, March 2016.

36 Chen, *Mutt*, 61.

37 Chen, 75.

38 Tom Williams, "Mutt," *Chicago Critic*, January 15, 2016, http://chicagocritic.com/?s=mutt.

39 Williams.

40 Williams.

41 Chen, *Mutt*, 33.

42 Lawrence Bommer, "A Seriously Stupid Screamfest," *Stage and Cinema*, January 14, 2016, http://www.stageandcinema.com/2016/01/14/mutt-stage- left-red- tape/. This author's emphasis.

43 Bommer.

44 Bommer.

45 Jeremy Diamond, "Trump: I Could 'Shoot Somebody and I Wouldn't Lose Voters," CNN, January 24, 2016, http://www.cnn.com/2016/01/23/politics/donald-trump -shoot-somebody-support/.

46 Diamond.

47 Trump biographer, Michael D'Antonio, notes that Trump's father, Fred, raised him to extol the benefits of being a "killer" and a "king." See Michael D'Antonio, "Donald Trump Believes He Was Born to Be King," *Los Angeles Times*, December 3, 2015, http://www.latimes.com/opinion/op-ed/la-oe-1203-dantonio-trump -race-horse-theory-20151203-story.html.

48 It is interesting to note that Chen never uses the word *creature* in reference to the mixed-race subjects in the play. See Nakashima, "An Invisible Monster," 174.

49 Lauren Whalen, "Mutt," *Chicago Theater Beat*, January 15, 2016, http:// chicagotheaterbeat.com/2016/01/15/mutt-review-stage-left-red-tape-theatre/.

50 "Playwright Christopher Chen Shares How His Identity Influences His Writing," *Singapore Repertory Theatre Blog*, May 9, 2019, https://www.srt.com.sg/article /interview-with-christopher-chen/.

51 I have used pseudonyms to identify the actors interviewed in this production.

52 *Hypodescent* refers to the assignment of a mixed-race individual to the race of the parent deemed socially subordinate. Consequently, mixed-race figures are compelled to identify as monoracials, who are only able to claim their non-white parentages.

53 Except for individuals of Native American Indian descent. In the case of Native Americans, the calculus is often more complicated as Native kinship rules collide with the White supremacist impulses of the one drop rule. See Circe Strum, *Blood Politics: Race, Culture, and Identity in the Cherokee Nation of Oklahoma* (Berkeley: University of California Press, 2002); Mikaëla M. Adams, *Who Belongs? Race, Resources, and Tribal Citizenship in the Native South* (New York: Oxford University Press, 2016); Theda Perdue, *Mixed Blood Indians: Racial Construction in the Early South* (Athens: University of Georgia Press, 2005); Celia Naylor, *African Cherokees in Indian Territory: From Chattel to Citizens* (Chapel Hill: University of North Carolina Press, 2008).

54 Autumn Walsh (actor) in discussion with the author, January 2016.

55 Nakashima, "An Invisible Monster," 177.

56 For further discussion on the "what are you" question, see Root, "A Bill of Rights for Racially Mixed People," 7; Teresa Kay Williams, "Race as Process," 191–210.

57 Carl George (actor) in discussion with the author, January 2016.

58 Walsh, in discussion with the author.

59 Root, "A Bill of Rights for Racially Mixed People," 9.

60 For a discussion on the casting history of *Miss Saigon*, see Glenn, "Racing and E-Racing the Stage," 4, 62–158; Lee, *A History of Asian American Theatre*, 177–199; and Moon, *Yellowface*, 163–165.

61 Paul King (actor) in discussion with the author, January 2016.

62 King.

63 Vanessa Stalling (director) in discussion with the author, April 2016.

64 Stalling.

65 Chen, in discussion with the author (March 2016).

66 Andrzej Lukowski, "The World of Extreme Happiness," *Time Out*, October 1, 2013, http://www.timeout.com/london/theatre/the-world-of-extreme-happiness.

67 Frances Ya-Chu Cowhig, *Lidless* (New York: Methuen Drama, 2011), 8.

68 Yen Lê Espiritu, *Body Counts: The Vietnam War and Militarized Refuge(es)* (Oakland: University of California Press, 2014), 40.

69 Cowhig, *Lidless*, 8.

70 Espiritu quoting Marianne Hirsch notes that the memory of the postwar generation can be thought of as "postmemory—secondary, mediated, and inherited memory of a long past." See Espiritu, *Body Counts*, 141–142.

71 Cowhig, *Lidless*, 36. This author's emphasis.

72 Cowhig, 40.

73 Chambers-Letson, *A Race So Different*, 3.

74 Cowhig, *Lidless*, 37.

75 Cowhig, 26–27.

76 Cowhig, 40.

77 Cowhig, 15.

78 Cowhig, 13.

79 Catanese, *The Problem of the Color[blind]*, 21.

80 Chen, *Mutt*, 67.

81 Chen, 67.

Chapter 6   Beyond Monoracial Hierarchies

bell hooks, "Marginality as a Site of Resistance," in *Out There: Marginalization and Contemporary Cultures*, ed. Russell Ferguson, Martha Gever, Trinh T. Min-ha, and Cornell West (Cambridge: Massachusetts Institute of Technology Press, 1990), 343.

Zora Neal Hurston, *Dust Tracks on a Road: An Autobiography* (New York: Harper-Perennial, 1996), 243.

1 Omi and Winant, *Racial Formation in the United States*, 13.

2 Young, *Embodying Black Experience*, 20.

3 Omi and Winant, *Racial Formation in the United States*, 14.

4 Omi and Winant, 14.

5 Glenn, "Racing and E-Racing the Stage," 2.

6 Thai, "The New Face of America."

7 Root, "The Multiracial Experience," 8–9

8 Lee, *Orientals*, 75.

9 Banerji, "Paratopias of Performance," 354.

10 Houston, *Thirst* (1990), 25.

11 Houston, "Notes from a Cosmopolite," 84.

12 Houston, 83–89.

13 George, in discussion with the author.

14 George.

15 The alliance is spearheaded by hapa performer Alex Chester, who is the founder and editor of Mixed Asian Media (MAM), a collective dedicated to the inclusivity and the ethical representation of the mixed-race Asian Americans.

16 Christopher Chen additionally won the Obie Award for Playwriting, along with playwright Lynn Nottage, in 2017.

17 Frances Ya-Chu Cowhig also won the prize for *Lidless* in 2009. For further discussion, see "Leah Nanako Winkler Wins 2018 Yale Drama Series Prize," *American Theatre*, March 29, 2018, https://www.americantheatre.org/2018/03/29/leah-nanako-winkler-wins-2018-yale-drama-series-prize/.

18 Basil Considine, "Interview: Leah Nanako Winkler on Parodying Stage Whiteness, the Kilroys, and More," *Twin Cities Arts Reader*, December 11, 2017, https://twincitiesarts.com/2017/12/11/interview-leah-nanako-winkler-two-mile-horror/.

19 Tim Dang served as the producing artistic director of East West Players from 1993 to 2016.

20 Snehal Desai (producing artistic director) in discussion with the author, November 2016.

Index

About the Author

RENA M. HEINRICH is an assistant professor of theatre practice in Critical Studies at the University of Southern California. She is a contributor to *Shape Shifters: Journeys across Terrains of Race and Identity* and *The Beiging of America: Personal Narratives about Being Mixed Race in the 21st Century*.